Heritage and Identity

Heritage and Identity explores the complex ways in which heritage actively contributes to the construction and representation of identities in contemporary societies, providing a comprehensive account of the diverse conceptions of heritage and identity across different continents and cultures.

This collection of thought-provoking articles from experts in the field captures the richness and diversity of the interlinked themes of heritage and identity. Heritage is more than a simple legacy from the past, and incorporates all elements, past and present, that have the ability to represent particular identities in the public sphere. A wide range of interconnected topics is discussed, including multiculturalism and globalization, local and regional identity, urban heritage, difficult memories, conceptions of history, ethnic representations, repatriation, ownership, controversy, contestation, and ethics and social responsibility.

Heritage and Identity places empirical data within a theoretical and analytical framework and presents an interdisciplinary approach to the study of the representation of the past, invaluable for anyone interested in heritage and museum studies.

Marta Anico and **Elsa Peralta** are Senior Lecturers in Anthropology at the Instituto Superior de Ciências Sociais e Políticas, Universidade Técnica de Lisboa, Portugal. Marta Anico's research interests include heritage, museums, cultural practices and representations, and culture politics. Elsa Peralta is currently researching the construction of Portuguese national identity and is also interested in comparative national memories in Europe, heritage and memory, tourism and museums.

Museum Meanings

Series editors

Eilean Hooper-Greenhill and
Flora Kaplan

The museum has been constructed as a symbol of Western society since the Renaissance. This symbol is both complex and multi-layered, acting as a sign for domination and liberation, learning and leisure. As sites for exposition, through their collections, displays and buildings, museums mediate many of society's basics values. But these mediations are subject to contestation, and the museums can also be seen as a site for cultural politics. In postcolonial societies, museums have changed radically, reinventing themselves under pressure from many forces, which include new roles and functions for museums, economic rationalism and moves towards greater democratic access.

Museum Meanings analyses and explores the relationship between museums and their public. 'Museums' are understood very broadly, to include art galleries, historic sites and historic houses. 'Relationships with the public' is also understood very broadly, including interactions with artefacts, exhibitions and architecture, which may be analysed from a range of theoretical perspectives. These include material culture studies, mass communication and media studies, learning theories and cultural studies. The analysis of the relationship of the museum to its public shifts the emphasis from the museum as text, to studies grounded in the relationship of bodies and sites, identities and communities.

Also in the series:

Museums and Community
Ideas, Issues and Challenges
Elizabeth Crooke

Museums and Education
Purpose, Pedagogy, Performance
Eilean Hooper-Greenhill

Rethinking Evolution in the Museum
Envisioning African Origins
Monique Scott

Recoding the Museum
*Digital Heritage and the
Technologies of Change*
Ross Parry

Museum Texts
Communication Frameworks
Louise Ravelli

Reshaping Museum Space
Architecture, Design, Exhibitions
Edited by Suzanne MacLeod

Museums, Society, Inequality
Edited by Richard Sandell

**Museums and the Interpretation
of Visual Culture**
Eilean Hooper-Greenhill

Re-imagining the Museum
Beyond the Mausoleum
Andrea Witcomb

Museum, Media, Message
Edited by Eilean Hooper-Greenhill

Colonialism and the Object
*Empire, Material Culture and the
Museum*
Edited by Tim Barringer and Tom Flynn

Learning in the Museum
George Hein

Liberating Culture
*Cross-Cultural Perspectives on Museums,
Curation and Heritage Preservation*
Christina F. Kreps

Pasts Beyond Memory
Evolution, Museums, Colonialism
Tony Bennett

Heritage and Identity

Engagement and Demission in the Contemporary World

Edited by

Marta Anico and Elsa Peralta

Routledge
Taylor & Francis Group

LONDON AND NEW YORK

First published 2009
by Routledge
2 Park Square, Milton Park, Abingdon, Oxon OX14 4RN

Simultaneously published in the USA and Canada
by Routledge
270 Madison Ave, New York, NY 10016

Routledge is an imprint of the Taylor & Francis Group, an informa business

Typeset in Sabon by
Book Now Ltd, London
Printed and bound in Great Britain by
TJ International Ltd, Padstow, Cornwall

British Library Cataloguing in Publication Data
A catalogue record for this book is available from the British Library

Library of Congress Cataloging in Publication Data
Heritage and identity : engagement and demission in the contemporary
world / edited by Marta Anico and Elsa Peralta.
    p. cm.
Includes bibliographical references.
    1. Cultural property—Protection—Case studies. 2. Cultural
property—Protection—Social aspects—Case studies. 3. Cultural
property—Protection—Political aspects—Case studies. 4. National
characteristics—Case studies. 5. Ethnicity—Case studies.
6. Social ecology—Case studies. 7. Collective memory—Social aspects—Case
studies. 8. Postcolonialism—Case studies. 9. Museums—Social aspects—Case
studies. 10. Museums—Political aspects—Case studies. I. Anico, Marta. II.
Peralta, Elsa.
    CC135.H45 2008
    363.6′9—dc22   2008025196

ISBN10: 0–415–45335–6 (hbk)
ISBN10: 0–415–45336–4 (pbk)
ISBN10: 0–203–88600–3 (ebk)

ISBN13: 978–0–415–45335–6 (hbk)
ISBN13: 978–0–415–45336–3 (pbk)
ISBN13: 978–0–203–88600–7 (ebk)

Contents

List of figures   vii

Notes on contributors   viii

Acknowledgments   xii

Introduction   1

PART I
Place and identity   13

1   What role can digital heritage play in the re-imagining
    of national identities?: England and its icons   15
    RHIANNON MASON AND ZELDA BAVEYSTOCK

2   Locating art: The display and construction of place
    identity in art galleries   29
    CHRISTOPHER WHITEHEAD

3   Place, local distinctiveness and local identity: Ecomuseum
    approaches in Europe and Asia   47
    GERARD CORSANE, PETER DAVIS AND DONATELLA MURTAS

4   Representing identities at local municipal museums:
    Cultural forums or identity bunkers?   63
    MARTA ANICO

5   Heritage according to scale   76
    LLORENÇ PRATS

PART II
Remembering and forgetting   91

6   Unsettling memories: Intervention and controversy over
    difficult public heritage   93
    SHARON MACDONALD

7   Public silences, private voices: Memory games in a
    maritime heritage complex   105
    ELSA PERALTA

8   The banalization and the contestation of memory in
    postcommunist Poland   117
    BARBARA A. MISZTAL

9   A landscape of memories: Layers of meaning in a
    Dublin park   129
    KATE MOLES

PART III
Domination and contestation   141

10 Labor and leisure at Monticello: Or representing race
    instead of class at an inadvertent white identity shrine   143
    ERIC GABLE

11 The ancient city walls of Great Benin: Colonialism, urban
    heritage and cultural identity in contemporary Nigeria   156
    FLORA *EDOUWAYE* S. KAPLAN

12 The past in the present: Towards a politics of care at the
    National Trust of Australia (WA)   169
    ANDREA WITCOMB

13 Yorùbá identity and Western museums: Ethnic pride and
    artistic representations   181
    ANNA CATALANI

    Index   193

Figures

2.1	Gateshead quayside, 2004	33
2.2	The 'Border Warfare' Room, 2007	34
2.3	Atmospheric décor changes to speed the shift through time and place, 2007	35
2.4	The eighteenth-century Coffee House, 2007	36
2.5	Mapping Newcastle's neoclassical architecture, 2007	37
2.6	John Charlton's *The Women*, shown within a diorama, 2007	38
2.7	The Twentieth-Century Room, including a scale model of the Tyne Bridge, 2007	38
2.8	The Twentieth-Century Room: 1960s fashion, 2007	39
3.1	Gavalachori Museum, Crete, 1998	48
3.2	Soga Old Village, China, 2005	54
3.3	Restored rice terraces, Kamiayama-guchi, Miura, Japan, 2003	55
3.4	Ecomusée de St Dégan. The farm, France, 1998	57
3.5	Restored farmhouse and terraced hillsides of Cortemilia, 2006	60
5.1	Social construction of heritage. Constituent elements	79
5.2	Local heritage. The forces involved and how they are structured. Distance and level of involvement	85
11.1	Posters for a Great Gospel Campaign near the Oba's Palace and around Benin City, 2005	157
11.2	View of remains of Benin City walls, 1984	161
11.3	Annual Benin community-wide Festival of Ewere, Ewere, 1989	163
11.4	Posted sign at a site of the Benin Moat, 2005	164

Contributors

Marta Anico is a Senior Lecturer in Anthropology at the Instituto Superior de Ciências Sociais e Políticas, Universidade Técnica de Lisboa. She co-organized the *First International Conference of Heritages and Identities* held in Lisbon in 2004 and is co-editor of the book *Patrimónios e Identidades: Ficções contemporâneas* and author of several chapters and papers in her research areas. Her main topics of interest include heritage, museums, cultural practices and representations, and culture politics.

Zelda Baveystock is a Lecturer in Museum Studies in the International Centre for Cultural and Heritage Studies, Newcastle University, UK. Prior to taking up this position, she was Senior Keeper of History for Tyne and Wear Museums, a museum service incorporating 11 museums and galleries in the north-east of England. Zelda is a long-standing committee member of the Social History Curators Group, which works to improve the status and provision of social history in museums. Her research interests revolve around the representations of minority groups and multicultural identities in museum displays, with a particular focus on how contemporary collecting theory impacts on history collections in practice.

Anna Catalani is a Research Fellow at the Center for Tourism and Cultural Change, Leeds Metropolitan University. Anna's current research interests are in the fields of museum studies, material culture, religion in museums, identities and diaspora.

Gerard Corsane is a Senior Lecturer in Heritage, Museum and Gallery Studies in the International Centre for Cultural and Heritage Studies at Newcastle University, UK. He is the Degree Programme Director for the taught postgraduate programmes in the Centre. His research interests relate to his work experiences in South Africa and revolve around issues of identity construction and representation in colonial and postcolonial heritage and tourism contexts. His research focuses on ecomuseums, community museology, 'new' museology, integrated heritage management, the value of intangible heritage resources, responsible heritage tourism and sustainable development.

Peter Davis set up the MA in Museum Studies at Newcastle University and helped found the International Centre for Cultural and Heritage Studies. His research interests focus on the relationships between natural and cultural heritage, and community-based approaches to heritage conservation and the related fields of cultural landscapes, identity and sustainability. Much of his recent work has been carried out in Italy, Sweden, Japan and China.

Eric Gable is currently Associate Professor at the University of Mary Washington, Virginia. He received his PhD in anthropology from the University of Virginia and his BA in anthropology from the University of California, San Diego. He has written extensively about his fieldwork among Laujé of Sulawesi, Manjaco of Guinea-Bissau, and Americans working in and visiting Monticello and Colonial Williamsburg. He is the author (with Richard Handler) of *The New History in an Old Museum: Creating the past at Colonial Williamsburg*). At present he is completing *Kinds of Cosmopolitans, or Anthropology and Egalitarianism* that draws on his fieldwork experiences in order to meditate on the problems of constructing theories and vernaculars of cultural difference in the era of globalization.

Flora *Edouwaye* S. Kaplan is an anthropologist, Professor *Emerita*, Faculty of Arts and Science, and founding director of the Museum Studies Program, New York University. She holds a PhD from The Graduate Center of the City University of New York and a Masters (archaeology) from Columbia University. A Fulbright Professor (University of Benin, 1983–1985), she publishes widely on Benin, religion, art, politics, gender and museum studies. Among her publications are some 70 articles and chapters in books and journals, and seminal works: *Images of Power: Art of the Royal Court of Benin* (1981); *Museums and the Making of 'Ourselves': The role of objects in national identity* (1994); and *Queen, Queen Mothers, Priestesses, and Power* (1998). *Benin Art and Culture* is forthcoming. In 1991, His Royal Highness, Oba *Erediauwa* of Benin, named her *Edouwaye* ('Your home is in Benin'), the first woman scholar in history to be so honoured, and equivalent to an Edo chieftaincy title.

Sharon Macdonald is Professor of Social Anthropology at the University of Manchester. She has research interests in identities, history and memory, heritage and museums, science and Europe. Her publications include *Reimagining Culture: Histories, identities and the Gaelic Renaissance*; *The Politics of Display*; *A Companion to Museum Studies*, and *Difficult Heritage: Negotiating the Nazi past in Nuremberg and beyond*.

Rhiannon Mason is a Senior Lecturer in Museum, Gallery, and Heritage Studies in the International Centre for Cultural and Heritage Studies, Newcastle University, UK. Rhiannon's research interests are: 1) national museums and national identities and 2) museological theory relating to issues of representation, communication, identity, diversity and history curatorship. In 2007 she published a book on the National Museums of Wales which explored the extent to which national museums have been involved in the articulation and definition of nationhood and national identities within Wales, both in the past and today. This work led to her current interests in Englishness and Britishness; the relationship between government, politics, museums, galleries and heritage; and how museums, galleries and heritage contribute to perceptions of place, belonging and identity.

Barbara A. Misztal is Head of Department of Sociology at the University of Leicester. She is the author of *Public Intellectuals and the Public Good: Creativity and courage*, *Theories of Social Remembering*, *Informality: Social theory and contemporary practice*, *Trust in Modern Society*, and co-editor of *Action on AIDS*. Her interest in memory is reflected in her articles: 'Memory and democracy'; 'The sacralization of memory', 'Durkheim and memory'. Her current writing projects include a book which aims to enhance sociological understanding of the concept of vulnerability.

Kate Moles is a Research Associate at Cardiff University. Her research interests are clustered around ideas of place and space, postcolonial and national identities and methods that facilitate interesting forays and creative insights into these issues. She recently completed her PhD, *Narratives of Postcolonialism in Liminal Space: The place called Phoenix Park* in the School of Social Sciences at Cardiff University.

Donatella Murtas trained as an architect and environmental engineer, and has worked in the United Kingdom for the Countryside Commission dealing with issues relating to landscape and its cultural and historical meanings. Based in Italy, her professional career has been devoted to ecomuseums and local development projects, with a special focus on landscape and community involvement. From 1999 she has been the coordinator of the Ecomuseo dei Terrazzamenti e della Vite in the south of Piemonte.

Elsa Peralta is a Senior Lecturer in Anthropology at the Instituto Superior de Ciências Sociais e Políticas, Universidade Técnica de Lisboa. She co-organized the *First International Conference of Heritages and Identities* held in Lisbon in 2004 and is co-editor of the book *Patrimónios e Identidades: Ficções contemporâneas* and author of several chapters and articles in her research areas: culture and identity, heritage, tourism and museums, and history and memory. She is currently researching the construction of Portuguese national identity and is also interested in comparative national memories in Europe.

Llorenç Prats is a Professor of Social Anthropology at the University of Barcelona. He is specialized in heritage studies and has developed a theoretical model of analysis applied to the study of heritage as a social construction. He has written several books, chapters and papers on these matters and is currently a teacher of the Masters in Cultural Management and Heritage Management at the University of Barcelona.

Christopher Whitehead is Senior Lecturer in Museum, Gallery and Heritage Studies at Newcastle University, where he is Director of the International Centre for Cultural and Heritage Studies. His research activities focus on both historical and contemporary museology. He has published extensively in the field of art museum history, with particular emphases on architecture, display and knowledge construction – notably with his monographs *The Public Art Museum in 19th Century Britain* and *Museums and the Constructions of Disciplines*. His second major strand of activity relates to education and interpretation practices in art museums and galleries, and includes considerable government-funded and policy-relevant research.

Andrea Witcomb is an Associate Professor at Deakin University in Melbourne where she contributes to the work of the Cultural Heritage Centre for Asia and the Pacific and the Research Institute for Citizenship and Globalisation. Andrea is a former curator with a background in history and cultural studies. Her research interests range across interpretation issues in both heritage sites and museums. Since her first book, *Re-Imagining the Museum: Beyond the mausoleum* (2003), Andrea has become known for her work on contemporary approaches to interactivity in the museum context. More recently she has been working on a history of the National Trust of Australia (WA) as part of an Australia Research Council Grant in partnership with the National Trust. On the museum front she is increasingly interested in how museums are responding to the policy imperatives currently forming around discourses of social cohesion.

Acknowledgments

This volume was made possible due to the contribution and the involvement of many people. First, we would like to address a special note of thanks to Flora Kaplan and Eilean Hooper-Greenhill, editors of this Museum Meanings series, for challenging us to present this editorial project. Of course this result would not be possible without our contributors to whom we express our deepest regards for their prompt replies and for their continuous patience with the editors. We would like to thank them all: Zelda Baveystock, Anna Catalani, Gerard Corsane, Peter Davis, Eric Gable, Flora *Edouwaye* S. Kaplan, Sharon Macdonald, Rhiannon Mason, Barbara A. Misztal, Kate Moles, Donatella Murtas, Llorenç Prats, Christopher Whitehead and Andrea Witcomb. A special word for Kate Moles and Andrea Witcomb, who joined us in a very advanced stage of development. We would also like to thank our editors at Routledge: Matt Gibbons, Amy Laurens and especially, Lalle Purgslove. Finally, a word of recognition for our families, for their comprehension and support. And also for our students, always a true source of inspiration.

Introduction

The title of this book comes as no surprise as it is common sense now that heritage has everything to do with identity. This is a rather straightforward relationship and there seems to be no question about it. The problem arises when trying to understand what identity is. The chapters included in this volume make it rather clear that identity is an elusive concept. It comprises identification as it is something that aggregates people, no matter how different their individual selves may be. But identity is not just about inclusion. It is also about exclusion. In order to identify with some, people also need do dis-identify with someone else. This makes a point to Bateson's words when he insightfully stated that 'it takes at least two some-things to create a difference' (1978: 78). Therefore, identity is not just identification: it is also the meaning ascribed to similarity and difference. In this sense, identity also comes close to – and is often confused with – culture. However, identity and culture are not synonyms as identity also entails action: the action of making and being part of.

'Being part of' requires a narrative in which we locate ourselves and are located in. These narratives, which are seldom of our own making, are constituted through representation and performance, conveying not only who we are but also who we will come to be (Somers 1994). This is to say that who we are very much results from what we have selected from the past and chosen to retain in the present. These choices and selections, which most of the times are not consciously captured, are the outcome of an implicated and engaged social agency. Identity is therefore intimately related with politics and power relations that publicly assert particular versions of who we are and who we are not.

Identities, in order to be effective, have to have some kind of materiality: the totems that symbolize the solidarity felt by generations of heterogeneous individuals towards a unifying narrative of belonging. In this context, heritage provides a rather effective material and symbolic support for these narratives, both serving as a resource for the representation of identities and a place for its performance. Through heritage, people not only experience community; they simultaneously legitimize and consent to the agendas of its builders and caretakers. Heritage, in this sense, is closely linked with power and is an influential device in the construction of nation-states as well as in the identity politics led by multiple groups that are globally situated.

This is probably why heritage has become so epidemic: everyone has to have one (Howard 2003: 6). Given its potential as a form of objectifying identity, this heritage epidemic comes close to identity politics. Through this, all kinds of minorities and cultural particularities previously marginalized from dominant narratives try to publicly affirm their difference. This is not to say that these particular narratives have taken over the hegemonic versions or that they always provide an example of a counter-narrative. It simply means that these narratives have become increasingly negotiated and multivocal, challenging the unilinearity and universality of the modern self.

In contemporary societies, difference has become so overwhelming narrativized that we can no longer rely on totalizing fictions. The keywords now are fragmentation, ambivalence, diversity, multivocality. In this context, heritage is more concerned with issues of contestation and contradiction and less with single, unitary and stable views of the past. Today, heritage is not able to provide us with stable meanings; it instead expresses the fragmented identities present in the contemporary world. This leads to a permanent struggle for asserting difference. More than ever, heritage is a social and cultural arena where disputes concerning the affirmation of identities take place. As a consequence, conflict emerges as a prominent aspect of contemporary heritage.

All of these complex dynamics have resulted in an increasingly discredited heritage. The use and abuse of heritage has emptied it of its meaning and banalized the identities it stands for. The manifest instrumentalization of the past through heritage, as well as its commodification, has turned it into a trivial domain. Paradoxically, the struggles and claims for affirmation have resulted in indifferentiation, as heritage no longer stands out for making a difference. In order to be meaningful, heritage has to be based on a credible memory collectively sanctioned and approved. In this early twenty-first century, people need more than just a flag to identify with. They need more than a physical heritage; they urge for references that represent their collective soul. This entails both engagement and demission towards the past. As some of the chapters clearly show this is not necessarily a state-sponsored process. There are a number of examples of memory activation by the state that are not followed and incorporated. Some are purely ignored while others are bluntly rejected by its citizens. Therefore, the politics approach to memory does not account for all the complexity of these matters. Instead, meaning seems to be found at the core of a more comprehensive approach of the processes implicated in the public representation of the past. Choosing to remember certain aspects of the past, as well as choosing to discard and demise others, is an act of engagement with an identity project. This, of course, poses several important issues regarding the moral and ethical concerns associated with the display of the past in the public sphere. These concerns are, perhaps, the more relevant matters arising in a critical reflection about heritage and identity in the twenty-first century.

The book begins with contributions that are essentially about place and identity. Centred in different scales and presenting diverse scopes of analysis, Part I provides an ideal starting point to a critical discussion of the key issues concerning the relationship between heritage and identity in contemporary societies. The chapters included in Part I offer a broad contribution regarding the multiple mechanisms through which heritage is able to construct and represent a wide range of identities. Providing a deep and analytic account of the different empirical cases described, the authors present an extensive reflection on the growing significance of local, regional and national affiliations in an increasingly globalized world, revealing the dynamics associated with the selection and activation of cultural referents of the past and their links to present interests and purposes.

Rhiannon Mason and Zelda Baveystock introduce an interesting reflection regarding the role played by digital heritage in the process of re-imagining national identities. Focusing on the British context, with its inherent multiculturalism and multiple levels of identities and affiliations, the authors reflect upon the means by which heritage, particularly digital heritage, can foster social cohesion and help define different perceptions of national identities. While discussing the 'Icons of England' online project, Mason and Baveystock emphasize the importance of the inclusion of previously marginalized subjects and popular ideas on national heritage in the production of an inclusive discourse that emerges as a mechanism to deal with and negotiate change. The authors' analysis acknowledges that the growing differentiation in people's sense of national identity is especially noticeable between the constituent nations within the United Kingdom and among different ethnic groups who often present fragmented perceptions of shared identities. As people's sense of Britishness weakens, the affiliations and identifications at the ethnic and local levels experience a considerable growth, providing the setting for the increased political interest and the recognition of the need to publicly debate the matters of heritage and national identity.

Created with the purpose of encouraging people's awareness and uses of heritage, the ICONS project is quite revealing of the ways by which government policy intersects with heritage and populist ideas. The diverse contents of the site clearly illustrate the difficulties and challenges in representing the identity of a nation, giving evidence of the eclectic and fragmented meanings that coexist and of the contradictory nature of the criteria that define and assert value to heritage. In this sense, multivocality and dissonance, as well as engagement and demission, are the main features that arise from this online public debate, a debate that entails many different meanings about what is considered national heritage.

For Christopher Whitehead, the discussion of the relationship between heritage and identity is centred on the local level and through the lens of the display of art. Analysing the topic of display and the construction of place identity in art galleries, Whitehead addresses relevant issues concerning people's sense of place-belongingness, by studying a particular display, *Art on Tyneside*, held at the Laing Art Gallery (Tyne and Wear Museums). Making use of spatial qualities, characteristics of the local inhabitants, local culture, local history and social aspects of the relations between local people, the author explains how this exhibition promotes and reinforces a particular narrative of place identity that enables people to locate themselves in a specific context. Whitehead argues that these processes are especially significant in places that have experienced a rapid and dramatic transformation of the landscape, with inevitable consequences for the construction of both local and self identities. Offering us a deep analysis of a particular display, Whitehead demonstrates how the exhibition incorporates and articulates histories of art and local social histories in order to present a discourse of belonging, achievement and pride, in a clear example of engagement with the representation of a specific version of the past.

This effort to locate art within constructions of local community may be described as part of the identity politics of the region, acting as a counterpoint to the difficulties and negative experiences triggered by the economic and industrial decline of the last decades. By introducing Lübbe's view of the museum as a compensatory institution, Whitehead explains how the *Art on Tyneside* exhibition, developed at a difficult moment in the history of the city and of the region, emerges as a positive referent that represents the familiar within the space of an art gallery, appealing to people that normally do not visit museums or art galleries, fulfilling a moral purpose in the present.

Place identity and local belongingness are also the topics discussed by Gerard Corsane, Peter Davis and Donatella Murtas through the study of different ecomuseum approaches in Europe and Asia. Just as Whitehead, the authors locate this debate within the context of globalization, which sets the basis for the growing appreciation of local distinctiveness and for the development of sustainable heritage projects that enable communities to create and identify with their own sense of place. Presenting study cases located in France, Italy, China and Japan, the authors debate how ecomuseums, with their holistic approach and community focus, can influence and produce changes in local communities, altering their perceptions, values and attitudes towards heritage and cultural resources. Each of the examples presented reveals different strategies and approaches to deal with questions of local differentiation, affiliation and identity, which are profoundly influenced by the social agency of local actors and social forces. The protagonism held by individual figures, and the dynamic relationships that characterize local networks of partners, collaborators and stakeholders, combined with the singularities of each specific case, also help to explain how the different choices and proposals offered by these ecomuseums contribute to legitimize the agendas of heritage builders and caretakers. As in Whitehead's approach, the authors also emphasize the link between heritage projects and the regeneration of places that have experienced economic and social difficulties. This has resulted in attempts to rescue local cultural referents considered to be threatened by local and global change, which ultimately aim to provide a better understanding of sense of place and local identity through the display of a heritage narrative centred on local identity, local pride and local engagement.

Marta Anico's contribution explores the relations between the uses of the past and heritage and the construction of place identities in local contexts that, as in Whitehead's analysis, have been submitted to considerable social, cultural and economic changes. In modern Portugal, heritage has played a decisive role in the definition and assertion of cultural identities and has therefore become increasingly present in the definition of cultural policies at the different levels of political authority. Anico shows how this growing visibility of culture and heritage in Portuguese society reflects a global trend that has given rise to heritage activation processes which are enacted through different practices and displays. For Anico, the study of a municipal museum network enabled her to illustrate the adjustments made by local cultural institutions to their changing surroundings, arguing that local heritage and local museums have become central to local political agendas due to their ability to define and celebrate the cultural identities of the different social groups present in these places.

The implications of globalization and the dramatic changes observed in this municipality of Loures over the last four decades have given a sense of urgency to the drive to capture and preserve the essence of traditional local communities, expressing a retrospective nostalgia in relation to a primordial past. However, it is interesting to note that this impulse to preserve the past is also accompanied by the urge to include the present. Anico's chapter shows how the same museums that celebrate endogamic identity narratives have also made considerable efforts to represent the different ethnic and social identities that coexist in their cultural landscape, in order to promote an effective and intercultural dialogue and the inclusion of diverse cultures in museums' displays and practices. Nevertheless, this balance between different meanings regarding culture, heritage and identities is difficult to achieve, and finally leads to dissonant perceptions of these cultural institutions, locally interpreted as being both identity bunkers and cultural forums.

This first section ends with a comprehensive theoretical insight provided by the Catalonian anthropologist Llorenç Prats with a discussion of the concept of heritage as a socio-cultural construction. The aim of this chapter is to reflect upon the ways by which heritage provides a means of establishing, sustaining and reforming a wide range of political and territorial identities. Prats discusses both the production of heritage and that of identity, pointing out the social dynamics that surround these processes. As argued by Flora Kaplan in Part II of this volume, Prats also defends heritage and identity as social arenas where political, economic and social issues are played out. Therefore, a discussion concerning heritage cannot work without a discussion on power and the different interests and purposes present in each specific context of analysis.

Prats looks at the modern concept of heritage as a social and ideological construction that has the ability to produce a symbolic connection to certain objects, places and realities based on their evocative power. Heritage is therefore an abstract construct that we seek to make real through activation processes that generate discourses of identity and belongingness. By giving examples of objects, sites and cultural manifestations, Llorenç Prats debates the power of these symbols to represent specific ideologies such as national, regional and local identities. Furthermore, discussion of the different interests associated with heritage activation processes is another central feature of his approach. According to this theoretical model, political authorities, experts in heritage management, the tourist sector and the general population are the main forces implicated in the social construction of heritage. Of course not all of these forces are driven by the same goals and purposes, and Prats clearly demonstrates how it is possible for them to coexist in a multivocal narrative without becoming overtly disruptive and dissonant.

The 'where' question is the most obvious one as heritage and identity are always inscribed in (or refer to) places. But as the embodiment of publicly selected memories that anchor identities in the past, heritage also concerns time. Part II of the book, 'Remembering and forgetting', brings out important questions on the way heritage simultaneously preserves and discards past events, constantly reshaping them in the present. Heritage is not the original event in the way it has occurred in the past; it is instead a representation of it. By this act of representation, which entails both remembering and forgetting, identities are asserted. Remembrance is a way of reaffirming an identity; forgetfulness is a way of sustaining it. This is, nonetheless, a troubling issue, posing several puzzling questions on the nature and value of both remembering and forgetting as well as on its importance in the creation of shared identities. Do we want to forget? Can we forget? Is there a need to remember? Should we remember? The answers to these questions are not straightforward as they very much depend on the context as the chapters included in Part II clearly show. However, taken together, these contributions offer an insightful reflection on matters such as the morality of the past – and of its representation in the present – and on the nature of heritage itself in this early twenty-first century.

Part II develops from Sharon Macdonald's remark that heritage has become a contested field, giving heed to the increasing unsettling of memories, narratives and heritage. Looking at two heritage controversies – the proposal to turn a major Nazi building into a shopping and leisure centre in Nuremberg, Germany, and the public display of the items found on a shipwreck implicated in transatlantic slavery in the United States – Macdonald shows how different visions over the same past can overlap and collide in one heritage site, as more and more groups seek for inclusion in the public space. Drawing from the theoretical insights of the Manchester School of Anthropology, controversies are viewed by the author as social dramas that instead of being disjunctive are rather productive interventions in a changing public sphere. Articulating power relations and poetics in social action, these controversies challenge the perceived forgetting and put 'difficult heritage' on the public agenda, when previous plans seemed to otherwise have eclipsed these uncomfortable histories. In the cases presented by Sharon Macdonald the eclipsing of the past is motivated mainly by commercial interests that seem to be above all ethics, contributing to the increasing discredit of heritage and putting it in the heart of a larger debate about commodification in the contemporary world. In this sense, these unsettlements can also be seen as a way of conferring a renewed ethical space to heritage, one that entrenches the representation of the past in moral imperatives. As Macdonald insightfully notes, 'it became no longer possible to simply forget the past', and this poses important theoretical challenges to the way we reflect upon heritage.

Elsa Peralta's contribution addresses more closely the question of forgetting as a collective act constitutive of a new identity when previous narratives seem to have collapsed. Drawing on field research conducted in a local heritage complex built upon maritime memories – cod fisheries – this chapter looks at the ways in which communities engage in forgetting not as a form of oblivion but rather as a way to cope with disruptive transformations. In fact, the representation of these fisheries only entered the public sphere when the whole activity was collapsing and when the locality was experiencing great social and economic transformations. Both at national and local level, cod fisheries were of great importance and their disappearance was not without some trauma. Moreover, this was an economic activity largely associated with Salazar's regime – the dictatorship that ruled Portugal for almost 40 years until 1974 – and, as such, had several ideological implications. Nonetheless, its representation in the public sphere is one of harmony and cohesion, leaving the ideological aspects behind. The social abyss that stood between captains and fishermen, as well as the inhumane conditions that the latter had to face are ostensibly forgotten in the public arena, perpetuating the past of those that occupied privileged positions in these fisheries. Elsa Peralta's argument is that these public silences are largely motivated by private voices that engage in order to be heard publicly, asserting their own identity versions. Despite this, evidence also shows that the private sphere and everyday life's accounts keep alternatives to the mainstream memory. However, these residual accounts do not operate as resistant strains against official and public versions of the past. These are just private voices that are kept private, as they do not engage in any kind of agency in order to assert an alternative version of the past in the public sphere. In this sense, public silences are consenting silences revealing a sort of amnesty towards the less pleasant aspects of the past and a way of denying the entry of its disruptive aspects into the social life.

Barbara Misztal's chapter goes deeper in analysing the social functions of remembering and forgetting, arguing that it is necessary to study both mechanisms of constructing the past. Starting from a critical review of the main theoretical perspectives on the role of social remembering and social forgetting, establishing important connections with the issues of justice, democracy and freedom, the chapter focuses mainly on memory in postcommunist Poland. Like Macdonald's account on the unsettling Nazi past, this contribution also points out the recent fascination with historical traumatic memories and with war guilt. In Poland, like in other postcommunist countries, there has been an institutionalized effort to restore the 'truth' about the communist past and to fill in the 'blank spots' that the previous communist regime had engendered about Polish history. However, just as before, in the newly established democracy some of these 'blank spots' – such as Polish anti-Semitism during the Second World War – were still not openly addressed. On the contrary, Polish postcommunist memory politics focused mainly on the restitution of truth about the communist past. As during the communist rule, the image of Poland that is again reified is one of heroism and victimhood, adding nothing new to the process of formation of new post-communist identities. As such, the debate over the communist past was ultimately banalized as most of the Poles consider it to lack any social significance. A new round of debates over the Polish past and Polish national identity was, however, inaugurated with the publication of Gross's book *Neighbors* about the Jedwabne massacre during World War II when a Polish community murdered nearly its entire Polish Jewish community. Misztal argues that the confrontation with the guilt and

7

shame of these events has caused an identity crisis and a great amount of political contestation in Poland, as it is this heritage of anti-Semitism, not the communist past, that disrupts the prevalent *ethos* of suffering and heroism in which Polish
national identity has been constructed for a long time. As in Peralta's chapter,
there are several issues here that concern a critical appreciation of the moral value
of the past in a context of great change and transformation where there is a need
for the construction of new identities.

Concluding Part II, Kate Moles reminds us again that remembering and forgetting
are not opposites. Contemplating the 'landscape of memory' – that is, the 'different topological, cultural and material monuments, events, people, words, stories
and meanings that come together to construct a particular place' – of Phoenix
Park, Dublin, Moles considers issues of national identity and heritage while also
bearing in mind that the shared national memories are always intertwined with
more personal accounts of the past. Drawing upon a three-year ethnography of the
area, Moles addresses these matters with two quite different examples of important events that took place in the park: namely the Papal Visit in 1979 and the
Phoenix Park Murders that occurred in 1882 as a result of a political clash. Both
of these events have left a physical mark on the park's landscape, despite the mark
of the latter being much less impressive than the one of the former. While the
Papal Visit seems to be actively remembered and easily integrated in the national
narrative, as it was a clear demonstration of cohesion and national unity, the
Murders seem on the contrary to be actively forgotten, at least by official accounts.
In the first case, the author shows that side by side with the official discourse there
are personal accounts that reveal both the integration of the dominant discourse
in personal memories and the influence of the mundane realities of everyday life
in the personal shaping of the past. In a different sense, the second example also
reveals the importance of personal trajectories in the meaning that is attributed to
the past. Being a polemic issue in Ireland's history, there are no official memorials devoted to the Murders in the place. Nonetheless, there are many different personal memories about this event, some of them standing in sharp contrast with
each other. There are in fact, as Moles shows, different layers of meaning in what
concerns memory. This gives evidence to the fact that memory cannot be totally
conventionalized by official narratives, as more personal imaginaries also account
for the way past events are remembered. In this sense, one important issue that
arises from all the chapters included in Part II is that of the inadvertent understandings of the past that arise beneath the official and purposeful memory discourses.

Despite being about legitimation – or maybe because of it – heritage is always a
contested field. Part III, 'Domination and contestation', and ends the volume with
a focus on the way heritage, as well as the identities it represents, is at all times
open to social revision and manipulation, operating under the pressures of challenges and attitudes of the present. Heritage always represents one linear unifying past and usually publicly enacts the vision and the interests of the ones that
have dominant positions in society. Nonetheless, sometimes the past that is represented through heritage does not convey the sense of past held by common people or by other interest groups that endlessly struggle to assert their own version
of the past. Being the product of collective agency, heritage sites are places where

identities contradict, revealing a tension between multiple political agendas and more personal aspirations. The chapters included in Part III give evidence of the transient and dynamic nature of heritage, as the past it represents and remembers is always open to contestation.

Part III opens with Eric Gable's wonderful ethnographic account on the way Monticello – a site representing the slave era and usually referred to as the home of Thomas Jefferson – produces national identity in the United States. The chapter starts with an insightful reflection about overlapping and misleading concepts such as identity and culture, stressing the importance of engagement with a common and shared past to the formation and maintenance of national identities. In a multiracial nation like the United States, the problem arises when trying to ascribe a common and shared past to a diverse and unequal society that was already diverse and unequal in the past. Giving evidence of the routines of identification that take place in Monticello, Gable notes that former and prevailing racial differences and class distinctions continue to pose identity problems. In spite of the efforts made by the staff to construct a more inclusive discourse towards African-Americans, the truth is that few Blacks visit the place. This happens, the author suggests, because despite intending to be an inclusive site and an arena of national identification, Monticello inadvertently is a white identity shrine, publicly conveying his-story (of Jefferson and white masters) instead of a shared history. This is, Gable argues, a race problem not a class one, because class distinctions are rooted in whiteness. Although there is not open contestation to the site and to what it represents in American history, there is nevertheless a demission from the identification it supposedly enacts. Memory, thus, can defy the exclusions and omissions of history itself.

Flora Kaplan's chapter makes it quite clear that we live in a world of competing cultural identities and agendas and as such heritage is more than ever opened up to revision and contestation. Focusing on postcolonial Nigeria where governments strive to unify the many competing ethnic groups that challenge the new nation's identity, Flora Kaplan's analysis is centred in the ancient city walls of the former Benin kingdom, a site listed among the 100 Most Endangered Sites by the World Monuments Fund. In a context where people have to struggle daily in order to survive, preservation and cultural heritage are not priorities. Moreover, despite the efforts made by the national museum system to integrate and represent Nigeria's ethnic groups and to create an all-encompassing national narrative, ethnicity and more recently religion seem to be more appealing for identitary purposes than nationality. As a result, the different factions that coexist in the territory do not seem to be the least interested in those elements that represent the nation's cultural identity and history. Instead, there is a will to demise Benin's ancient traditions and belief systems, which are equated in negative terms. Paradoxically, the ones that continue to support and identify with Benin and publicly assert its history and cultural unity are those long-time expatriates that live abroad, especially in the United States.

Change is also crucial in Andrea Witcomb's contribution. This chapter makes it quite apparent that the value attributed to the past, as well as the way we relate to it, largely depends on present concerns and agendas. Focusing on Western Australia, Andrea Witcomb looks at the National Trust of Australia's involvement in two quite different heritage battles: the battle for the Barracks Arch and the battle for the Burrup Peninsula. These battles took place at different moments of time and thus express different agendas and different ways to relate to the past. In the Barracks case, a site built by convicts in 1863 that once housed pensioner guards, what is at stake is the preservation of a major landmark of the city of Perth and a symbol of national identity, as the building is closely associated with the first development of the colony and with the initial settlement period. When the government manifested its intention to demolish it to build a freeway, the Trust immediately advocated for its preservation, initiating a public campaign in order to mobilize public opinion and civic participation. The battle against the government was ultimately won due to the lobbying exerted by the Trust, but mainly as a result of the engagement of the citizens of Perth in this process. This case occurred in the 1960s. The past that was debated and conflicted here was a white past. Later, in the 1990s and early 2000s, the Trust engaged again in a fight against the government's ongoing participation in destroying the Aboriginal heritage situated in the Burrup Peninsula, Western Australia, due to economic and development interests. The Trust's involvement in the fight to stop industrial development in the peninsula and thus preserve what is left of that heritage also expresses a progressive political attitude towards the Aboriginal people. If in the former case what it meant to be Australian was to be white, in the Burrup case what it means to be Australian includes Aboriginal people. In both cases, the chapter stresses the way the Trust facilitated citizens' involvement in the struggles for the preservation of sites against dominant development ideology led by the government. Heritage, as Andrea Witcomb notes, 'had become a right' and a place of engaged citizenship.

These questions regarding heritage as a civil right are also present in Anna Catalani's discussion of the representation of the cultures ethnic minorities in Western museums. Anna Catalani's reflection on ethnic pride and artistic representations in Western museums poses interesting questions regarding the nature of the culture clashes that may arise when different cultures and societies become in contact. Drawing on her PhD research conducted with the Yòrubá communities living in Leicester and Nottingham, Catalani approaches matters such as the historical and social changes that have occurred in the interpretation of non-Western objects, and the perceptions of the Yòrubá people towards their ethnic identity and the display of their material culture in Western museums. The author situates these reflections within the broader context of postcolonial societies, presenting evidence of the ways by which museums have been involved in the construction and display of social, cultural and economic ideologies, focusing specifically on the idea of 'Africans' and 'African cultures'. Depicted as centres of colonial policy and promoters of imperialist interests in the nineteen and early twentieth centuries, museums have changed their own identity and redefined their mission as a means to enhance and celebrate cultural diversity. Catalani demonstrates how this change has resulted in considerable efforts to actively engage the communities represented through the establishment of a more interactive and cooperative dialogue. These changes also explain how African material cultures have shifted from the category of ethnography to that of art. However, there is evidence of a clear dissonance between museum representations and the communities' perceptions, values and attitudes towards the specimens of their material culture. The members of the Yòrubá diaspora in Britain show an increased and stronger sense of communal identity, asserted by a feeling of ethnic pride that can be observed in their relation regarding the cultural objects displayed in British Museums. Nevertheless, this is an uneasy relationship due to the inconsistency between the ways the Yòrubá see and feel these objects, and the ways they are presented in museums, which raises important moral and ethical issues concerning museums' cultural authority and authorship.

This chapter, as well as the previous contributions, shows evidence of a new status for heritage, one that poses important critical and theoretical reflections. Heritage in the contemporary world incorporates different layers of meaning, which give way to new forms of engagement – and demission – depending on how people, as in the Yòrubá case, see and feel their heritage.

Bibliography

Bateson, G. (1978) *Steps to an Ecology of Mind*. New York: Bantam.

Howard, P. (2003) *Heritage: Management, interpretation, identity*. London: Continuum.

Somers, M. (1994) 'The narrative constitution of identity: A relational and network approach', *Theory and Society*, 23(5): 605–49.

Part I

Place and identity

What role can digital heritage play in the re-imagining of national identities?: England and its icons

Rhiannon Mason and Zelda Baveystock

> So let me be equally blunt in my challenge to the heritage sector: if you are not part of the solution to this crisis of Britishness, you are part of the problem.
>
> (Lammy 2005)

> Heritage is not an artifact or site. It is a process that uses objects and sites as vehicles for the transmission of ideas in order to satisfy various contemporary needs. It is a medium of communication, a means of transmission of ideas and values and a knowledge that includes the material, the intangible and the virtual. Heritage is a product of the present yet drawing upon an assumed imaginary past and an equally assumed imaginary future.
>
> (Ashworth 2007: 2)

'Heritage' is increasingly invoked in Britain by politicians and policy-makers as one means of repositioning British national identity to foster social cohesion. The first quotation, for example, is drawn from a speech in 2005 by David Lammy, MP, who was at that time Minister for Culture in the British Government's Department for Culture, Media and Sport (DCMS). The speech, entitled 'Where now for Britain's shared heritage?', was delivered in an event hosted by the Heritage Lottery Fund at the British Museum. This chapter will explore how heritage is being defined within such contexts, and being deployed as a resource for reframing relationships between identities and nations. We will discuss both 'Britain' and 'England' in recognition of their continual conflation and interdependence. The study will also explore Ashworth's argument that heritage can be understood as a 'medium of communication' which draws upon not only the material and intangible but also the virtual 'in order to satisfy various contemporary needs' (2007: 2).

This study is premised on the idea that 'national heritage' is enlisted as part of the process of 'governmentality' and the first section examines this in the current British context. The second section outlines recent research findings which suggest changes in perceptions of national identities in Britain and the relevance of this for heritage. The final section considers the 'ICONS of England' online project and what it reveals about the way that governmental discourses intersect with the wider heritage sector and populist discourses.

By examining a selection of so-called icons of Englishness from the site, we argue that this example of contemporary digital heritage illustrates some of the conflicting responses invoked by the process of defining Englishness and how these definitions continually refer back to ideas of Britishness. The process of redefining Englishness is, we argue, an essential step in the diversification of public notions of national heritage and of collective identity. This process is as important as the inclusion of previously marginalized groups and identities into the 'national historical narrative'. We conclude that this website offers an alternative forum in which the central suppositions underpinning England's and Britain's national heritage can be problematized and unpicked. At the same time, we identify certain problems relating to the medium and its ability to generate an effective dialogue about national heritage.

Before looking at the case study, it is useful to revisit some pertinent themes in recent literature. Heritage can be defined in numerous ways (Graham and Howard 2008). At its simplest, it 'can be defined as properties and artifacts of cultural importance handed down from the past' (United Kingdom's DCMS website). At its broadest, Lord Charteris of Amisfield, as Chair of the National Heritage Memorial Fund, stated that 'heritage is anything you want' (quoted in Hewison 1987: 32). Laurajane Smith has argued that 'there is, really, no such thing as heritage' (2006: 11). Smith's point is that nothing is inherently 'heritage'; 'there is rather a hegemonic discourse about heritage, which acts to constitute the way we think, talk and write about heritage' (2006: 11). As Smith argues, the process of identifying, recognizing and managing heritage is always political, partial and contested. Ashworth and Graham use the term 'dissonant heritage' to refer 'to the discordance of lack of agreement and consistency as to the meaning of heritage' (2005: 5).

Heritage is dissonant because it is always held in tension between the competing pull of the universal and the particular, the collective and the individual (Ashworth and Graham 2005). While much attention focuses on the official and institutional aspect of heritage, its personal appeal is equally powerful. Bella Dicks attributes the popularity of what she terms 'vernacular heritage' to its personal dimension and its ability to enable individuals to situate their sense of identity and past within a collective memory. Heritage 'provides a means of appreciating the intersection between individual biographies and wider social and cultural changes' (2003: 126). Dicks sees this as symptomatic of a broader shift towards the 'diffusion of an identity-centered relationship with the past' (2003: 125). This understanding of heritage as a process and a mechanism for negotiating change is shared by Smith (2006: 308).

Although interest in heritage can be seen as a reaction to change, gaining acceptance of alternative definitions of heritage is often contested. This is especially so where they conflict with what Smith calls the 'authorized heritage discourse': the official and publicly sanctioned – hegemonic – discourses of heritage. Like Smith, Stuart Hall has long drawn attention to the operation of hegemony in relation to what he terms 'The Heritage' particularly around the lack of representation of race and empire in Britain's 'national story' (2005).

National heritage, in this sense, is part of what Bennett has termed the 'public cultural and historical sphere' (quoted in Karp *et al.* 2006: 9). As part of the public cultural and historical sphere, national heritage is enlisted as part of the process not just of government but of 'governmentality'. Hall describes this as 'how the state indirectly and at a distance induces and solicits appropriate attitudes and forms of conduct from its citizens' (2005: 24). It is in this sense that we can read Ashworth and Graham's observation that 'heritage is simultaneously knowledge, a cultural product and a political resource' (2005: 8).

Although national heritage can be seen as both constituted and enlisted by processes of governmentality, like the idea of 'the nation', it is equally 'flagged' and materialized through 'banal' everyday, unofficial practices, customs, and habits (Billig 1995; Palmer 1998). For example, it is notable that people's use of the English flag at sporting events has increased in recent years alongside calls for the official promotion of St George's day as a day of national celebration. The point here is that heritage is constructed at an individual, personal and everyday level and is as much to do with immediate social groups and family context as with larger national frameworks and public, institutional practices. Indeed, Ashworth and Graham caution against overstating the hegemonic dominance of 'official heritage' particularly in relation to ideas of identity and sense of place. They argue that 'the peoples, the identities, the images and the purposes are just all too plural to be reduced simplistically in this way' (2005: 4).

National heritage in the British context

Many of these issues can be seen in debates about Britain's and England's national heritage and identity particularly in recent years. The creation since 1999 of separate, semi-autonomous, devolved political bodies in Scotland, Wales and Northern Ireland has brought about many changes in the areas of politics, media, education and health, and the cultural and heritage sectors in the various countries of the United Kingdom (Mason 2007). In particular, it has problematized the position of England in the United Kingdom's parliamentary system and is testing the bonds of the Union especially in relation to the independence movement in Scotland. In 2007, Gordon Brown, a Scottish MP, became Prime Minister and head of the UK Government in Westminster. The year 2007 also marked the three hundredth anniversary of the Act of Union which joined the Kingdoms of Scotland and England into the United Kingdom of Great Britain.

Brown is a strong advocate of the Union and has given many speeches promoting the concept of Britishness and outlining what he sees to be British values. He has defined these as 'British tolerance, the British belief in liberty and the British sense of fair play' (speech at the Commonwealth Club, 27 February 2007) and 'hard work, doing your duty and always trying to do the right thing' (Labour Party Conference, 24 September 2007). In January 2006, Brown proposed the idea of a national British day to mark 'shared common values' and to be 'a celebration of who we are and what we stand for' (speech at the Fabian Society Conference, 14 January 2006).

National identity is also currently high on the political agenda because of concerns over domestic security and social cohesion, particularly following the bombings by home-grown terrorists in London in July 2005 and the attack on Glasgow airport in 2007. Although recent events have heightened concerns, multiculturalism has been a topical issue for some time; for example, since riots broke out in 2001 in the northern English towns of Oldham, Burnley and Bradford. In September 2005, the chair of the Commission for Racial Equality, Trevor Phillips, triggered public debate by claiming that Britain was 'sleepwalking our way to segregation' (Phillips 2005). Phillips argued that policy had overemphasized differences between ethnic groups at the expense of their commonalities, although this is disputed by others (Modood 2005). Debates have been further underscored by changing patterns of immigration to Britain since the expansion of the EU membership in 2004 and 2007 to include 12 additional nations, principally in Eastern Europe (Vertovec 2006).

Shifting loyalties

A raft of studies by policy bodies and think-tanks suggest that Britishness generally may be in decline or in transition, with growing differentiation between people's sense of national identity in the United Kingdom's constituent nations and amongst different ethnic groups (ETHNOS 2005; NatCen 2007; Stone and Muir 2007). The reports suggest a growing identification with Englishness and Stone and Muir warned that this was frequently defined in a narrow, ethnic way rather than a more civic, inclusive fashion, albeit identification varied according to class, generation and educational background. A report on diversity and citizenship in relation to the English school curriculum found much confusion and negativity surrounding ideas of British and English national identity and heritage; it identified this as a central barrier to the promotion of diversity and citizenship (DfES 2007: 30).

Stone and Muir's report further argued that there had been an increase in people's sense of identification at the most local level – their locality or town (56 per cent) – as opposed to the national (25 per cent) across all generations (2007: 13). It reported a shift towards defining Britishness in terms of values such as free speech, justice and tolerance and less with state public figures and traditional institutions, with the exception of the BBC and the National Health Service.

This discursive shift correlates with Brown's attempt to redefine and promote Britishness as a set of values. Despite this, the overall findings suggest that those wishing to reinvigorate public enthusiasm for Britishness 'will have to reverse a current trend and that their endeavors will not be equally well received in different parts of the UK' (Stone and Muir 2007: 10). A study into constitutional change and identity, which examined attitudes held by Scottish and English people living in Scotland, concurred that '[t]here remains substantial evidence that British nationals, let alone newcomers, do not have much shared understanding of the term' (Bechhofer *et al.* 2006).

Most of these reports focused on Britishness but all inevitably discussed Englishness because national identity can only be understood relationally. This is particularly acute in the case of England because the distinction between Britishness and Englishness is less clearly articulated than with Scottishness or Welshness and Britishness. By contrast, some historians have cautioned against overstating this apparent 'identity-crisis' by pointing to a long precedent of complex and multiple identities within Britain's constituent nations (Kenny *et al.* 2008). Notwithstanding this, the evidence above suggests a convergence of factors which is currently intensifying public and political concern about national identity and national heritage in the United Kingdom.

National heritage and social cohesion

Against this backdrop, David Lammy's challenge to the heritage sector that 'if you are not part of the solution to this crisis of Britishness, you are part of the problem' assumes its full resonance (2005). During his time as Minister for Culture (2005–2007), Lammy spoke widely about Britishness, empire, race, slavery, black and minority heritage and social cohesion. His speeches often draw on his own experiences as British-born, growing up in Tottenham, London, with parents who were 1950s' migrants from the former British colony of Guyana. He also speaks about his experiences of talking to different ethnic groups within Britain about their own sense of heritage and is explicit about the link between heritage and national identity.

> Heritage comes from the same root as inheritance. It's about what we want to pass on to future generations. Our responsibility for heritage extends not just to the preservation of ancient bricks and mortar but to the custodianship of a legacy of ideas about Britain and Britishness.
>
> (Lammy 2005)

While Lammy brings a particularly personal note to the subject, previous holders of this post have been equally quick to promote Britain's diversity (Smith 1998). Indeed, concerns over multiculturalism and national heritage precede the current debates by at least three decades (Littler and Naidoo 2005: 15). From the 1990s, in particular, a number of reports have increased awareness of structural differences between the perceptions and experiences of Britain's heritage held by different groups of visitors and non-visitors along lines of race and ethnicity (Desai and Thomas 1998). The results are too numerous to cover here but it is fair to say that there have been many initiatives which have addressed cultural diversity in the UK museum context, prompting organizations, particularly those with public funding, to review their collections, exhibitions, marketing, audiences, recruitment and workforce training.

This activity has produced commendable results. However, much of the activity around diversity and heritage so far has been about diversifying the national story by attempting to include those previously marginalized. While evidently a necessary step, if the core is left unchallenged, the centre/periphery hierarchy remains intact. Stuart Hall, for example, has argued that

> the majority, mainstream versions of the Heritage should revise their own self-conceptions and rewrite the margins into the center, the outside into the inside. This is not so much a matter of representing 'us' as of representing more adequately the degree to which 'their' history entails and has always implicated 'us' across the centuries, and vice versa. . . . The first task, then, is re-defining the nation, reimagining 'Britishness' or 'Englishness' itself in a more profoundly inclusive manner.
>
> (Hall 2005: 31)

Re-imagining 'England's heritage' online: Displaying dissonance

Recognition of the need to profile these debates publicly has motivated some large-scale projects. One of these is the ICONS of England website (www.icons.org.uk), on which members of the public can nominate, comment on and vote for items perceived to be symbolic of England's national heritage. Given its participatory nature and its attempt to question mainstream ideas of Englishness, it represents a particularly apt way to examine competing discourses surrounding national heritage. It also illustrates the continual slippage between Britishness and Englishness even on a site explicitly designated to be about England.

Clearly, the representativeness of ICONS should not be overstated. Methodologically, many of the same issues which pertain to the analysis of museum-visitor books apply (Macdonald 2003). Contributors will be self-selecting while many users will visit but never post a comment. Some visitors/users may come from cultural backgrounds which inhibit their inclination to contribute and the use of websites requires a certain amount of cultural capital, technological resources and web literacy, all of which relate to levels of income and education. As is so often the case in visitor books, comments will arise in response to other, comments so that particular threads will be foregrounded and other, potentially relevant points may be neglected. This issue is particularly pertinent in the case of this website, which is specifically organized around the principle that users should read and respond to other people's comments. Despite the need for caution, we consider this website worthy of study as it so clearly illustrates many of the debates outlined above and because it offers a rare opportunity to see the processes of 'heritage-making' made public.

ICONS was initially envisaged as an online collection of 'England's most cherished cultural treasures' (Culture Online 2007), and in this way could potentially be viewed as a digital museum of England. In 2007, it promoted itself as 'a living portrait of a country, a people and a way of life'. ICONS was commissioned as a £1.1 million flagship project by Culture Online, a DCMS initiative which funded projects in England only. From the outset the ICONS Advisory Board discussed whether the site should become ICONS of Britain and not just of England, but found itself restricted by the funding arrangements (Minutes of 13 October 2005).

The ICONS of England project is interesting for what it reveals about the way that government policy intersects with both the heritage sector and populist discourses. Culture Online was launched by DCMS in 2000 with the aim of building engagement with arts and culture through technology, with a particular emphasis on working with 'hard-to-reach' groups. ICONS thus originally had the dual aims of encouraging awareness and use of real heritage sites, including museums and galleries, alongside a technological agenda to increase web literacy. However, importance was also placed on the interactive and collaborative potential of the Internet; the site was intended to create an open forum in which discussions on the nature of contemporary Englishness could be played out and debated.

How ICONS works

The website operates on several levels. There are nominations for icons posted (and commented on) by members of the public, celebrities or specific institutional partners such as the National Trust or English Heritage, and then a 'top tier' of nominations which have been agreed by the Advisory Board to be an approved part of the ICONS 'collection'. These 'approved' ICONS contain extended web content, including associated historical and contextual information, suggestions for places to visit, games, lesson plans, curriculum links and further resources. The weighting of the website in its first 18 months of operation (from January 2006) was thus unequally balanced between the approved collection of less than 100 icons, and 1,165 would-be icons-in-waiting. While the editorial and moderation processes of the site will be the subject of further research (the 1,165 nominations listed were in themselves selected from nearly 8,000 nominations received in all – see Holden 2007), the site can be seen to reflect both the processes of heritage authorization from the 'top down' and the dissonant nature of heritage 'in the making'.

The extent and variety of content on the site illustrates the diversity of reactions to this challenge of representing a nation iconographically. The site does not attempt to segment or disaggregate the ICONS into categories. We have therefore drawn on a study conducted by ETHNOS into *Citizenship and Belonging* which set out to categorize popular responses to the question 'What is Britishness?' into eight 'dimensions' (2005: 6). We have utilized these dimensions to loosely group what is seen to represent England and Englishness as articulated on the ICONS site. A brief outline of the categories follows, with examples of some approved icons, to indicate the project's scope. Readers not familiar with British history and culture may find it helpful to consult the detailed explanations of each icon on the website. We have also anonymized respondents while indicating their locality as provided on the website:

- *Geography*: Landscape and topography feature strongly in both the approved and unapproved icons, with the former including the Peak and the Lake Districts, the White Cliffs of Dover and the Thames. Given the underlying aim to encourage visitation of cultural heritage sites, there is also a strong emphasis on traditional-built heritage: from Stonehenge to Blackpool Tower. Some content is generic rather than specific: the hedge, the parish church, the pub and the phone box.

- *National symbols*: These include the flag of St George, the oak tree, the rose, the bobby (policeman), the bowler hat, the robin and the V-sign.

- *People*: The ICONS Advisory Board took the decision that people would be expressly excluded from the site, 'so that current day pop stars did not skew the vote' (Minutes of 13 October 2005). However, mythical and literary figures such as Robin Hood, Doctor Who, Sherlock Holmes and Alice in Wonderland are all featured.

- *Values and attitudes*: Only one English value – the stiff upper lip – makes it onto the approved list. Unapproved nominations also include good manners, a sense of humour, working too hard and queuing. However, it is arguable that the underlying significance of many ICONS is their partial representation of other English values or attitudes: for example, Monty Python is commended as 'the supreme expression of English eccentricity' (comment posted by R1 from Australia).

- *Language*: The English language is represented by the *Oxford English Dictionary*.

- *Cultural habits and behaviour*: Aside from geography, this is possibly the largest category of nominations, ranging through various sports (cricket, rugby, Wimbledon and the FA Cup) to food and drink (cheddar cheese, cup of tea, fish and chips, the pint, roast beef and Yorkshire pudding) to cultural practices such as fox hunting and Morris dancing.

- *Achievements*: Technological, scientific, literary and creative achievements include specific works, like the *Origin of Species*, *Pride and Prejudice* and the Lindisfarne Gospels; works of art (the Haywain and Holbein's portrait of Henry VIII); inventions and industrial designs (the Spitfire, the Mini, the Rolls Royce); and popular songs (*Jerusalem* and *Sergeant Pepper's Lonely Hearts Club Band*). Also symbols of particular eras in English history, for example, the Domesday Book and Magna Carta.

Problematizing national heritage

The apparent randomness of this eclectic list supports the initial discussion of heritage. It reinforces the comments of both Lord Charteris and Laurajane Smith in that heritage can be whatever people choose to identify as such, and anything has the potential to become heritage if it is identified and sufficiently acknowledged as heritage in a publicly recognized forum. It is also an unusually explicit example of 'heritage in the making' and the authorizing of national heritage. The nomination process operates to sift and shift (or not in some cases) the icons from the status of personal choice to publicly sanctioned national heritage through a double mechanism of individual, public user-voting and collective, private committee selection.

There is further evidence of an 'authorized heritage discourse' at work, in particular with the extensive amount of traditional-built heritage vying for position in the nominated listings. In this section of the site it appears every professional heritage manager, marketer or supporters' group in the country has nominated their own site, monument or museum. The approval of only a limited number of these may point to an English spirit of fair play, but is more likely to be a deliberate (and deliberated) attempt by the Board to ensure an even geographical distribution in the collection.

This is evidenced most clearly in the 'ICONS Atlas' section of the site where stylized pictorial icons are depicted on a map of England divided into its regions. Stonehenge thus stands for the south-west, the Angel of the North for the north-east and Blackpool Tower for the north-west. Cornwall is represented by the Eden Project, a highly successful ecological visitor attraction opened in 2001 as a means of regenerating a former clay pit. Eden is architecturally and technologically innovative, but its inclusion appears to point most closely to the original aims of the project to promote 'take-up' of official cultural resources from both local residents and tourists. The heritage-as-tourism dimension is reinforced by subsequent levels of information offered via the 'Atlas'. If users click on each region on the map they are led to a list of standard museums, galleries, heritage sites and visitor experiences, only some of which are directly or tangentially related to other ICONS.

In this way, the site acts as a portal to the official heritage sector and tourist industry exemplifying how national heritage is invariably bound up with tourism. This means that the site addresses many different 'publics' simultaneously. The mix of official/collective and unofficial/personal heritage again refers back to issues raised earlier, namely that heritage continually blurs boundaries of public and private, official and unofficial, state and personal, collective and individual, institutionalized and informal. This is arguably always the case but is particularly explicit in the Web 2.0 context.

Amongst users' comments, most frequent debate is elicited on the definitions of Britishness and Englishness. Many of the examples above are argued by contributors to be the former rather than the latter. Other contributors perpetuate the elision of the terms by positively affirming icons as typically British (rather than English), without apparently realizing this is not the overall purpose of the site. These tensions are apparent throughout, but are particularly noticeable in some of the choices of the historic environment. London, for example, is represented by the Tower of London, Westminster Abbey and Big Ben, all of which are arguably symbols of the British state (in the guise of monarchy, church and parliament). Big Ben received a comparatively high number of comments (40 published), most of which agree that the building is internationally recognized, but dispute whether it is a 'symbol of England' or 'a key British icon'. Debates over the Englishness of the London icons perhaps support Stone and Muir's observations of the growth of local identity over national; several correspondents from outside of London complain about the dominance of the capital in the national imaginary. As one contributor from 'glorious Devon' writes:

> I was under the impression we were voting for English Icons? London is a tiny little bit of it, and quite insignificant to most people, apart from those who live there. London and all it contains is not an icon .... Could this sad city not have its own site and stop cluttering up this one???

Other common debates foreground the divide between ethnic and civic definitions of nationalism, demonstrating not only dissonance but contributors' efforts to assert competing definitions, embrace or refute change, and invoke criteria to justify inclusions or exclusions. A vocal minority of users stringently refutes all the attempts to include multicultural elements as part of the English national heritage stating that they are simply not 'from' England. Such comments appear to be premised on a definition of Englishness which for some respondents is not merely white, but also exclusively Anglo-Saxon in origin. Thus, the Tower of London is castigated for being 'a symbol of Anti-Englishness', the home of 'swaggering invaders' with 'un-Anglo-Saxon' architecture. One extremist even comments that for this reason the Tower 'should be demolished' – a radical approach to dealing with dissonant heritage, which if pushed to its logical conclusions would see the end to vast swathes of heritage, preservation. Interestingly, Hadrian's Wall is not similarly criticized as the cultural product of an invading Roman force, but is rather accepted as a World Heritage Site with only three uncontroversial public comments.

Attempts to 'rewrite the margins into the center', by flagging up the centrality of multiculturalism to England's heritage, are received equally controversially and rarely demonstrate the kind of inclusive 're-imagining' of Englishness as envisioned by Stuart Hall. The *SS Empire Windrush* and the Notting Hill Carnival are both in the collection, inspiring some of the more divergent and heated responses. Those with a more ethnic nationalist perspective condemn the inclusion of these events as politically correct and see them as revealing forces of authority at work behind the site. Those of a more apparently civic nationalist persuasion seem prepared to admit them as icons, but argue that they are British and not English. Only a very few perceive the symbolic power of these icons to lie in acceptance of multiculturalism per se, as evidence of a British/English value of the sort championed by Gordon Brown. For one contributor, the Carnival is a symbol of

> how 'Englishness' has, contradictorily, come to be defined by our ability to assimilate and celebrate the best that immigrants have brought to our society. It is this open-mindedness that I am most proud of when I tell people I'm English.
>
> (posted by R2 from Nottingham)

For another commentator:

It represents the vibrance [sic], color and positivity of modern England. It shows how people can feel comfortable in England to express themselves and celebrate their identity, and not oppressed by a requirement to conform to some imagined norms. It also shows that everyone's welcome at the party in England.

(posted by R3 from London)

In general, what is lacking from much of the public commentary is an understanding of the longer history of multiculturalism: the fundamental interconnectedness of English heritage with other nations and peoples. This runs counter to the political aspirations of the site. In a speech on 'Capturing the Public Value of Heritage' made shortly after the site's launch, David Lammy lauded the ICONS project's ability to 'unpick' traditional heritage and reposition it within a broader, more culturally inclusive discourse. Identifying the cup of tea as an English icon, Lammy stressed its potency as a multicultural symbol. In his words, 'it was the tea-pickers of Sri Lanka and the Lascar dockers of Woolwich as much as the tea-merchants of Surrey who established the Englishness of a cup of tea' (Lammy 2006). But while the cup of tea does indeed feature in the ICONS collection, the vast majority of public comments reference the symbolism of the *act* of tea drinking and not its complex social history. This is expressed most eloquently in the following contribution:

Isn't it obvious? It is the way we deal with disaster, fear, war, death. It is the way we welcome a friend or stranger, it is how we express love, sympathy, compassion, it is our condolence in hard times, our pick-me-up when we're tired, our anodyne when we are sick and our comforting cup when go to bed. Tetley, PG Tips, Yorkshire, Barry's, Tesco's, whatever you drink, it is our old standby, or friend, and a true national icon.

(posted by R4 from London)

This example reiterates the plurality of meanings that people attach to heritage and how these draw on their own suppositions, perceptions and contexts, often contrary to what might be anticipated by those involved in the 'managing' of national heritage. Tellingly, given that ICONS has chosen to represent specifically a cup of tea (rather than the more common mug), other contributors point out the implicit class distinctions of tea as cultural practice in Britain. Commentators debate social protocols such as whether milk should be put in first or last, as well as the propriety of having two teapots (a chipped one for the family and a 'good' one for company). Ultimately, tea is viewed as an inclusive icon not because of its multicultural history, but because of its universal consumption: 'it is enjoyed by English of all classes, races and creeds' (posted from R5 from Birmingham).

The contradictory nature of the criteria by which heritage is judged is further illustrated by comparing the legitimacy of tea against another culinary icon, chicken tikka masala, which is not perceived to be legitimate by many commentators. In many ways, this curry dish is equal in symbolism to the humble 'cuppa' in terms of its coupling of popular consumption with representation of the history of Empire. In 2001, the then foreign secretary, Robin Cook, famously declared chicken tikka masala to be 'a true British national dish, not only because it is the most popular, but because it is a perfect illustration of the way Britain absorbs and adapts external influences' (Wintour 2001).

While 13 public comments on ICONS hardly amount to a representative sample, nearly half are resolutely against the nomination. Despite ICONS' presentation of the astonishing statistic that 'Marks and Spencers sells more than 18 tonnes of it as sandwiches every week' and that it is 'the most ordered dish across our nation's 8,000 curry houses', at the time of writing 75 per cent of responses through the 'vote' function of the site equally rejected it as an icon of England. In this case, ubiquity of consumption does not appear to equal acceptance as a national cultural habit. Further research is needed to understand why tea is so readily accepted as an English icon, but curry is not. These two products have similar histories so why do they elicit such drastically different responses? Is it an expression of the comparative recentness of the curry eating habit in Britain, or the fact that despite being a dish invented for the English, it is still predominantly served up by those who might be perceived by some as immigrants or 'others'?

Heritage online: Forum or soapbox?

The degree of dissonance shown between nominations on ICONS leads us to question how this example of digital heritage operates in terms of providing a forum for dialogue, and the extent to which it is able to promote debate and understanding rather than merely function as a public platform for airing diverse views. While Lammy (2006) stressed the role of heritage in helping to 'build a Britain at ease with its present because it understands, values and is able to access its past', the comments written on the site could be read as indicative of a limited understanding or valuing of differing points of view. It appears that the necessity of moderation may result, on the whole, in a series of unconnected public comments rather than a genuine exchange of ideas. However, it is important to recognize that this relates to the nature of the medium; fragmentation is an inherent feature of online asynchronous communication of the kind utilized here. In many ways the design of the website lends itself best to browsing rather than in-depth exploration and follows the conventions set by other online forums in this respect. Further assessment of the success or otherwise of websites in supporting debate of such kinds will require an innovative methodology attentive to the characteristics of the medium.

In the meantime, what ICONS confirms is that as a medium for public debates about heritage, the Web has both advantages and disadvantages. It creates new opportunities for participation and multivocality but is accompanied by the risk of producing fragmentation and a cacophony of viewpoints. Indeed, we might question the appropriateness of attempting to conduct this kind of national debate via a global medium. It is important to note that users contribute from all over the world, thus further complicating both the parameters of this discussion of national heritage, and the aspiration that the project would speak to tensions in the United Kingdom. It confirms how challenging it is, in practice, to enlist or position heritage in relation to national identity in a Web 2.0 context. ICONS also exemplifies how public understanding of heritage is continually being remade and always inflected by the specificity of the medium.

At the same time, it is important to remember that there are multiple audiences who may be visiting the site and reading the comments. What we are unable to judge, as yet, are the reactions of those who read but do not otherwise contribute by posting their views. The publicists for ICONS have assumed that '[d]ifferent communities will learn a lot about each other's icons, bringing people closer in understanding' (press release, 10 January 2006). While the first half of the statement is undoubtedly possible, it will require further research before we can assess the likelihood of concomitant understanding.

Despite the technological challenges, ICONS represents a timely opportunity to see the processes by which national heritage is defined, articulated, and contested in action and in public. Viewed in the broader context of recent public debates about shifting national loyalties in Britain, this case study also illuminates the interconnectedness of national heritage, politics and governmentality. Whether digital heritage of this kind is really able to play the kind of socially cohesive role envisaged for it remains the subject of further study.

Acknowledgements

Our thanks to Areti Galani and Chris Whitehead.

Bibliography

Ashworth, G.J. (2007) 'On townscapes, heritages and identities', paper presented at Institute for Advanced Studies Colloquium on Urban-Rural: Flows and Boundaries, Lancaster University, January 2007. Available online at: http://www.lancs.ac.uk/ias/annualprogramme/regionalism/docs/Ashworth_paper.doc (accessed 4 October 2007).
Ashworth, G.J. and Graham, B. (eds) (2005) *Senses of Place: Senses of Time*. Aldershot: Ashgate.
Ashworth, G.J., Graham, B. and Tunbridge, J.E. (2000) *A Geography of Heritage*. London: Arnold.
Bechhofer, F., Kiely, F. and McCrone, D. (2006) *Whither Britishness? The accounts of Scottish and English people living in Scotland*. Edinburgh: Institute of Governance.
Billig, M. (1995) *Banal Nationalism*. London: Sage.
Brown, G. (2006) 'The future of Britishness', speech presented at The Fabian Society New Year Conference, 14 January 2006. Available online at: http://fabians.org.uk/events/new-year-conference-06/brown-britishness/speech (accessed 2 October 2007).
Brown, G. (2007) 'Britishness', speech presented at the Commonwealth Club, 27 February 2007. Available online at: http://www.hm-treasury.gov.uk/newsroom_and_speeches/speeches/chancellorexchequer/speech_chx_270207.cfm (accessed 2 October 2007).
Brown, G. (2007) 'Strength to change Britain', speech to the Labour Party Annual Conference, 24 September 2007. Available online at: http://www.labour.org.uk/conference/brown_speech (accessed 2 October 2007).
Culture Online (2007) 'In production'. Available online at: http://www.cultureonline.gov.uk/projects/in_production/icons/ (accessed 2 October 2007).

Desai, P. and Thomas, A. (1998) *Cultural Diversity: Attitudes of ethnic minority populations towards museums and galleries*. London: BRMB International.

DfES (2007) *Curriculum Review: Diversity and citizenship*. London: Department for Education and Skills.

Dicks, B. (2003) *Culture on Display: The production of contemporary visitability*. Buckingham: Open University Press.

ETHNOS (2005) *Citizenship and Belonging: What is Britishness?* London: Commission for Racial Equality.

Graham, B. and Howard, P. (eds) (2008) *The Ashgate Research Companion to Heritage and Identity*. Aldershot: Ashgate.

Hall, S. (2005) 'Whose heritage? Un-settling 'the heritage', re-imagining the post-nation', in J. Littler and R. Naidoo (eds) *The Politics of Heritage: The legacies of 'race'*. London: Routledge, 23–36.

Hewison, R. (1987) *The Heritage Industry: Britain in a climate of decline*. London: Methuen.

Holden, J. (2007) *Logging on: Culture, participation and the web*. London: Demos.

Karp, I., Kratz, C.A., Szwaja, L. and Ybarra-Frausto, T. (eds) (2006) *Museum Frictions: Public cultures/global transformations*. Durham, NC: Duke University Press.

Kenny, M., English, R. and Hayton, R. (2008) 'Beyond the Constitution: Englishness in post-devolved Britain'. Institute for Public Policy Research (IPPR/IPPR North). February 2008. Available online at: http://www.ippr.org/ipprnorth/publicationsandreports/ (accessed 12 May 2008).

Lammy, D. (2005) 'Where now for Britain's shared heritage?', 25 October 2005. Available online at: http://www.davidlammy.co.uk/da/24528 (accessed 4 October 2007).

Lammy, D. (2006) 'Capturing the public value of heritage', 26 January 2006. Available online at: http://www.davidlammy.co.uk/da/29386 (accessed 4 October 2007).

Littler, J. and Naidoo, R. (eds) (2005) *The Politics of Heritage*. London: Routledge.

Macdonald, S. (2003) 'Accessing audiences: Visiting visitor books', *Museum and Society*, 3(3): 119–36.

Mason, R. (2007) *Museums, Nations, Identities. Wales and its national museums*. Cardiff: University of Wales Press.

'Minutes of ICONS of England Advisory Board Inaugural Meeting', 13 October 2005. Available online at: http://www.icons.org.uk/introduction/iconfolder.2006-04-21.0869811214/advisory-board-meeting-one (accessed 2 October 2007).

Modood, T. (2005) 'Remaking multiculturalism after 7/7', *www.openDemocracy.net*, 29 September. Available online at: http://www.opendemocracy.net/conflict-terrorism/multiculturalism_2879.jsp (accessed 28 September 2008).

NatCen (2007) *Perspectives on a Changing Society: British social attitudes, 23rd report*. London: National Center for Social Research.

Palmer, C. (1998) 'From theory to practice: Experiencing the nation in everyday life', *Journal of Material Culture*, 3(2): 175–200.

Phillips, T. (2005) 'After 7/7: Sleepwalking to segregation', speech at Manchester Town Hall, 22 September 2005. Available online at: http://www.rima.org.uk/Default.aspx.LocID-0hgnew07r.RefLocID-0hg00900c001001.Lang-EN.htm (accessed 2 October 2007).

Smith, C. (1998) *Creative Britain*. London: Faber and Faber.

Smith, L. (2006) *Uses of Heritage*. London: Routledge.

Stone, L. and Muir, R. (2007) *Who Are We? Identities in Britain, 2007*. London: Institute for Public Policy Research.

Vertovec, S. (2006) 'The emergence of super-diversity in Britain'. Working Paper no.25. Oxford: Center on Migration, Policy and Society.

Wintour, P. (2001) 'Chicken tikka Britain is new Cook recipe', *The Guardian*, 19 April 2001.

2

Locating art: The display and construction of place identity in art galleries

Christopher Whitehead

This chapter will address the relationships between art on display in museums and galleries, identity and geographic location with reference to concepts of place identity. It will focus on the ways in which place identities are constructed in displays of art, building upon the notion of place identity as a political and social construction (and in this case specifically a curatorial one) intended to allow people to make sense of their connectedness to place in ways which inform identity construction. Within this conceptual framework I will discuss *Art on Tyneside* (AOT), a display dating from the early 1990s but still (at the time of writing) in existence today in the Laing Art Gallery in Newcastle upon Tyne (which, along with the neighbouring town of Gateshead, forms a large post-industrial urban centre in the north-east of England). The display makes explicit reference to local places and appeals to visitors' place identities, and provides a platform to address the questions: why and how are place, community and identity actively connected in this gallery display? What rhetorical means are used to do so and what does this say about institutional views of audiences, community and belonging? Also, what are the relationships between the gallery itself as place and the external places which are the focus of its displays? The chapter then examines the representation of place in displays as prompts and suggestions for visitors' own constructions of place identity. This is seen to relate, tacitly, to the wider historical context of late twentieth-century Tyneside as a place of (amongst other things) social, economic and psychological hardships. The exploration of AOT will show how the interplay of political actions at institutional, museological and disciplinary levels functioned as an attempt to broker new forms of access to new audiences, through prompting visitors to engage in place-based identity construction processes, effectively locating themselves within time, space and (art) history.

Museums, place and place identity

'Place identity' is a topic which has become increasingly prominent over the last three decades or so in fields as varied as environmental psychology (Proshansky *et al.* 1983; Rowles 1983), social psychology (Dixon and Durrheim 2000), geography (Keith and Pile 1993), sociology (Degnen 2005), anthropology (Low and Lawrence-Zúñiga 2003), planning (Hague and Jenkins 2005) and, to a lesser extent, heritage studies (Ashworth and Graham 2005; Smith 2006: 74–80). It is a contested term (and some of the authors mentioned do not use it at all), but refers in general to two interrelated human practices. First, it concerns the imposition of constructed identities on place (and different people and groups may confer quite different identities on individual places, as in Neill's 1999 study of the different readings of the physical environment of Belfast by unionists and nationalists). Second, it concerns the construction of identities for ourselves through reference to place, ranging from the immediate habitat (the domestic, leisure and work places of our lives) to civic, regional and national places (e.g. Newcastle upon Tyne, the North-East, England) and geographical notions of place (e.g. 'northernness'). Our self-consciousness within cultural (and physically real) places and our choice to inhabit or avoid them can also be linked to the political operation of cultural capital, as we define ourselves in relation to the places in which we feel at ease or ill at ease – the museum, the greyhound track, the fitness club and so on, each with their own codes to be understood or resisted (this can be considered in relation to Bourdieu and Darbel's 1969 discussion of 'Cultural works and cultivated disposition').

One aim of this chapter is to introduce place identity into the field of museum studies, and in particular to bring it to bear on considerations around the display of art. This is also an opportunity to point to the surprising paucity of studies employing notions of place identity in relation to museums of any kind, and not only art museums. Of particular relevance here are 'city' museums (e.g. the Museum of London, the Kölnisches Stadtmuseum or Museum of the City of Cologne, etc.) and the many technology, transport and social history museums whose collections and displays have regional or local geographical emphases, such as Newcastle's Discovery Museum, one of whose permanent displays is (at the time of writing) dedicated to the natural and social history of the River Tyne. It is arguable that the presentation of material cultures and indeed oral testimonies associated with histories of work connected to specific locales can be understood as prompts for the construction of place identity on the part of visitors who – it is envisaged – are likely to identify themselves within the cultural-geographical landscapes and pasts represented in display. This understanding relates to the current preoccupation of many UK museums, and certainly those administered by local authorities, to appeal strongly (although not exclusively) to local communities. For example, the UK Government Museums, Libraries and Archives Council have a policy on 'Delivering for Local Communities' (MLA 2006).

I argue that this relates closely to the ways in which those responsible for museum displays are likely to envisage visitors, and I will use this concept of the envisaged visitor or envisaged audience throughout this chapter. While related to antecedents such as the constituted and positioned subject from structuralism or the 'implied reader' from reader response criticism and reception theory, the 'envisaged visitor' includes the further dimensions of the visitor's anticipated habitus, behaviour and movement-within-space (in this case the space of the gallery), which form key curatorial concerns in the development of displays. I also need to make further clarifications here. First, the following analyses make no reference to visitor studies as the field is commonly understood; that is, I have not sought to understand the views and experiences of 'real' visitors to AOT. Second, in considering curatorial acts in which visitors are envisaged, we must attend to the possibility that these are not monolithic and shared fully by all those involved in the production of a display, for as Macdonald's ethnographic study of exhibition work at the Science Museum shows us, 'the process which is sometimes called "encoding" in cultural studies can be just as multi-faceted and disjunctive with cultural texts as "decoding" by audiences' (2002: 8). My own decoding of AOT is, of course, a personal one with specific theoretical inflections, and will illuminate the display from a specific angle, leaving much in shadow. While there is value in this, it is clear that these clarifications point to further avenues for study which are beyond the scope of this chapter.

The focus on provision for local communities by way of displays about local place involves making an appeal to envisaged audiences (who may indeed be envisaged as in some way 'local') to *locate* themselves in cultural place, both in literal and metaphorical senses. Discourses of belonging, achievement and pride and often human characteristics which are seen to be shared by place inhabitants (e.g. hardiness, resourcefulness, industriousness, community spirit and so on) can be formed through such displays. With this, place-based 'communities' are invoked and projected onto contemporary inhabitants (some of whom – even if only a small proportion – will visit the displays in question).

Seen from a different angle, displays about local place envisage audiences who form interpretive communities with shared cultural repertoires based on their feelings of 'place-belongingness' (Korpela 1989: 246) in which 'human actors are cast as imaginative users of their environments, agents who are able to appropriate physical contexts in order to create . . . a space of attachment and rootedness, a space of being' (Dixon and Durrheim 2000: 29). Histories of place may also appeal (and be intended to appeal) to what Rowles terms 'autobiographical insideness' (1983: 302), which arises from individuals' sense of their existence within place over time and the figuring within this of incidents and events (social, economic and personal events, which may indeed be historicized in the museum). While such feelings ('belongingness', 'insideness') may be present within the individual, studies in place identity have, latterly, begun to examine their *social* construction and operation and the relation in this context of the psychology of the individual to that of the group. For example, Danziger has discussed the play of place identity from the cognitive and affective processes inside the individual's head into 'the interpersonal space of conversation' (1997: 411), and Amundsen has identified four perceptions of place which amount to a common cultural repertoire for use within the construction of place identity. These are as follows:

1   Spatial qualities that distinguish the place from others – for example, location, but also infrastructure, communication and architecture;
2   Characteristics or qualities of the inhabitants that distinguish them from inhabitants of other places – for example, values, customs, physical appearance;

3   Social conditions and social relations between the inhabitants; and
4   Culture and/or history, seen as a unifying element that again connects the
     inhabitants to tradition and again distinguishes them from 'the other' (Hague
     and Jenkins 2005: 13).

Notwithstanding the growing sophistication of place identity studies in relation to
individual and social psychologies, it is notable that little attention has been paid
to the importance of public media in promoting and consolidating specific place
identities. For example, it is possible to envisage a careful study of aspects of place
identity in the north-east of England through television and film (*The Likely Lads,
Auf Wiedersehen Pet, Our Friends in the North, 55° North* – all drama series
based or partially based in Newcastle and which foreground its urban environment), local news transmissions such as *Look North*, literature (the historical novels of Catherine Cookson set on Tyneside) and, of course, museum display.
Historiographical media such as museum display and historical novels take on
particular significance here, for, as noted by Haartsen *et al.*, since the future is not
yet known, perceptions of place identity 'always lean on the past' (2000: 2). The
historical dimension of place identity perception is significant for additional reasons. As Dixon and Durrheim (2000: 36) point out, place identity is sometimes
defined as a psychological structure of which people are only partially conscious,
and is 'brought to consciousness' in individuals who experience the rapid transformation of places through which they have constructed self identities. This is
especially pertinent in the adjoining urban conurbations of Newcastle and
Gateshead, whose once industrial landscapes have changed dramatically over
the past three decades. One particularly emblematic transformation is that of the
Gateshead–Newcastle quaysides in the early 2000s (the River Tyne itself is the
boundary between the two cities) from industrial riverscapes to cultured leisure
destinations (Figure 2.1), most especially through the redevelopment of the Rank
Flour Mill building into the BALTIC Center for Contemporary Art and the new
development of the Sage Gateshead music venue in a vast, hi-tech building
designed by Norman Foster. These two responses (from a focus group conducted
by the present author) show in different ways how individuals construct their identities in relation to the transformation of familiar places:

> 'Well I'm 68 years old. I was born just along . . . further along, past that
> bridge, a little bit further along, and I know all about the Tyne. And it was
> fascinating when I was a little girl, and you know when you come down
> now and you see the BALTIC and the Sage and that, and I think back to
> what the Quayside was like . . . it was brilliant the Quayside, it was full of
> intrigue. And that sticks in your mind, you don't lose that you know, but
> it's wonderful to see all these changes, and life is changes, isn't it?
>
> [To me] this [BALTIC Center for Contemporary Art] is the Rank Flour Mill.
> And when I'm in it, I'm picturing all these men working, and all the
> machines, it's going through my mind, you know, what were they doing and,
> you know, all the work they had. And to me it's still a Rank Flour Mill'.
>
> (Newman and Whitehead 2006)

Figure 2.1 Gateshead quayside, 2004. The BALTIC Center for Contemporary Art is on the left; the Sage Gateshead Concert Hall, shown still in construction, is on the right.

Photo: Gerard Corsane

Art on Tyneside

Art on Tyneside is a permanent display at the Laing Art Gallery, the only gallery within Tyne and Wear Museums (TWM) in the city of Newcastle upon Tyne. The Gallery itself was opened to the public in 1904 and has rich collections of paintings and decorative art, primarily from the eighteenth to late twentieth centuries. AOT was primarily intended for local audiences and followed a series of displays and exhibitions focusing on aspects of north-eastern art history (Millard, pers. comm.). It is a succession of environments, each of which represents an epoch 'in the story of art on Tyneside over some 300 years' (Millard 1992: 32) moving up to the present day (or at least the present day as it was when AOT opened in 1991), although in fact the geographical purview of the displays is initially wider (the story begins with the Border Wars, taking place in what is now north Northumberland and south-eastern Scotland – much further north than 'Tyneside'). The order is generally chronological and there is a linear visitor route. As the then curator John Millard explained, AOT replaced 'a shanty town of new and old cases which had been gradually installed over a fifteen year period, giving rise to displays which were disjointed and lacked focus' (1992: 32). These older displays segregated works of different artistic media from one another; one primary intention of AOT was to bring such works together in a coherent and non-hierarchical fashion. This, as we shall see, was an important and highly publicized part of TWM's self-positioning within the museums sector. It is an approach which disrupted the respective conventions of the museum display of art and of social history, calling into question what objects can or should be thought of as 'art' or thought of in the context of 'art history', and what history can be seen through art. As an attempt at a form of disciplinary fusion, it was pioneering, with few imitators at the time.

Figure 2.2 The 'Border Warfare' Room, 2007.

Photo: The author

It is now worth providing a brief walkthrough of AOT. This walkthrough represents AOT as it was for much of its lifespan and not as it is now, nearing the end of its days, since so much of its complex apparatus (in particular electronic and audio-visual elements) has been removed over the course of its 16-year lifespan. (Charting the gradual adulteration of a 'permanent' display like this would make a fascinating institutional study in itself.) On entering AOT, the visitor finds him/herself in a dark environment comprising a diorama concerning Border Warfare. The visitor's eye is first drawn to a mannequin representing a man making off through the ruins of a building (possibly representing one of Northumberland's many castles) with a chest, presumably containing valuables

Figure 2.3 Atmospheric décor changes to speed the shift through time and place, 2007.

(Figure 2.2). He looks over his shoulder and when we follow his gaze we see a hanging taking place on the hill behind him. An audio track plays, suggestive of the chaos of pillage, for, as a text panel explains, with some melodrama:

> The sounds you hear set the scene for the turmoil of the border wars, when the North of England and Southern Scotland were disrupted by constant battles and disputes over land and property.
>
> Among the clans involved in this warfare were the Armstrongs, the Fenwicks and the Douglasses. These names rang with steel well into the seventeenth century.

On the other side of the room, the diorama fades away and we find the first museum objects (in the conventional sense) – a historic map of the region and a sword in a display case, neither of which is conventionally interpreted as art – for example, in relation to their aesthetic or decorative qualities (the label for the sword informs us only that 'backswords had single-edged blades, used for hacking at the enemy'). To represent the shift from the Hobbesian turmoil of the Border Wars to genteel society, around the corner we encounter a female mannequin in a rich but somewhat austere domestic interior behind glass. From here, by means of atmospheric décor changes (Figure 2.3), we move into an eighteenth-century Coffee House in which bewigged mannequins appear to chatter (there is another audio track) over a copy of the *Newcastle Courant* (Figure 2.4). On the walls engravings are hung and conventionally interpreted by way of text labels; inset into one wall is a selection of historic coffee pots.

Figure 2.4 The eighteenth-century Coffee House, 2007.

Photo: The author

Following this are similar semi-immersive interiors representing plein-air sketching in artists' picturesque tours of the north and a generic craft studio – a chance to showcase the work of the local Beilby glass, enamel and engraving workshop and the work of the engraver Thomas Bewick, celebrated for his illustrations of animals. Along the way we also encounter a mock neoclassical interior with a light-up map (Figure 2.5) of Newcastle's neoclassical architectural landmarks and a magnetic board on which visitors can experiment with the elements of a neoclassical façade; a Victorian gallery, based on nineteenth-century precedents in Newcastle; and a diorama showing the rescue of a fishing boat at the nearby coastal village of Cullercoats, the backdrop to which is John Charlton's celebrated painting *The Women* (depicting the Cullercoats lifeboat being hauled from the sea, mostly by women, after a rescue in 1861). This display forms a neat example of the incorporation of histories of art and local social histories which, in the process, upsets the modernist convention wherein paintings are intended to be focal points unencumbered by

Figure 2.5 Mapping Newcastle's neoclassical architecture, 2007.

other display matter (Figure 2.6): in fact the painting cannot be scrutinized closely, for as well as being placed in the same case as a mannequin it is hung at an obtuse angle with respect to the viewer. The penultimate room represents twentieth-century, modernist Tyneside, combining a large model of a portion the Tyne Bridge, clothes from the 1930s and 1960s, modernist painting and sculpture, ceramics and interactive elements such as the 'Talking Tug Boat', which gives visitors answers to a quiz via audio-phones (Figures 2.7 and 2.8). Throughout, audio forms an important aspect of the display, ranging from ambient background noise to the introduction of historical characters to whose fictional oral histories one can listen via audio-phones (e.g. 'I'm Mary Beilby from the Beilby family workshop, and folk seem to like the glass and silverware that I design and make').

The final room acts as an acclimatization zone and readies us for our delivery from history into the present. This space is given over to exhibitions of contemporary

Figure 2.6 John Charlton's *The Women*, shown within a diorama, 2007.

Figure 2.7 The Twentieth-Century Room, including a scale model of the Tyne Bridge, 2007.

Figure 2.8 The Twentieth-Century Room: 1960s fashion, 2007.

Photo: The author

work, often by school or other local groups. For many years a looped video was also screened here which played a key interpretive and rhetorical role, closing the display as a whole. The video was presented by north-eastern actor Tim Healy, most famous for his role in *Auf Wiedersehen Pet*, a popular TV series running for over 20 years from 1983 about the life, work and escapades of a group of itinerant construction workers, three of whom (including Healy's character) were from Newcastle. The series, although often comedic, functioned in a sense as a deep study of the poetics and psychology of place and displacement, with themes like leaving home (repeatedly) and homecoming being central to the emotional substance of the extended narrative. Shot partly on location in Tyneside, the series arguably led Healy to assume a quasi-metonymic value in relation to place, abetted by his unshakeable regional accent. The choice of Healy as presenter of the AOT video, and interlocutor with the AOT visitor, was therefore a resonant one.

The video shows Healy leaving the Laing Art Gallery, after which he looks over his shoulder and addresses the visitor/viewer, partly in local dialect, and in terms which reflect the expectation that visitors will be local or have local affiliations:

> 'Oh . . . there you are. What did you think of that, nice eh? Bit proud, are ye?'[1]
>
> [. . .]
>
> 'Let's have a look round town. Howway.'[2]
>
> (Transcript in AOT records[3])

Healy then proceeds to tour the city of Newcastle, pointing out notable sights and continuing to address the viewer(s) in the first person, often employing the first-person plural and possessive adjective ('our best known architect John Dobson'), thereby aiding the construction of a common community and a bond, based on place, between Healy and his viewers. In an intertextual play upon Healy's association with the theme of home and homecoming, links are made between the historical art on display in AOT and the city and riverscape outside the gallery in an explicit invocation of place identity, acting as a rhetorical appeal to the viewer/visitor to locate him/herself within the places depicted:

[the photography directions read:]

'cut to from [Thomas] Bewick woodcut of a bird to birds/seagulls on the Tyne – cut to Tim watching them.'

'Just like me they know where to come back to . . . The River Tyne. When I see these bridges, famous symbols of Tyneside, and these two churches I know I'm home.'

Premised on a groundwork of first-person-plural dialogue, Healy's scripted act of self-location – an affirmation of Korpela's 'place-belongingness' – functions as an implicit appeal to the envisaged visitor to adopt a commensurate or comparable subject position and to experience, as the curator John Millard puts it, a 'feeling of ownership of the art heritage' in contrast to the impersonal histories of art narrated in TV broadcasts such as Kenneth Clark's *Civilization* (pers. comm.). It is tantamount to interpellation, working through notions of natural habitat and indigenousness and creating a complex nature–culture bind (consider Healy's identification with the native fauna, and then consider how this itself is identified with a native history of art represented metonymically by the Bewick engraving). But what appeal, if any, is made to those without local affiliations – to those who do not or cannot 'locate' themselves on Tyneside and are possessed of 'outsideness'? As outsiders, perhaps such visitors are envisaged as looking in or looking on, consuming the constructed history of the region much as they might a tourist information brochure, and taking away their impressions of this place of others. Or perhaps visitors as outsiders are simply 'disinherited' from the heritage on display, in that it is presented as 'someone else's' (Ashworth and Tunbridge 1996: 21), and are not envisaged, interpellated or appealed to at all.

Place, display, politics

AOT was very well funded for a display of its type, in part through considerable competitively won public funds (AOT records). It formed an important aspect in the positioning of TWM in the early 1990s as a radical service, committed to winning over new audiences (Millard 1992: 32) and prepared to rethink museum practice at a time when the tenets of the New Museology were only just beginning to pervade. AOT was opened with some pomp by Tim Renton, then

Minister for the Arts, on 23 July 1991, with historic re-enactment and regional folk music performances. What is noteworthy here is that such a large financial, political and promotional investment was made in a display about art and (local) place, or rather, about locating art within place and within constructions of local community and regional and civic identity. In a way this may be seen to reconnect to entrenched traditions in the practice of art history, in which the geography of artistic production has acted as an important organizational, taxonomic and investigative apparatus – for example, in the identification and study of regional 'schools' of painting or constructs such as 'Sunderland glass', 'Derby pottery', and so on.

This geographical tradition is not apolitical in nature. For example, the characteristics of given schools of painting have often been equated with the characteristics of the peoples who produce them (in 1857 Ruskin noted that Dutch painting reflected the 'quiet and cold' temperament of the Dutch people (Whitehead 2005: 42). Also, the scholarly, *a posteriori* identification (construction?) of place-based 'schools' of painters can confer cultural prestige on an area, bestowing benefits which go beyond that of scholarly attention. Such schools are often persuasively linked to local place. The Cullercoats School, for example, included indigenous painters and others, attracted by place characteristics such as, typically, 'the special atmosphere and changing light' (this is from the AOT text panel on 'Artists at Cullercoats'). But it is still rare to find work within, or related to, such traditions in which the identity politics of a region and its inhabitants are so explicitly and forcefully bound up as in the case of AOT. Within this 'binding up' are interesting tensions concerning the understanding of the universal or contextual qualities of art as a category of material culture and experience: when is art 'of' place and/or constitutive of place and when, alternatively, does art transcend place? In a similar vein, one can contrast 'objectified' histories of art with 'humanized' ones. In the former, objects are abstracted away, or extricated, from specific places into the museum as *heterotopia* – a place for the placeless display of objects, informing a long tradition of criticism of the art museum as an agent of the dislocation and decontextualization of objects. The latter, on the other hand, necessarily connects objects with, and represents, the places of habitation and work as physical, emotional and psychological loci for the production and consumption of art. In a letter to the *Museums Journal* in February 1992 (another example of the political and rhetorical self-positioning of TWM, this time for the attention of a professional audience), the TWM Director David Fleming touched on this theme in a response to an article written by the museums critic Kenneth Hudson in a previous issue:

> Hudson wonder[s] where the revolution, where the 'humanization' of art museums will begin . . . the good news is, Mr Hudson, that the revolution has begun, at the Laing Art Gallery in Newcastle upon Tyne. Come and have a look at *Art on Tyneside* and you may see, notwithstanding some predictably adverse comment from the more reactionary end of the art historical profession, the shape of the future.
>
> (Fleming 1992: 56)

41

Discomfort

AOT was widely promoted in the early 1990s as a groundbreaking display, knowingly overturning more conventional approaches to the presentation of art (Millard 1992). As Fleming indicated, a small number of critical voices objected to the collapsing of boundaries between art and social history, to the breakdown of tacit rules of display and to the confusion of modes of address and experience (the cross-contamination of codes, as this could also be termed). The critic Richard Dorment, for example, stated as follows:

> Poor in design and vacuous in content [,] *Art on Tyneside* proved to be the most abysmal museum installation I've ever encountered.
>
> But it was clear from the visitor's book that, with some sectors of the public [,] *Art on Tyneside* has been popular. I suppose one must accept this. If some visitors are so unimaginative that they need half-baked gimmicks to make history come alive, then by all means let them have them.
>
> But not in an art museum.
>
> (1993: 42)

Embedded within this elitist position is an interest in the maintenance of the political project of distinguishing and holding separate different types of knowledge through institutionalization. In some ways TWM defined itself in opposition to such views with recourse to AOT. Millard noted that AOT was an 'attempt to appeal to people who would not normally go to an art gallery' in terms which relate closely to the operation of place identity within that of cultural capital:

> The Laing has an imposing portico and marble halls, which were meant to create a hallowed atmosphere for art when it opened in 1904. This sort of intimidating atmosphere is familiar enough, but it now suggests to many that art and art galleries are 'not for the likes of us'. The Laing, as Newcastle's city art gallery, cannot afford to project such an exclusive image. Newcastle suffers from problems of inner city deprivation and unemployment, and saw riots last summer.
>
> (1992: 32)

The first issue of interest here is the envisaged visitor with anticipated stocks of cultural capital, intimidated by the gallery as place. To this visitor an appeal is made through reference within display to the *external* places of the city and its environs. These places work as pre-known triggers for self-recognition, allowing a self-identification within locations which, although familiar, can be seen anew as 'art' or in some way as part of 'art history'. This is, in a sense, the provision of a key to help the notional visitor decode the unfamiliar spaces and conventions of the gallery while simultaneously aggrandizing the geographical reference points of the individual.

The second important issue which this quotation introduces is the relationship between AOT as a display which celebrates the relationships between art and local place and the general historical context of its development, at a moment when heavy industry and shipbuilding had been in serious decline for some time. This led to significant levels of unemployment and to the decay of some of the urban fabric, in particular the industrial landscapes and the residential areas connected to them located (literally) on Tyneside. The riots mentioned here were the Meadowell Riots of September 1991, just a short time after AOT opened earlier in the summer, in which over 400 protesters clashed with police after the deaths of two car thieves in a high-speed police chase. It is evident, then, that AOT was developed in a difficult moment in the history of the city and also the region (e.g. the gradual closure of the coal mines continued until the mid-1990s), and it is possible to view the display as – at least on some level – a counterpoint to negative experience and representation of the region, with the focus on art working to construct possibilities for local pride through the presentation of the region's history as, in fact, a *history of art*, with the cultural prestige this bestows. As Millard, discussing one of the curatorial imperatives, notes:

> We felt that the North East was not associated with culture and that it should be. The display was meant to say that people in the North East could take pride in their art and architecture.
>
> (Millard pers. comm.)

Here we might adapt Hermann Lübbe's view of the museum as a compensatory institution. As Andreas Huyssen paraphrases:

> Lübbe argues that modernization is accompanied by the atrophy of valid tradition, a loss of rationality and the entropy of stable and lasting life experiences . . . In Lübbe's theory the museum compensates for this loss of stability. It offers forms of cultural identity to a destabilized modern subject, pretending that these cultural traditions have not been affected themselves by modernization.
>
> (Huyssen 1994: 26)

In the case of Tyneside, the loss of stability is not incurred through the kind of shift implicated in industrialization (to which Lübbe alludes) but through that implicated in industrial to post-industrial decline. In this view, AOT becomes a suggested negotiation of difficult pasts and the (potentially, to some) uncomfortable present, opening the possibility of a secured and comfortable identity position emerging within and through a comforting view of place and history. Art in AOT is presented as a category of material culture and a mode of experience which is both positive and distinctive, and here we can recall that for Amundsen the *distinctiveness* of place forms a key part of the repertoire of place identity. Notably, the design brief for AOT stated that 'the keynote of the display is *the qualities of Tyneside art*' (AOT records, original emphasis). This attempts to counter both the negative view of Tyneside as post-industrial wasteland and another, of this place losing what were perceived as its special characteristics and becoming *atopia*, threatening to destabilize and dislocate identities. Notable parallels emerge here in studies of dialect in the north-east: Beal (2000: 343), in her analysis of 'Geordie' literature, shows that 'the prominence of local forms in dialect literature may represent an assertion of local identity in the face of the perceived threat of cultural and linguistic homogenization'. Consider the destabilization of place identity in the following quotation about the removal of the distinctive cranes from the riverside in Wallsend – a posting to a recent online forum concerning the demise of shipbuilding on the Tyne:

> I think school trips visiting Segedunum [an archaeological museum in Wallsend] as part of their history lesson, should also be given priv[i]lege of seeing where there [sic] fathers and grandfathers worked [who] made this river one of the beacons of light for all mariners the world over. COZ WEN TH[E] CRANES GAN THATS IT THERES NEE MARE WAALSEND.[4]
>
> (Martin 2007)

In this context, it is interesting to consider how AOT eschews the topic of shipbuilding. In the process of recasting social history objects as art and/or design (pushing objects over contested boundaries), it is notable that neither Newcastle's shipbuilding history nor the ships as designed objects figure in displays or in the planning for displays. Curators did, as Millard states, 'discuss the boundaries of what might be included in the display', but ultimately 'drew quite a tight line round fine art, decorative art and architecture' (pers. comm.). AOT's redrawing of the disciplinary map of art history was – while pioneering – done through reference to a limited survey of material culture, drawn largely from the Laing's own collections. This material culture, already labelled as 'art' through institutional accession, was simply repositioned, while material from TWM's history collections proper were bounded elsewhere. Thus, the inter-institutional politics of disciplinary mapping (in which museums and groups of museums are key players) was formative within the construction of cultural geographies and place histories.

Conclusions

This chapter has explored the ways in which AOT appeals to envisaged audiences through making connections between art and place identity. Seen in historical context, the development of AOT relates both to industrial and economic decline in the region and to the political and museological positioning of TWM within the museums sector, at a time when access and audience development were important drivers. AOT disrupted museum conventions, merging display practices from social history and art, creating an experience intended to align with, and prompt, visitors' identity construction processes through representing the familiar, external environment and its material culture within gallery space. This outside–inside dynamic characterized an attempt to offer a form of access to those who, because of their cultural dispositions, find it difficult to negotiate, or identify themselves in relation to, the gallery as a place in itself. In recasting familiar places as art or places of art, and therefore associating them with high cultural achievement, AOT envisages the visitor act of negotiating a comfortable and comforting location of the self within place and time. In this, AOT programmes the rescripting of visitors' own autobiographical stories, and the reactivation of feelings of 'insideness', through reference to pride, ownership and belonging.

The notion of the museum as map or as cartographic space has emerged towards the closing of this chapter. It is a notion with some currency. Kirschenblatt-Gimblett discusses the nature of the museum as an 'undrawn map' whose contents, spaces and itineraries are indexed to travel, to other places and to collecting (1998: 132). In this sense, all museums are about place, although the extent to which place is purposefully invoked and evoked can differ markedly. Another cartographic notion which has emerged here concerns disciplinarity and knowledge, and once again this has relations with other fields of thought. For example, Elkins experiments with historiography by drawing visual maps of the history of art (2002: 1–11), and Gieryn (1999) has developed the notion of cultural cartography as a means to account for the ways in which boundaries of 'science' shift over time. This chapter, we may conclude, has discussed the double-mapping of knowledges and places, creating a terrain in which the visitor is placed as local traveller.

Acknowledgements

I am grateful to Zelda Baveystock for her comments on a draft of this chapter, to Rhiannon Mason for introducing me to Hermann Lübbe's view of the museum as a compensatory institution, to Julie Milne and Sarah Richardson of Tyne and Wear Museums for granting me access to, and for allowing me to quote from, the 'Art on Tyneside' records held at Tyne and Wear Archive Service and to John Millard at National Museums Liverpool, who was Curator of the Laing Art Gallery in 1991, for providing helpful answers to my many questions about the display.

Notes

1 'Ye' means 'you'.
2 'Howway' means 'come on'.
3 The AOT records are held at Tyne and Wear Archives Service.
4 The final sentence is in dialect and can be translated thus: 'Because when the cranes go that's it, there will be no more Wallsend.'

Bibliography

Ashworth, G.J. and Graham, B. (eds) (2005) *Senses of Place: senses of time*, Aldershot: Ashgate.

Ashworth, G.J. and Tunbridge, J.E. (1996) *Dissonant Heritage: the management of the past as a resource in conflict*, London: John Wiley.

Beal, J. (2000) 'From Geordie Ridley to Viz: popular literature in Tyneside English', *Language and Literature*, 9: 343–59.

Bourdieu, P. and Darbel A. (1969; 1997) *The Love of Art: European art museums and their public*, Cambridge: Polity Press.

Danziger, K. (1997) 'The varieties of social construction', *Theory and Psychology*, 7: 400–16.

Degnen, C. (2005) 'Relationality, place and absence: a three-dimensional perspective on social memory', *Sociological Review*, 2005, 53(4): 729–44.

Dixon, J. and Durrheim, K. (2000) 'Displacing place-identity: a discursive approach to locating self and other', *British Journal of Social Psychology*, 39: 27–44.

Dorment, R. (1993) 'Are galleries losing art?', *The Daily Telegraph*, 9 September 1993, p. 49.

Elkins, J. (2002) *Stories of Art*, London: Routledge.

Fleming, D. (1992) 'Letter from Newcastle upon Tyne', *Museums Journal*, 2: 56.

Gieryn, T.F. (1999) *Cultural Boundaries of Science: credibility on the line*, Chicago: University of Chicago Press.

Haartsen, T., Groote P. and Huigen, P.P.P. (eds) (2000) *Claiming Rural Identities: dynamics, contexts, policies*, Assen, The Netherlands: Van Gorcum.

Hague, C. and Jenkins, P. (eds) (2005) *Place Identity Participation and Planning*, London: Routledge.

Huyssen, A. (1994) *Twilight Memories: making time in a culture of amnesia*, London: Routledge.

Keith, M. and Pile, S. (eds) (1993) *Place and the Politics of Identity*, London: Routledge.

Kirshenblatt-Gimblett, B. (1998) *Destination Culture: tourism, museums and heritage*, Berkeley, CA: University of California Press.

Korpela, K.M. (1989) 'Place-identity as a product of environmental self-regulation', *Journal of Environmental Psychology*, 9: 241–56.

Low, S.M. and Lawrence-Zúñiga, D. (eds) (2003) *The Anthropology of Space and Place: locating culture*, London: Blackwell.

Macdonald, S. (2002) *Behind the Scenes at the Science Museum*, Oxford: Berg.

Martin, B. (2007), 'Demise of Swan Hunter'. Available online at: http://www.bbc.co.uk/tyne/content/articles/2006/11/23/swan_hunter_23112006_feature.shtml (accessed 24 September 2007).

Millard, J. (1992) 'Art history for all the family', *Museums Journal*, 2: 32–3.

MLA (2006) *Museums, Libraries and Archives and the Local Government White Paper Strong and Prosperous Communities: A Discussion Paper*. Available online at: http://www.mla.gov.uk/website/policy/Communities (accessed 24 September 2007).

Neill, W.J.V. (1999) 'Whose city? Can a place vision for Belfast avoid the issue of place identity?', *European Planning Studies*, 7(3): 269–81.

Newman, A. and Whitehead, C. (2006) 'Fivearts cities: an evaluative report on the impact on over 50s people of participation in activities related to British Art Show 6', unpublished report. Gateshead: BALTIC Centre for Contemporary Art.

Proshansky, H., Fabian, A.K. and Kaminoff, R. (1983) 'Place-identity: physical world socialization of the self', *Journal of Environmental Psychology*, 3: 57–83.

Rowles, G.D. (1983) 'Place and personal identity in old age: observations from Appalachia', *Journal of Environmental Psychology*, 2: 299–313.

Smith, L. (2006) *The Uses of Heritage*, London: Routledge.

Whitehead, C. (2005) *The Public Art Museum in 19th Century Britain: the development of the National Gallery*, Aldershot: Ashgate.

3

Place, local distinctiveness and local identity: Ecomuseum approaches in Europe and Asia

Gerard Corsane, Peter Davis and Donatella Murtas

Introduction

The small village of Gavalochori lies in the foothills of mountains above Souda Bay on the northern shores of the Mediterranean island of Crete. The village's survival was once dependent on agriculture, growing a variety of crops including fruit, vines and olives, and rearing sheep and other livestock. However, it has gradually adapted to the influence of tourism, which is now the mainstay of the island's economy. Other Europeans have settled there or built second homes, the village has acquired new *tavernas*, and enterprising locals have explored ways of motivating tourists to stop and explore. The rich cultural heritage of the village has been central to their actions, with signposts encouraging visitors to discover for themselves the Venetian buildings, ancient village wells, threshing floors and Roman tombs. The revitalization of local crafts (including pottery, needlework, painting, cookery and the distillation of raki) has been encouraged by a women's cooperative. These craft goods are sold in a local *taverna* which is also run by the cooperative. The women act as guides to the Gavalochori Museum which conserves material culture linked to their village history and promotes an identity to the outside world.

Basil Fronikakis, a local man, was responsible for initiating the idea of a local museum. As President of the local community he recognized that the village's cultural assets could be used to assist in the development of local identity and the local economy. The introductory panel in the museum records his words:

> I had started collecting books of a medieval, ethnographic and historical nature for the creation of an ethnographic and medieval museum. Since then a long time has elapsed full of effort, and in 1965 as President of the Community, as is known, I disregarded everything. I put aside every other thought which did not have to do with communal development. I made every effort for the revival of our old village, and started a very systematic and intensive cultural campaign. I collected medieval and ethnographic material of the wider region of our community and I looked after the preservation of local customs.

Fronikakis' work was continued by other village Presidents, and a small house in the village square became a temporary exhibition area for the collections. Then,

Figure 3.1 Gavalachori Museum, Crete, 1998.

Photo: Peter Davis

in 1983, George and Maria Stilianakis donated a house to the village that had been built during the Venetian period, and later modified following the Turkish invasion. Vasilios Fronimakis (1904–1983), the President of the Community at the time, realized that this was a potential home for the collections and records of village life, and took responsibility for its conversion to a permanent museum. The Gavalochori Museum (Figure 3.1) opened in 1992 and describes itself as a 'historical folklore museum'. The building, with its arched interior, mezzanine living space, balcony and shady courtyard has been carefully restored to provide pleasant exhibition areas. The oldest part of the house has been restored to demonstrate the traditional room configuration of kitchen, bedroom and store rooms, complete with original furniture and household goods. The remainder of the museum is devoted to craft skills, notably silk weaving, pottery, 'kopaneli' (lace-making), masonry and woodcarving; a small section is devoted to Cretan history and the exploits and heroism of local people during military actions.

This small museum emphasizes that in a globalized world, there is a perceived, even urgent demand by small communities to appreciate and demonstrate their own history, distinctiveness and identity. It is acknowledged that all museums – whether they are city museums, national museums, regional museums – through their collections and exhibitions have close links to the identity of a place and its people. However, what makes a museum such as Gavalochori special is that it was initiated by local people and is maintained by the community. It has a carefully defined territory, links to other sites in the vicinity that have been preserved *in situ*, is part of a greater cooperative venture and supports local economic development. Here local people, not trained specialists, have made decisions about how to define and sustain their identity. Interestingly, although it does not use the title 'ecomuseum', its genesis and practices demonstrate close links to the ecomuseum concept, which will be discussed later. For ecomuseums or other community-led museum and heritage projects, such as Gavalochori, an important starting point is to attempt to audit the heritage and cultural resources of the place, to begin to define what is special about it, and to determine which features lend the place 'local distinctiveness'.

Defining your place – Local distinctiveness

What do small local communities value most about their environment, the features of their natural and cultural landscape for which they share communal ownership and responsibility? What is it about our local environment that provides a feeling of belonging, a sense of place, the knowledge that we inhabit somewhere with distinct characteristics? Meinig (1979) suggests that (Western) people categorize their landscape as nature, as habitat, as an artefact, as a system, as a problem, as wealth, as ideology, as history, as place or as aesthetic. The feelings of people in a community in relation to their environment will inevitably represent this diversity of views, and poses a real challenge to those individuals responsible for interpreting it. Meinig's view of landscape as place is especially interesting. He states that:

> It is landscape as environment, embracing all that we live amidst, and thus it cultivates a sensitivity to detail, to texture, color, and all the nuances of visual relationships, and more, for environment engages all our senses, the sounds and smells and ineffable feel of a place as well . . . . Such a view is . . . central ground to the geographer . . . [who] . . . will see in the landscape a variety of patterns and relationships . . . [which] . . . take on meaning only when interpreted with some understanding of history and ideology . . . . Those interested in particular localities share a belief that one of the greatest riches of the earth is its immense variety of places . . . [and] that the individuality of places is a fundamental characteristic of subtle and immense importance . . . that all human events *take place*, all problems are anchored in place, and can ultimately only be understood in such terms.
>
> Meinig (1979: 45)

49

This holistic view of landscape as place is a commonly held one, and is consistent with a new – also holistic – paradigm for museology (Corsane and Holleman 1993: 121). It provides a strong indication of the importance of place, not simply for the elements within it, but how they relate to one another and how they link us with the past. It is the meanings attached to these tangible elements that provide a sense of continuity and identity.

However, the idea of place needs to be treated with care, as it embodies much more than physical components, for each individual it is a unique experience. For example, Buttimer (1980: 173) suggests that her home in rural Ireland allows her to experience 'a sense of being in tune with the rhythmicity of nature's light and dark, warmth and cold, sowing and harvesting'. She adds, 'it is the style of life associated with place which is still far more important for me than its external form' (Buttimer 1980: 178). Relph (1976: 29) quotes Donat's warning that '[P]laces occur at all levels of identity, my place, your place, street, community, town, county, region, country, and continent, but places never conform to tidy hierarchies of classification. They all overlap and interpenetrate one another and are wide open to a variety of interpretations'. Davis (1999: 18) when exploring place within the context of eco-museum philosophy, concluded that 'place is a chameleon concept, changing color through individual perception, and changing pattern through time'. However, despite these complexities, there is no doubt that the elements of place – tangible and intangible – are vital in helping people to understand their own and other places in the world; they provide us with our cultural identity.

The need to recognize and appreciate the richness of individual places has been promoted in the United Kingdom by the organization Common Ground. They stress that it is important to value the detail and the commonplace in the landscape, the characters that give 'local distinctiveness', defined by Clifford and King (1993: 7) as 'that elusive particularity, so often valued as "background noise" ... the richness we take for granted'. They suggest that it is 'as much about the commonplace as about the rare, about the everyday as much as the endangered, and about the ordinary as much as the spectacular'. Human beings appreciate subtle distinctions and detail, the difference and richness of places, and we appreciate them even more when we are in danger of losing them, but as yet no official mechanisms have evolved to protect the smaller, but no less significant features of the cultural landscape. Clifford and King (1993: 8–9) note: 'Apples, bricks, sheep and gates, all of which have had generations of careful guided evolution creating qualities related to conditions of locality and need, no longer show the differentiation that whispers ... where you are'. To Common Ground

> local distinctiveness is about everywhere, not just beautiful places; it is about details, patina and meaning, the things which create identity. Importantly it focuses on locality, not on the region. It is about accumulation and assemblages ... accommodation and change .... It includes the invisible as well as the physical; dialect, festivals, myths, may be as important as hedgerows, hills and houses.
>
> (Common Ground 1996)

Common Ground regard small-scale approaches to be essential – locality rather than region – and have applied their ideas in carefully defined geographical localities, most often the smallest British bounded unit – the parish. They have developed two interesting techniques to list and quantify the aspects of place that individuals and communities attach deep significance to. They have helped local communities to produce illustrated A–Z posters – 'illuminated alphabets' – and pictorial Parish Maps to identify the 'cultural touchstones' that help to define the special nature of place. These may be significant landscape features, or small things – the design of farm gates, the type of stile encountered on a footpath, a particular breed of sheep, a local personality from the past or the present. These two techniques have been widely used by ecomuseum activists (especially in Italy) and by local communities in England (Leslie 2006) as a starting point for heritage projects.

The range of features that emerge from these exercises is fascinating. Maps and alphabets include vernacular architecture, art, civic buildings, dress, accent, pastimes, food and drink, societies, festivals, attitudes, people, past achievements, natural features, traditions, events, song and a sense of history. Buried within them is a unique combination of past and present, of traditions and new ideas, of appearance and language, the potent symbols and tangible structures that help to provide a specific localized identity.

All museums embrace, reflect and celebrate these through their activities, and hence their significance to cultural identity. In terms of preservation, conservation and documentation of the cultural and natural landscape they have played an important role. However, this has largely been achieved by removing artefacts (large and small) from the natural and built environment into galleries and storerooms. Open-air museums, industrial museums and other museums have used different approaches to conserve elements from the past, often *in situ*, whilst countryside and urban interpretation has helped to proclaim the significance of sites, adding labels, signposts or other markers in the process that has witnessed the 'musealization' of the environment. 'Experts' who attach their own meanings to sites or objects have largely carried out these processes, not the people who experience them. It might be argued that the complexity of place and what it represents to individuals and communities makes it evident that the traditional museum can never capture its elusive qualities. It is impossible for the curator to acquire place, carefully label it and store it in an acid-free container. Museums can acquire fragments of place, and exhibit them together to re-create their version of place, but that is all. The essence of place lies beyond the museum, in the environment itself, and is defined by the individuals and the communities that live there.

If museums are going to play a major role in conserving places, in protecting the environment, then a new kind of museum is required with two important attributes. The first of these, the realization that the museum extends beyond the physical barrier of its walls, has been largely accepted by museums. The second attribute, community empowerment, despite the demands for social inclusion, still has a long road to travel. From the 1970s, ecomuseum practitioners have attempted to use their new philosophy to try to reach these goals, having at their core the need to represent their place, their past and the cultural identity of their inhabitants.

Ecomuseum philosophy

We suggest that the 'traditional' museum, trapped within its walls and glass cases, is not necessarily the ideal means of capturing local distinctiveness or the spirit of places, but that a new museum model that goes beyond the confines of the museum and empowers local communities might be advantageous. The ecomuseum is such a paradigm, whose origins, development and diversity has been described by Davis (1999). Before considering the key principles of the ecomuseum ideal, it is useful to gain a basic understanding of the differences between the 'traditional' museum and the ecomuseum. These differences have been very concisely illustrated by Rivard (1984: 43–53; 1988: 123–4) and Boylan (1992). They state:

> Traditional Museum = building + heritage + collections + expert staff + public visitors

and

> Ecomuseum = territory + heritage + memory + population.

More recently (2004) the 'Long Network' of ecomuseums developed in Europe provided a concise definition, namely that, '[a]n ecomuseum is a dynamic way in which communities preserve, interpret, and manage their heritage for sustainable development. An ecomuseum is based on a community agreement', *Declaration of Intent of the Long Net Workshop*, Trento (Italy), May 2004.

Ecomuseums demonstrate remarkable diversity, yet despite these variations, Davis (1999) suggested that the following list of attributes can be applied to most of them:

- The adoption of a territory that is not necessarily defined by conventional boundaries;
- The adoption of a 'fragmented site' policy that is linked to *in situ* conservation and interpretation;
- Conventional views of site ownership are abandoned; conservation and interpretation of sites is carried out via liaison, cooperation and the development of partnerships;
- The empowerment of local communities; the involvement of local people in ecomuseum activities and in the creation of their cultural identity; and,
- The potential for interdisciplinarity and for holistic interpretation is usually seized.

This list, and the characteristics identified by Corsane and Holleman (1993), have recently been further developed and utilized to assess how far ecomuseums and similar heritage management projects reach the tenets of the philosophy (Corsane 2006; Corsane *et al.* 2007). It would seem that the guiding principles for ecomuseums should enable them to conserve local heritage resources in a democratic manner and effectively capture local distinctiveness. Ecomuseum principles have now been deployed in many countries throughout the world, and in a variety of ways, responding to local physical, economic, social, cultural and political environments in order to manage the full range of environmental and heritage resources through processes that encourage public participation. Where these ecomuseum principles are utilized there is often an emphasis on self-representation; full community participation in, and ownership of, heritage resources and the management processes; rural or urban regeneration; sustainable development; and, responsible tourism.

So have ecomuseums achieved their potential, and are they able to represent and celebrate local identity? The following section discusses some recent examples from Europe and Asia to assess their impact.

Ecomuseums in practice

China – The Soga ecomuseum

In June 2005 there were seven ecomuseums in China, all of which are dedicated to sustaining ethnic minority groups: four are located in the south-western province of Guizhou. These ecomuseums were established after the concept was introduced to Chinese museologists in 1994 by the Norwegian ecomuseologist John Aage Gjestrum, with support and funding for these ecomuseum projects coming through a Sino-Norwegian agreement (An and Gjestrum 1999). The starting point for this development was the formation of an agreed set of principles for ecomuseum establishment, which became known as the Liuzhi Principles from the name of the prefecture where the meetings took place (Davis 2007).

The Soga Miao Ecomuseum (Figure 3.2) is located 208 kilometres west of the capital of Guizhou Province, Guiyang. The ecomuseum, centred in Longga Village, connects 12 villages of the Qing Miao people in the remote rural mountainous area of the Liuzhi Prefecture in the Liupanshui Municipality. This ecomuseum was to become the first in China when it was officially opened in October 1998. Its key feature is an Information Centre that houses the local 'Memory Project', which sought to document collective memories of the village inhabitants through oral recording in their own language; the Miao have no written language of their own. The memory project has since grown to include the documentation of village practices and rituals through the collection of photographs and material culture. The Information Centre also houses a professional exhibition about aspects of the Qing Miao and their culture, and from here the visitor is free to roam through the old village, meet local people and purchase craft souvenirs.

The ecomuseum project led to significant improvements for local people, with the renovation of houses and the provision of piped water and electricity, a new school and medical facilities. It appears that in all the developments of ecomuseums in these remote rural areas of China there have been major tangible benefits for the indigenous cultural minorities concerned. Every effort has been made to

53

Figure 3.2 Soga Old Village, China, 2005.

Photo: Peter Davis

make interventions in a sympathetic manner with respect for local people, their customs and beliefs, making effective use of the Liuzhi principles (Davis 2007). The conservation of the distinctiveness of local culture is central to these projects. However, ecomuseum development in China is not without risk. The focus on ethnic minorities in China's ecomuseums is fraught with potential problems, particularly the danger of transforming living cultures into mere exhibitions, with the potential loss of authenticity and cultural identity.

Japan – Miura Peninsula ecomuseum

The Miura Peninsula lies in the south-east of Kanagawa Prefecture, to the west of the urban conurbations of Yokohama and Tokyo. Traditional industries in agriculture and fishing still prosper there, but the peninsula increasingly acts as a dormitory and recreation area for people working in Yokosuka and Yokohama to the north. The ecomuseum consists of scattered natural and heritage sites across the peninsula, brought together by the Kanagawa Foundation for Academic and Cultural Exchange (K-Face). K-Face has acted as facilitator, ignoring conventional governmental boundaries: it sees the ecomuseum as a way of conserving regional cultural resources.

Figure 3.3 Restored rice terraces, Kamiayama-guchi, Miura, Japan, 2003.

Photo: Peter Davis

The network (currently five sites) includes the Yokosuka City Museum, and its branch museum at the Tenjin-jima 'marine biological garden'. This small museum adjacent to the beach houses displays material related to traditional fishing methods and boatbuilding, and has a classroom for educational visits.

The third ecomuseum site, in the Kamiayama-guchi area, is a renovated terraced rice paddy (Figure 3.3). The work on this traditional farming site brought together a team of enthusiasts who now work together to grow other traditional economic crops (such as bamboo and reeds used in vernacular housing, fruit trees and potatoes), and who seek to regain skills in crop management and in traditional fishing methods such as seine-netting. Hayama Town – in which Kamiayama and Shibasaki are located – has supported ecomuseum activities and has written the site into its local plan, central to its environmental objectives. In its role as facilitator, Hayama encouraged the ecomuseum activists to form their own Association in May 2002, and this now has the status of a non-profit organization.

The intertidal zone at the seashore site at Shibasaki has been declared a 'national treasure' by Hayama Town and is the fourth ecomuseum satellite. The site is species-rich in marine algae and invertebrate animals, and the marine rangers who work at the site monitor the life on the shore, act as guardians against poachers and provide educational tours for the public and visiting school groups. The fifth ecomuseum site in Miura is the traditional farming area of Koyasu village, which is set in a wooded undulating landscape; traditional long-roofed barns and modern buildings stand side by side. The emphasis there has been on preserving traditional methods of agriculture, and its associated material.

Although Miura ecomuseum is still at an early stage in its evolution, it is evident that the local activists have real enthusiasm for the concept, recognizing the advantages of working together, sharing expertise and training, jointly marketing their enterprises and beginning to share databases. The involvement of a major local museum in the ecomuseum network is of real significance: not only is it prepared to accept that small associations of local people have a basic right to be involved with their heritage (that heritage is not just for curators) but also it wishes to be actively involved in a larger enterprise, one with a different, more democratic vision.

Whether this ecomuseum will have meaning for all local people and visitors has yet to be tested, simply because it is a new enterprise. For the casual visitor the sites would probably be seen as isolated examples of heritage preservation, and not as an integrated effort. Many of the sites are not even signed or advertised, and most tourists (and locals) would probably pass them by unnoticed.

France – Écomusée Saint Dégan

The village of Saint Dégan lies adjacent to the River Loc'h that empties into the Gulf of Morbihan in Brittany. Founded by an association in 1969, the museum opened in 1971 and changed its name in 1978 to the 'Écomusée de Saint Dégan, Nature et Traditions du Pays d'Auray'. It is housed in a group of renovated farm buildings dating from the seventeenth to the early twentieth centuries where furniture, everyday objects, tools and machinery are displayed to provide a glimpse of rural life in the nineteenth century in the region of Auray. Rural crafts are well represented, including clog-making, thatching, blacksmithing, basket-weaving and spinning. The reconstruction of kitchens and living rooms in the old buildings provides such an authentic atmosphere that the visitor is left feeling that the original inhabitants have simply made a quick exit and may return at any moment.

Peron (1984) listed the three basic aims of the ecomuseum:

1 To make better known the richness of the heritage within the Auray region;
2 Within an educational environment, to inform young people of the heritage they have received from the past; and,
3 To enable visitors to understand better the natural beauty and soul of the region.

These aims are achieved within a very special setting (Figure 3.4). The main farmhouse buildings have been beautifully restored on site – the Association was awarded the Prix de la Fondation des Pays de France in 1984 and the Prix René Fontaine in 1986 for their work – and house wonderful collections of objects, mainly donated by local people. There are very few labels on show, as guided tours are the key interpretive methodology. Exclusively in French, they are led by

Figure 3.4 Ecomusée de St Dégan. The farm, France, 1998.

Photo: Peter Davis

enthusiastic and knowledgeable local people, members of the Association who give accounts of the special features of local architecture, furniture, machinery, tools, costume and skills. Footpaths run from the museum into the surrounding countryside and encourage further exploration.

In many ways Saint Dégan is a model ecomuseum. It was created by local people, and is run by them on a purely voluntary basis. Through their activities they have preserved a delightful site, carefully researched and documented its history, and collected and catalogued the material culture of Morbihan in a professional manner.

Italy – Ecomuseo dei terrazzamenti e della vite, Cortemilia

The potential to create an ecomuseum in Cortemilia was recognized by one of the authors of this article (Murtas) in 1995, when a new law was passed that enabled the creation of ecomuseums in this region of Italy. Because of her direct involvement, we have thought it appropriate to give here a more detailed account of its origins and the techniques used in its delivery as a means of exploring how inclusive ecomuseum processes can revitalize local identity.

The mid-1990s was an opportune moment for change because of the appalling environmental, social and economic situation in the Bormida Valley. The area, which benefited from a strategic geographical location between the coast and the hinterland, was once renowned for its high-quality agricultural produce, but had suffered, like many other rural areas in Europe, from economic decline, emigration and the consequent abandonment of farmland. However, the Cortemilia area had two other major environmental problems which affected people's lives, namely pollution and flooding. From 1889 to 1996, the valley had been heavily polluted by a chemical factory located 30 kilometers from Cortemilia. Pollutants had been discharged directly into the Bormida River, and noxious fumes from the plant spread into the valley. These pollutants affected soils, crops and the health of local people. The once-famous wine, vegetable and cheese production ceased, and over time the remarkable terraced agricultural landscapes were abandoned, reverting to partial woodland. In 1994, a terrible flood emphasized the fragility of a cultural landscape that had lost its purpose. The terraced hillsides lay partly ruined at the bottom of the valley, a visual metaphor for environmental and social erosion.

In 1996, the factory closed, but only after several years of lobbying by the local inhabitants. The townspeople of Cortemilia now had an opportunity to assess their options for the future. Would they simply accept the collapse of local culture, or be willing to accept the challenge of creating a new future by utilizing the town's local distinctiveness with its links to history, landscape, economy and environment? It was at this point that an ecomuseum approach was suggested. Although ecomuseum theory and the potential for a new way of working were not very easy to explain to local people, perhaps most importantly an ecomuseum project – if accepted by the region – would attract funding and could deliver real benefits.

The Cortemilia proposal was chosen for support by the region, but the project immediately had to counter a significant legacy. The town had seemingly lost confidence in itself. Local people felt they had no previous experience with cultural projects or in cooperating at local, regional or national levels. As well as this perceived lack of skills there were no museums, no public library and little collective awareness about local heritage. When local people were asked about the special and distinctive attributes of the area, most inhabitants struggled to find an appropriate answer. Some suggested the town's main church and its medieval tower; most were silent. It appeared that the thousands of tangible and intangible elements that make the Cortemilia area distinctive and special were invisible to local eyes.

The ecomuseum team had to make choices about where to begin, and the area's terraced landscape was chosen as the key ecomuseum theme, not only because the terraces are at risk, but because they give a sense of continuity in time and space. Murtas (pers. comm.) suggests the terraced hillsides are 'like a territorial skeleton, supporting human activities and dreams'. They link people and places and element with element; they are inclusive and not exclusive; they are a good example of a sustainable approach towards local and available resources; most important, they were built by the community and not by an architect or engineer; the terraces have no individual signature but are a collective enterprise in harmony with nature, following natural laws and not fighting them. All the project's aims – the contemporary interpretation, preservation and enhancement of the elements of local distinctiveness and community values – were linked to the terraced landscape.

The project coordinators realized that a gradual approach would be necessary to encourage local potential and the empowerment of the community. It was recognized that the conservation, maintenance and rebuilding of the terraced landscape would never happen without a revolution in perception and attitudes, and that the ecomuseum's role was to give strength, self-confidence, good practical examples and contemporary values to local heritage and local distinctiveness. The adoption of a 'traditional museum' project was not deemed appropriate to deal with a landscape with a very strong character. The need for a more dynamic and revolutionary approach was seen to be of strategic importance. Within the framework of the ecomuseum paradigm, practical work with the community began by using three different approaches, all of them related.

The first dealt with values and meanings, providing the community with tangible examples of other terraced places in the world and offering a contemporary interpretation of them. This message was then distributed using interpretative exhibits (using stories written by children about how the terraces had been formed), local newspapers, summer work-camps, learning visits and welcoming external groups who have a similar approach towards democratic and participative local development.

The second approach sought to overcome local skepticism and pessimism through building projects. Emphasis was on dialogue, discussion and action, not on ecomuseum theory. Structures were chosen because of their position, qualities, state of abandonment and potential for interpretation. None of them were restored just for the sake of conservation, but always linked to collective re-use. The ecomuseum has renovated three main structures, located in different part of the Cortemilia area. An historical building in the old village centre has been transformed into an interpretation centre, library and temporary exhibition space. It has facilities for video projection and meetings, and acts as the ecomuseum headquarters. This prize-winning restoration has encouraged similar projects; other buildings located in the same square have been restored. The square itself, once a car park, is now a charming pedestrian area, paved with stone and used for exhibitions, theatre and film.

Another building is a farm with its vineyard and orchard (Figure 3.5). Sitting on a superb terraced hilltop, the farm and its terraced fields had been abandoned for more than 30 years. Despite the complexities of multiple land ownership, the ecomuseum project acquired it and additional money was found for its restoration. After a year the structure, even if not totally restored, was opened to the local community and now hosts schools, specialist groups and training courses. The vineyard has also been restored and the ecomuseum has its own niche production of wine. Local, ancient varieties of vegetables and fruit are grown on the terraced fields, creating an important link to the past while acting as an important gene bank. A third building is a small traditional store for chestnuts. Located in a hamlet belonging to the Cortemilia area, it was semi-derelict, but its special rounded shape makes it unique. The restoration, aided by a local expert, used traditional dry stone techniques. The inauguration of this small building became a major local event: everyone from the village came to the celebration, a clear

Figure 3.5 Restored farmhouse and terraced hillsides of Cortemilia, 2006.

Photo: Donatella Murtas

message of a revitalized sense of belonging. Now, one year later, the chestnut hut is being used for its original purpose, for storing, drying and packing an important local crop. Murtas refers to the restoration of these buildings as a 'sleeping beauty effect' – long forgotten buildings being brought back to life.

The third approach taken by the ecomuseum team relates to community building through activities designed to bring people together and build collective values and projects. Sustainable local development and enhancement of local heritage is at the core of this group of projects, which often focus on intangible heritage, on local knowledge and traditions. Central to these discussions was the production of a Parish Map for the village, used as a means of stimulating local discussion and promoting pride in place. Efforts were made to revitalize traditional events such as the carnival, the midsummer night feast and seasonal local markets. The number and qualities of these initiatives have now grown, and offer an opportunity to strengthen the local economy by links to local produce.

The ecomuseum project has enabled a growing interest in the Cortemilia area. Schools and adult groups are beginning to show a real interest in local heritage; local producers are cooperating and promoting their wares using the 'terraced landscape' as a marketing asset and as a logo. In addition, although less overtly, the ecomuseum is creating a memory bank of recorded histories, capturing the unwritten past of the area, and producing publications and films about the town.

After a dark past of pollution and misgivings about the future, the people of Cortemilia have found a way, through ecomuseum processes, of shaping a future and of ensuring sustainable local development. They have found a new vision and new ways of living, demonstrating that quality of life and sense of belonging to a specific place are strongly dependent on an understanding and appreciation of local heritage.

Conclusion – Ecomuseums and local identity

So have ecomuseums, with their holistic approach and community focus proved to be a new museological *utopia*? Do ecomuseums demonstrate the authenticity of place, a foundation for collective understanding and involvement and a better means of representing local identity? The ecomuseums described above all have strengths and weaknesses, but essentially the local people involved in them are motivated by a perceived need to conserve heritage and cultural resources as expressions of their local identity. They are democratic institutions that serve the local community and present an identity to visitors. It is evident, however, that they are all very different, each having found its own approaches to deal with questions of local distinctiveness and identity; each has its own network of connections and stakeholders, created relationships with a variety of partners or collaborators to provide funding and expertise. It is also clear that all these enterprises face risks and challenges – changes in political or social climates, loss of funding or changes in personnel could have a profound impact. But what would have happened to these extraordinary places, to local identity and distinctiveness, without these community interventions? Their future would not have been assured by a conventional museum approach, even if local museums had demonstrated an interest.

Heron (1991), whilst recognizing ecomuseum diversity, suggests that the three principal features of ecomuseums are their strong sense of local pride in traditions, customs and vernacular architecture, a link with economic regeneration and their attempts to save a threatened culture. In our experience, the one characteristic that appears to be common to all ecomuseums is their pride in the place that they represent. This is true whatever the nature of the ecomuseum, whether it be a rural farming community in mainland China, a scattered group of heritage sites on a Japanese peninsula, an old farm settlement in Brittany or abandoned terraces in northern Italy. This pride is expressed in a variety of ways. It can be seen in the careful design of an exhibition, in the sheer pleasure people take in performing local music and dance, the pride in demonstrating weaving skills or delivering bold and imaginative interpretation. Ecomuseums encourage dialogue with local people as well as inviting visitors to explore their territory, which can only promote a better understanding of sense of place and local identity.

Inevitably, many ecomuseums are not 'professional' establishments, and it has to be said that buildings and collections are not always well conserved – indeed larger objects frequently appear abandoned – and hand-written labels are commonplace.

This gives many ecomuseums a charm of their own, a welcome contrast to a museum world dominated by slick presentation and marketing gloss. Ecomuseums are often simple and accessible, and especially effective when interpreted through third-person interpretation by local people. The key to their success is the drive and enthusiasm of the people who are responsible for their operation and their ability to capture, appreciate and interpret their own heritage.

Bibliography

An, L. and Gjestrum, J.A. (1999) 'The ecomuseum in theory and practice: The first Chinese ecomuseum established', *Nordisk Museologi*, 2: 65–86.

Boylan, P. (1992) 'Ecomuseums and the new museology. Some definitions', *Museums Journal*, 92(4): 29.

Buttimer, A. (1980) 'Home, reach and the sense of place', in A. Buttimer and D. Seamon (eds) *The Human Experience of Space and Place*, London: Croom Helm, 166–87.

Clifford, S. and King, A. (1993) 'Losing your place', in S. Clifford and A. King (eds) *Local Distinctiveness: Place, Particularity and Identity*, London: Common Ground.

Common Ground (1996) *Common Ground, Promotional Leaflet*. London: Common Ground.

Corsane, G. (2006) 'Using ecomuseum indicators to evaluate the Robben Island Museum and World Heritage Site', *Landscape Research*, 31(4): 399–418.

Corsane, G., Davis, P., Elliot, S., Maggi, M., Murtas, D. and Rogers, S. (2007) 'Ecomuseum evaluation: Experiences in Piemonte and Liguria, Italy', *International Journal of Heritage Studies*, 13(2): 101–16.

Corsane, G. and Holleman, W. (1993) 'Ecomuseums: A brief evaluation', in R. De Jong (ed.) *Museums and the Environment*, Pretoria: Southern Africa Museums Association, 111–25.

Davis, P. (1999) *Ecomuseums: A Sense of Place*, London and New York: Continuum.

Davis, P. (2007) 'Ecomuseums and sustainability in Italy, Japan and China: Adaptation through implementation', in S. Knell, S. MacLeod and S. Watson (eds) *Museum Revolutions: How Museums Change and Are Changed*, London: Routledge, 198–214.

Davis, P., Maggi, M., Su, D., Varine, H. de and Zhang, J. (eds) (2006) *Communication and Exploration, Guiyang, China, 2005*, Trento, Italy: Provincia Autonoma di Trento.

Heron, P. (1991) 'Ecomuseums – a new museology?' *Alberta Museums Review*, 17(2): 8–11.

Leslie, K. (2006) *A Sense of Place: West Sussex Parish Maps*, Chichester: West Sussex County Council.

Meinig, D.W. (1979) 'The beholding eye: Ten versions of the same scene', in D.W. Meinig (ed.) *The Interpretation of Ordinary Landscapes*, New York: Oxford University Press, 33–50.

Peron, J. (1984) *Écomusée St. Dégan en Brec'h*, Auray, France: Association Nature et Traditions du Pays d'Auray.

Relph, E.E. (1976) *Place and Placelessness*, Pion: London.

Rivard, R. (1984) *Opening up the Museum*, Quebec City. [Typescript at the Documentation Center, Direction des Musées de France, Paris].

Rivard, R. (1988) 'Museums and ecomuseums – questions and answers', in J.A. Gjestrum and M. Maure (eds) *Økomuseumsboka – Identitet, Økologi, Deltakelse*, Tromsø, Norway: Norsk ICOM, 123–8.

4

Representing identities at local municipal museums: Cultural forums or identity bunkers?

Marta Anico

Introduction

Heritage has played a decisive role in the definition and assertion of cultural identities, becoming increasingly prominent in the field of cultural policies. In post-industrial and postmodern societies, heritage is frequently described as a cultural legacy which is both 'good and necessary', something that should be cherished and preserved, celebrated and promoted for its ability to represent a wide range of social and cultural identities. This growing appreciation of cultural manifestations and collective legacies is an identifiable global trend and has resulted in the rise of heritage processes where cultural visibility is enacted through various practices, politics and displays. There are several reasons that account for this situation: postcolonialism, globalization, migration, cultural diversity, and transnational and local identity movements are just some examples of the significant changes observed in contemporary societies that contribute to the dramatic increase of heritage. In a global scenario of rapid movement, fluxes and changes, heritage arises as a particularly effective resource for asserting continuity and stability which enable societies to define and anchor their identity.

The encounters between past, present and future, the global and the local, between different cultures and societies have turned heritage into a central concern for many social groups, leading to the promotion of local, regional, national or ethnic singularities that help to represent and assert difference and distinctiveness in a world of increasing similarity. However, we must not forget that heritage is, and has always been, an ideological and symbolic construction, submitted to and influenced by the historical, political and social frameworks in which cultural meanings are produced and interpreted (Kaplan 2006). Therefore, it emerges as a socio-cultural discourse based upon highly valued cultural referents that have the ability to enact and reinforce a shared feeling of connection and belonging to a place, a time, a community. Cultural practices and displays such as museum exhibitions, the collection and documentation of fragments of material culture, cultural performances, cultural theming, as well as public references to the past, or to the local are some of the strategies designed to make people aware and informed of their cultural legacies, made visible, legible, and in many cases visitable (Dicks 2003).

This chapter is premised on the assumption that culture, cultural heritage and museums have become central to political agendas due to their ability to define, celebrate and also question the cultural identity of social groups. It specifically aims to discuss the connections observed between heritage, museums and local identities in places that have experienced significant changes associated with social and economic hardships, and where populations are increasingly mobile and multicultural. We propose to do so by studying the case of the Museums of Loures, located on the outskirts of the city of Lisbon, Portugal, which integrates two distinctive museological units, the Municipal Museum of Loures (MML) and the Ceramics Museum of Sacavém (CMS), as well as several other local heritage referents that form part of the municipality's cultural landscape.

The underlying argument is that the display of local heritage in municipal museums results in a fragmented and hybrid cultural discourse composed of two separate but complementary narratives related with the contrasts between different times and cultures and the fragmentation of local memories. The ideas and values displayed in municipal and other local museums frequently act as a protective strategy, promoting an essentialist and primordial identity paradigm based on the existence of a mythical local community and a vision of a past of authenticity, solidarity, place and local distinctiveness. There are considerable risks regarding this retrospective nostalgia that excludes, ignores and sometimes depreciates the new configurations of the present. Focusing on an imagined past, which vaguely resonates with the experience of only a few, may transform local and municipal museums into identity bunkers. While concentrating their heritage discourses on territorially based cultural referents and on a particular community whose origins are supposedly rooted in the place, other communities may experience feelings of exclusion and dis-identification, thus making it very difficult for local museums to achieve the aims of social cohesion and cultural integration.

However, and paradoxically, the same museums that celebrate these endogamic versions of identity also incorporate many of the trends that define postmodern museological practices and displays. Therefore, the representation of the local and of the place also deploys culturally diverse heritage as a means to promote an effective dialogue between a great diversity of cultures, topics and social groups that establish their presence in the new territories of postmodernity. This strategy also enables museums to respond to the main problems and issues that affect contemporary societies, such as multiculturalism, social marginalization, cultural exclusion and ethnic conflicts. While contrasting different perceptions regarding the definition of culture, heritage and identity, the same museums that may be described as cultural bunkers, can also act as cultural centres, where social and cultural aspects tend to be captured and reframed at a deeper and comprehensive level. This does not conceal the fact that these displays are social, cultural and historical constructions which make an explicit use of comparative analysis and contact zones insights (Clifford 1997).

If this is a general trend observed in local museums, it is therefore pertinent to ask, do the museums of Loures operate as identity bunkers, as cultural forums or both? To answer this central question we will address other aspects such as:

Which social groups do they represent? Whose cultures? And how do they do so? We will first look at the social, economic and political changes that have occurred in the municipality of Loures over the past 30 years and then observe how these transformations have been perceived and displayed in museums.

Recent transformations in Loures

Loures is the fifth largest municipality in the country in terms of population, with approximately 200,000 inhabitants. Situated on the outskirts of Lisbon, Loures forms part of the Lisbon Metropolitan Area and reflects some of the characteristics present in other regions of the Portuguese national territory: a growing movement of population from the interior regions to the cities of the littoral coast and the demographic concentration in urban districts. Comprising 18 administrative districts, the municipality of Loures includes a mixture of rural, industrial and urban landscapes. Although the rural districts located in the northern area of the municipality are also the largest in terms of territorial dimension, they are the least populated (approximately 4,000 inhabitants). In contrast, the districts situated in the south-west, in the administrative border of the municipality of Lisbon, are smaller and more populated (approximately 20,000 inhabitants). This demographic concentration and development pattern must be seen in the context of the influence exerted by the capital city, Lisbon. This means that Loures, as well as other municipalities located in the administrative borders of the capital, has grown and developed due to its relation and connection with Lisbon. Let us now look at the interplay between the political, social and economic interests that are present in this specific context of analysis.

Founded in 1886, the municipality of Loures experienced a slow demographic growth throughout the first half of the twentieth century (1890–1950) followed by a considerable increase between 1950 and 1991, particularly significant during the 1970s and 1980s. In its origins, Loures was a rural territory that supplied Lisbon with agricultural products and goods, benefiting from the proximity to the city and from the existence of good communications and accessibility routes. If this was true for the northern areas, industry was taking its place more to the south, closer to the rivers Trancão and Tejo. Both agriculture and industry have been of great significance in the municipality due to their economic and social implications. If the northern areas have been traditionally described as rural, industry has also taken a specific place in districts such as Sacavém, which have been heavily industrialized for decades. This is a trend that goes back to the nineteenth century, when populations from different regions of the country first began to come to Loures in response to the labour demands of the industries located in the industrial riverside area.

Even though these aspects help to explain some of the demographic growth experienced in Loures, they do not account for all the dimensions of this phenomenon, particularly if we take into consideration how the agricultural production dwindled and how many industries experienced a considerable decline during the twentieth century. Some of the factories closed down, others considerably reduced their production with a corresponding decrease in the number of jobs that were available. However, this does not mean that the population has followed this same declining trend, on the contrary. Loures geographical position, located in the suburbs of Lisbon, therefore explains the constant and persisting movement of internal migration from the interior regions of the country. At the same time, new international migration patterns were emerging. The de-colonization processes that followed the Revolution of April 1974 led to the return of thousands of people from Portugal's former and recently independent colonies. These additional population flows brought diversity and change, transforming the cultural landscape into a multicultural and plural one. This diversity, with all of its consequences, was amplified and reinforced by a second wave of immigrants from Eastern Europe and Brazil that came to Loures in the 1980s and the 1990s. Still, the transformations occurring in Loures were much more complex than this demographic growth can account for.

The Revolution of April 1974 and the consequent political democratization brought considerable changes to Portuguese society, on the political scene, as well as in the social, cultural and economic spheres. The country gradually opened up and experienced a delayed modernity with the democratization of education and culture, the emergence and affirmation of middle classes, social mobility and the expansion of consumption, aspects that were later on consolidated when Portugal joined the European Economic Community in 1986. Portuguese civil society soon realized that knowledge, culture and information were important instruments of empowerment and therefore invested in the improvement of educational standards and in the development of the service sector. However, the country experiences an intermediate stage of development, described as a state of multidirectional and unfinished modernity (Machado and Costa 2000).

Loures is currently experiencing a new configuration that comprises different social and cultural identities and is considerably different than the one from which it originally derived. Approximately 73 per cent of the population works in the service sector, leaving behind the traditional agricultural and industrial activities. Educational standards have also improved, and the number of people attending secondary and university levels has increased from 14 per cent in 1991 to 34 per cent in 2001. But what is notable is that this modernization has not only affected Loures' social and economic structure but has also produced significant consequences in the cultural landscape of the municipality, influencing and changing local ways of life, thus resulting in the emergence of a new social and cultural configuration. Even the physical landscape has changed making rural and urban areas increasingly indistinctive. All of these recent transformations have resulted in the coexistence of traditional cultural practices with modern and postmodern ones, incorporating and reflecting the diversity, plurality and syncretism of post-industrial, postcolonial and postmodern societies.

Heritage and municipal museums: The production of local narratives

Rapid population growth, multiculturalism, and the restructuring of local economies triggered by social and economic decline are some of the forces that frequently lead to heritage activation processes. These forces provide a means to promote new forms of belonging through the creation of local identifying discourses that usually result in general approval and consensus (Prats 1997). In fact, when cultural and social identities become uncertain or ephemeral, there are a wide range of symbolic resources which emerge and form part of the construction of new identity discourses. It is precisely when identity boundaries become increasingly weak, indistinctive and fluid that the effort to assert the 'authenticity' and 'distinctiveness' that enables cultural validation of identity and political claims of all kinds escalates. This is particularly important in places such as Loures, with multiple communities and cultural references that permanently question the differences and similarities between 'us' and 'them'.

As part of a discursive realm, identity needs something that simultaneously allows its versions to be represented but, above all, that allows them to be objectified. In order to make these discursive fictions appear real, individuals and collectives turn to heritage for its ability to create and promote a narrative of singularity, similarity and unity that conveys a particular version of identity in the public sphere. In this sense, heritage is more than a simple legacy from the past. It is a product of the present appropriated by different social groups as an instrument for the creation of new identification referents that articulate a sense of belonging to a distinctive place, group or cause.

Heritage is therefore a social construction based upon symbolic structures. It is clearly an ideological construct which derives from the interplay of complex historical, political and social dynamics that determine which structures and referents should be selected, combined and interpreted in order to acquire new meanings as identity symbols. There are always choices implicit in these processes. While selecting and interpreting cultural referents from the past and the present, many others are ignored and excluded, and when this happens conflicts may arise and integration may give way to exclusion. For all these reasons it is safe to argue that heritage is an inherently political process. To reflect upon it implies a serious discussion regarding power: the power to choose the ideas, values and knowledges displayed in heritage discourses and narratives (Peralta 2006).

When I started my research in Loures, my intent was to find answers to a multitude of questions. For instance, if local museums represent local communities, their culture and ways of life, how do they address the current cultural diversity present in their landscape? If populations are increasingly mobile and submitted to the influence of global flows, how does this incorporate in the definition of local singularity and place distinctiveness? And which communities do these museums represent: the original and mythical ones from the past, or those hybrid and fragmented ones from the present? Finally, I was also particularly interested in uncovering both the continuities and ruptures in the heritage discourse displayed in the museums of Loures throughout their history, as well as the cultural mechanisms by which they have adjusted to the current shape and configuration of the municipality. The main question behind all of my reflections was an attempt to comprehend the motives which sparked choices that were made during different historical moments of these museums. What was excluded or included and why?

Heritage and museums are powerful tools in meaning-making processes, as vehicles for the transmission of ideas and values (Ashworth 2007) and as cultural resources for reframing relationships between the universal and the particular, the global and the local, the collective and the individual, the past and the present. However, as human products of different times and places, they tend to incorporate and reflect the dominant values in each moment, and in each society. They represent cultural ideologies and as such they are political in all senses. However, this does not mean that they are necessarily hegemonic or univocal. Museums and heritage have the ability to negotiate and create new identities, values and understandings (Smith 2006), promoting unique cultural experiences which enable audiences to actively construct their own meanings and interpretations. However, this is not a simple task. It implies a paradigm that often falls into a wider political debate regarding the social role of these processes.

Museums are relational institutions, and the Museums of Loures are no exception. They reflect and influence their surroundings and their survival depends on the capacity to adapt to shifting contexts and on the ability to negotiate change. This implies the redefinition and reinvention of the museum's identity and the abandonment of a set of obsolete values inherited from their institutional past. The future entails many possible paths. The difficulties arise in choosing the most appropriate one for each particular context.

In the case selected for this study, it is possible to identify three distinctive moments in the creation of a local heritage discourse which reveal how these local museums have established their priorities and purposes in each phase of their history. The first of these moments began in 1979 with the promulgation of the Local Government Act which determined the competences and responsibilities of City Councils in Portugal in the aftermath of the Revolution of 1974. This legislation established the guidelines for local authorities' interventions and explains how and why many local municipal museums were created and developed. From this moment onwards, local administrations have assumed the task of promoting culture as a fundamental political responsibility and the municipality of Loures has followed this trend.

In Portugal, municipal councils are the main promoters of local heritage and local museums, a tendency that may be explained by different factors. If it is true that there has been a public demand for cultural projects and activities, it is also true that the acknowledgement of this need was actively promoted by local politicians that soon realized the benefits they could derive from intervening in the cultural sector (Anico and Peralta 2007). Culture and cultural projects, such as local museums, frequently achieve high levels of consensus and seldom attract conflict and contestation. This explains why they have assumed an active role in the construction and promotion of a discourse that enhances the importance and relevance of culture as a symbol of local progress and development, which in turn translates into electoral benefits for its political promoters.

But the year of 1979 was also decisive for another reason: it was when local political authorities decided to acquire a symbolic building of both historic and architectonic value – Casa do Adro. The building and adjacent structures were considerably degraded requiring an architectonic rehabilitation project that was designed with the purpose of accommodating a cultural centre that would incorporate the Cultural Department of the City Council, a municipal library and a local museum.

While this rehabilitation took place, the professionals of the future museum proceeded to conduct an extensive field research composed of heritage inventories and the creation of a small and incipient collection. This finally resulted in the creation of the MML which opened to the public in 1985 with three exhibition rooms destined to represent local ethnography, archaeology and history. Despite the transformations of the Museum from its origins to the present day, it is safe to argue that its core identity has been the same throughout the years. It is a local museum that reflects the municipality's ethnographic, historic and archaeological heritage, an assumption that has always been present, operating as a guideline for future developments.

The year of 1985 and the inauguration of the Museum set the standard for the beginning of a second phase characterized by the definition of a museological plan, which determined the topics, purposes and goals of this project, as well as the definition of audiences and communication strategies. During this period, the museums' professionals were less concerned with research and collection management and more focused on achieving the support and collaboration of local groups such as schools, ethnographic and heritage associations, and also that of the immigrant collectives that were just then arriving in Loures. This strategy was designed in order to determine which were the most relevant cultural references present in the municipality with the help and involvement of the local population, a strategy that has contributed to the creation of an emotional and affective attachment that has extended its influence to the present, and that we could observe in many of the interviews conducted with local informants.

These efforts persisted throughout an entire decade and its results became public with the celebrations of the tenth anniversary of the Museum in 1995, a symbolic commemoration that made way for a new stage, one of consolidation and validation of the work previously accomplished. It was the year in which the information concerning the Museum's transfer to another building was made available to the public. The Museum had experienced a considerable growth. Its physical and symbolic dimension was no longer compatible with a small space in a shared building with other City Council Departments. After many efforts and requests from the museum professional team, local political authorities finally responded by offering a 'new' Municipal Museum to Loures. This achievement must be associated with the fact that during its first decade of existence, the MML had been awarded with several national and international prizes. The award for Best Educational Services (1993) granted by the APOM (Portuguese Association of Museology), and the special mention from the European Museum of the Year Award, attributed by the European Museum Forum (1993) were both received with great enthusiasm and locally interpreted as a symbol of distinction and recognition for the high standards of the MML practices and displays.

The project for this 'new' museum, located in a sixteenth-century convent, was therefore presented by local authorities as a reward for the excellence of this cultural institution which actively contributed to promoting Loures and making the locality visible by placing it on a global cultural map. However, Loures had changed dramatically and with the transformations came the need to expand the scope of the museological interventions. This resulted in the definition of a Municipal Museological Plan (MMP) in 1999 that included new proposals such as the CMS (opened in 2000), José Pedro's Museum (opened in 2005), the Wine Museum (still in project), and the concept of 'Exterior Heritage', a cultural route through the territory of Loures that encompasses different cultural referents associated with the local historic, archaeological, industrial and rural heritage. Emerging in a difficult moment in the history of Loures, the MMP acted as a counterpoint to negative and destabilizing experiences, offering a comprehensive view of the region's present cultural landscape. New cultural themes such as gender, vernacular heritage, rural and industrial legacies, multiculturalism and new museological practices were deployed in order to create an inclusive and representative local museum network.

If the MML was designed to celebrate the municipality's ethnographic and archaeological legacies, the CMS was created with the purpose of preserving the industrial heritage which also represents a fundamental cultural reference for place identity. Located on the former site of a ceramics factory of international artistic, social and economic relevance, with more than 150 years of continuous labour (it was founded in 1856), this Museum was soon awarded the Luigi Michelitti Prize (2002) for its contribution to the memorialization and representation of the factory's artistic production and social history, as well as for its efforts in obtaining the participation of the local community. This museum presents a particularly interesting case study of the cultural dynamics which arose to preserve the memory of a local referent that had physically disappeared from the landscape, after a polemic bankruptcy process. This ultimately acted as a starting point for a heritage project that aims to define some of the qualities that determine the special nature of the place. The initial fear of losing the history and memory of the industrial past has therefore been resolved in the creation of a museum designed as a compensatory strategy (Lübbe quoted in Huyssen 1994) destined to revive and restructure place identity that can also be described as a process of musealizing frustration (Prats 2005).

Despite this intimate relationship with the Ceramics Factory of Sacavém the museological program of this museum also takes into account the display of other topics which portray the vast industrial heritage of Loures, since there were many other industrial units located in this territory that have exerted their influence on local ways of life. Validated by professional authorities and largely supported by the local population and local politicians, the museum has also tried to incorporate the more recent changes in the municipality, expanding the scope in which topics concerning industrial heritage have been approached.

Continuities, changes and variations in local representations

These three moments in the history of the Museums of Loures reveal some continuity in reference to the dominant ideas and values that have been communicated over the years, such as the narrative emphasis on the rural and industrial local heritage, but they also reveal variations regarding the museums' fundamental discursive lines. The growing concern for the inclusion of topics related to the representation of the working classes, gender or multiculturalism, represents some of the innovations observed in the meaning-making processes of these local museums, reflecting a global museological trend that has been locally incorporated in the exhibitions, catalogues and in the different cultural performances developed in Loures. The collaboration of former workers from the Ceramics Factory in artistic workshops, the presentation of exhibitions concerning women's role in local industry and local society, and the display of ethnic cultural performances in moments such as the inauguration of an exhibition centred on migration are some of the examples of the more recent discursive variations.

These innovations can be interpreted as an adjustment to the transformations that have affected the social and cultural fabric of Loures over the past 30 years. Changes such as the ones previously described have posed considerable challenges to these local museums, resulting in multiple strategic adjustments destined to enhance the museums' ability to respond to the cultural diversity of the present. There are many examples of initiatives developed in order to achieve this goal of negotiating change that may be grouped into four different categories, following Hooper-Greenhill's (2000) definition of the postmuseum: the introduction of new professional roles and competences, the segmentation of audiences, the presence of different voices and narratives and the flexibility of the museums' cultural borders and physical frontiers.

Introducing new professional roles

Museums in Loures have come a long way from the Casa do Adro and the earlier practices and displays of the 1980s. This is particularly evident in terms of their internal organization. Today, they comprise four distinctive functional areas: Research, Collection Management, Educational Services, Documentation Centers, Communication and Promotion. This structure contributes to the specialization of roles and competences, and has been positively assessed by the museums' professionals. The observations made in the field reveal that this segmentation results in the creation of interdisciplinary teams, specifically designed for particular projects, generating a cultural and professional dynamic that enables these professionals to simultaneously develop different tasks and routines associated with the different projects in which they participate (exhibitions, research, conferences, brochures, cultural activities, etc.). Each area is responsible for implementing specific projects and for the presentation of annual reports and accounts which show precisely how their activities have contributed to the museums' overall cultural and social mission. More recently, and given the institutional changes experienced by museums worldwide, the Museums of Loures have created a new department considered to be fundamental for achieving their purposes, that is, the Fundraising and Development Sector, responsible for international contacts and projects with other museum and cultural institutions, most of them presented within the framework of the European Union Funding Programmes.

The segmentation of audiences

The observations and inquiries made in the field have also revealed that these local museums have a broad comprehension of their audiences. There is no such thing as 'the public'. There are many different audiences, with different characteristics and needs that have led the museums' professionals to design specific cultural activities for each segment. The museums' visitors include groups from local schools and associations, private collectors (in the case of the CMS), informants and other collaborators, as well as visitors who come from varying places and backgrounds, with no previous knowledge about Loures, or its local cultures and population.

As in many museums, schools represent one of the most significant groups of visitors in Loures and there are many projects which are specially designed to diversify the offer of cultural and educational activities for this particular group. These activities include artistic and pedagogic workshops, conferences, guided tours and an initiative entitled 'Heritage School Projects', in which they have largely concentrated their efforts and resources since the 1980s. This initiative consists of the definition of a set of themes and topics related to Loures' cultural heritage, establishing the guidelines for the presentation of research projects of schools from the municipality. The professionals of the museums' educational team are then responsible for selecting the schools, determining which kind of support will be assigned, for managing this support, following up the projects and evaluating their final reports. It is interesting to note that these projects may or may not include visits to the museums. In many cases, representatives from the museums visit the schools, presenting some of the objects from their collections, giving lectures explaining how the different professional areas operate, or offering technical and research assistance.

Local schools are not the only audience that receives the museums' attention. The emergence of social movements in defence of civil rights represents an important feature of contemporary societies which has experienced a considerable growth in recent decades. Museums have been confronted with increasing demands from all over the world to incorporate the cultural and educational rights of groups that have been traditionally excluded from these institutions' cultural practices and displays.

Both the MML and the CMS have assumed this challenge as a central concern regarding their social role. This ethical and social assumption has resulted in the presentation of inclusive museological experiences that aim to be global and involve senses and emotions with the purpose of creating different possibilities of exploration. These concerns have translated into architectonic adjustments, catalogues in Braille, catwalks for the visually impaired, objects that can be touched and manipulated, headphones for guided tours, and accessible workshops designed to expand the options offered when visiting these museums.

Different voices and narratives

The museums' efforts to enhance familiarity with their visitors and their broader socio-cultural context have resulted in the combination of different voices and narratives in the creation of local heritage discourses. When questioned about the museums' social responsibility, the professionals always refer to these concerns regarding the diversification of themes and topics that have been addressed over the years. Exhibitions centred on women and their role in local and national history, the representation of the lives of the rural and industrial working classes, as well as displays about the cultures of different ethnic communities that form part of Loures' social and cultural fabric are frequently highlighted as a response to contemporary social concerns.

This response is obviously linked with the democratization of culture and of cultural institutions. Diversifying topics, amplifying the scope of analysis of subject matters and including multiple voices in museums' practices and displays are some of the mechanisms set in motion by the professionals as an answer to the representational demands of different groups. The publication of bilingual catalogues, the mailing of invitations to the exhibitions and events that take place in the museums, the formal letters thanking the collaboration of local institutions and individuals, the municipal medals and cultural merit awards are all examples of communication instruments which are designed to reciprocate the support received from the different communities and local social actors, thus recognizing their fundamental role, as well as stimulating an emotional involvement that sets the basis for further collaborations. Many of these informants have never visited a museum. Some never will. This is especially the case of the older inhabitants of Loures and Sacavém, as well as some of the migrant groups whose contribution is always made public through references in catalogues, panels or oral discourses.

The flexibility of museums' cultural borders and physical frontiers

Local museums, and Loures museum network is no exception, have also been confronted with another kind of challenge. The constant fluxes of people, culture, information, and economic resources have influenced museums, making them aware of the necessity to become more flexible in order to adapt to their global and local surroundings. This consciousness has led these cultural institutions to the establishment of specific measures that allow them to go beyond the limits and constraints imposed by their cultural borders and physical frontiers. The survival of museums in contemporary societies depends upon their ability to adapt and this frequently requires them to leave the actual building and to present innovative proposals.

In the municipal museums of Loures, these proposals include the definition of a communication strategy that comprises different supports, such as the publications that derive from research developed by the museums' professionals, the exhibition catalogues, the creation of a specialized journal entitled *Museums*, the websites and CD ROMs, as well as the participation in museums networks and international forums and the partnerships established with government and private institutions. These are some of the solutions designed by the Museums of Loures with the purpose of becoming available to larger and more diversified audiences thereby resulting in more traditional initiatives such as the ones referring to the dialogues with local informants, institutions and communities.

Conclusions

This chapter set out to analyse the interplay between local identities, heritage and museums in places that have experienced recent significant changes, in order to discern whether they act as identity bunkers or cultural forums. The observations conducted in the field have led us to conclude that the heritages and identities displayed in the Museums of Loures reveal an eclectic and fragmented nature, in consonance with the hybridism and diversity of the cultural landscape that surrounds them. This should come as no surprise given that it is very common in localities that have undergone significant and sometimes traumatic transformations. The abandonment of traditional activities and local occupations produces social and cultural implications that usually result in a sense of loss and disappearance of local cultural referents. In this context of change and decline (Hewison 1987), heritage emerges as a cultural resource that allows a socially and culturally deprived place to assert its distinctiveness and uniqueness in a global context of increased homogenization. This frequently encompasses the creation of local museums, a phenomenon that may be described as a strategy designed to compensate for social, cultural and economic losses, in which political forces and museum professionals both play a decisive role.

Museums are governmental institutions (Bennet 1995). They are submitted to the influence of historic and political circumstances, especially those museums that are government funded and managed. In Loures, as in many other municipal councils, local authorities have designed a cultural policy concerning heritage that is more concerned with the political benefits they may derive from their investments than with the promotion and validation of local culture. In this context, museums have emerged as particularly effective institutions, since they are perceived as symbols of modernity, cosmopolitism and cultural dynamism, assigning visibility and prestige to the municipality and to the agents responsible for their creation and maintenance. Recognized for their strong attachment to the place, municipal museums such as the Museums of Loures emerge as important instruments for the cultural and social regeneration of localities. They contribute to their positioning in the global space, affirming and promoting new ways of imagining the place.

However, the representation of a local heritage discourse that aims (and claims) to be inclusive and multicultural reveals some contradictions and could be best described as ambivalent. It is true that considerable efforts have been made to include social groups that tend to be excluded from the displays and practices produced, communicated and consumed in these cultural institutions. But these manifestations and celebrations of diversity have been permanently accompanied by a narrative centred on the representation of a specific version of local identity that turns to local history with the purpose of celebrating a poetic and imagined past, one that seeks to validate a fictional memory that is perceived as being in danger, facing the risk of disappearance due to the transformations brought by the present. Therefore, the municipal museums of Loures are in the process of trying to achieve a difficult balance between the past and the present, the local and the global, and this process entails many versions of local heritage and local identity, thus reflecting the fragmented nature of their cultural landscape. This is why the Museums of Loures can be described as being both identity bunkers and cultural forums.

Acknowledgements

I am grateful to Elsa Peralta and Amber Hall for their helpful suggestions and comments on a draft of this chapter, and to the Museums Network of Loures for providing all the information necessary for the reflections presented in this chapter.

Bibliography

Anico, M. and Peralta, E. (2007) 'Political and social influences affecting the sense of place in municipal museums in Portugal', in S. Knell, S. MaCleod and S. Watson (eds) *Museum Revolutions. How Museums Changed and Are Changed*, London: Routledge, 189–97.

Ashworth, G.J. (2007) 'On townscapes, heritages and identities', paper presented at Institute for Advanced Studies Colloquium on Urban-Rural: Flows and Boundaries, Lancaster University, January 2007. Available online at: http://www.lancs.ac.uk/ias/annualprogramme/regionalism/docs/Ashworth_paper.doc (accessed 11 November 2007).

Bennet, T. (1995) *The Birth of Museum. History, Theory, Politics*, London: Routledge.

Clifford, J. (1997) *Routes. Travel and Translation in the Late Twentieth Century*, Cambridge: Harvard University Press.

Dicks, B. (2003) *Culture on Display. The Production of Contemporary Visitability*, Maidenhead: Open University Press.

Hewison, R. (1987) *The Heritage Industry: Britain in a Climate of Decline*, London: Methuen.

Hooper-Greenhill, E. (2000) *Museums and the Interpretation of Visual Culture*, London: Routledge.

Huyssen, A. (1994) *Twilight Memories: Making Time in a Culture of Amnesia*, London: Routledge.

Kaplan, F. (2006) 'Making and remaking national identities', in S. Macdonald (ed.) *A Companion to Museum Studies*, Oxford: Blackwell Publishing, 152–69.

Machado, F. and Costa, A. (2000) 'An incomplete modernity. Structural change and social mobility', in J. Viegas and A. Costa (eds) *Crossroads to Modernity. Contemporary Portuguese Society*, Oeiras: Celta, 15–40.

Smith, L. (2006) *Uses of Heritage*, New York: Routledge.

Peralta, E. (2006) 'Memória do mar: património marítimo e (re)imaginação identitária na construção do *local*', in E. Peralta and M. Anico (eds) *Patrimónios e Identidades. Ficções Contemporâneas*, Oeiras: Celta, 73–82.

Prats, L. (1997) *Antropología y Patrimonio*, Barcelona: Ariel.

Prats, L. (2005) 'Concepto y gestión del patrimonio local', *Cuadernos de Antropología Social*, 21: 17–35.

5

Heritage according to scale[1]

Llorenç Prats

The social construction of heritage[2]

When we talk of heritage, we generally refer to it as something that simply 'exists', that is a part of our society; naturally, then, the questions we raise about the management of heritage generally stem from this premise. However, heritage is *not* a naturally occurring phenomenon, nor is it universal or eternal. It is in fact a socio-cultural construction, born at a specific moment in history, and which has clear objectives that it pursues along symbolic lines that can be easily analysed. In this respect, reflecting on the nature of heritage is not a theoretical exercise, removed from the day to day study and dynamics of heritage management, but rather a necessary clarification that places the relevant issues in a clearer, more manageable context.[3]

In order to analyse the nature of heritage, or 'patrimony', we should start from the Latin form, referring to inheritance from the father (which, in a society that has been patriarchal since the dawn of history, is essentially the same as family inheritance). Patrimony is the inheritance from the father, the family inheritance distributed between brothers from generation to generation, and which constitutes the source of their wealth – wealth that these heirs conserve, augment, lose, squander, convert and, in turn, pass on. The notion of inheritance has been understood in the context of family for a large part of our history. Even the concepts of land and vassalage, debts and opprobrium, have at one time formed part of this family inheritance. But there can be no notion of collective inheritance without the more basic notion of collectivism, a concept that did not clearly emerge until the bourgeois revolutions and the fall of the *ancien régime*. When society is capable of looking at itself as a historical subject, it can also begin to consider heritage as a collective inheritance that is passed down through the generations. This does not change the nature of heritage; it simply means that in addition to the family inheritance, there also exists a collective inheritance that the new generations manage according to the principal demands of their society. In other words, collectivism is a necessary condition in order to arrive at the notion of heritage that we are interested in, and which we understand to a certain extent, if not fully.

To understand the modern concept of heritage, in its denominations as *natural* or *cultural heritage*, we cannot simply turn to the generic idea of collective inheritance. We must also consider a more complex mechanism, perhaps as old as humanity itself, by which we feel an attachment or symbolic connection to certain objects and certain places, not for their tangible properties, but for the way in which they evoke other people and places, other times and realities. This is the basic mechanism of the mental association of ideas (and, by extension, symbolism), of metaphor and metonymy, through which determined referents evoke content that is not present, through similarity in some cases, or through contact and belonging in others. Not all of these symbolic referents have the same evocative power; metaphor can be differentiated from metonymy by the fact that metaphor maintains a formal relationship between referent and content, whereas metonymy maintains a *real* relationship, which makes it generically far more powerful. We are dealing with the concept of relics, whether religious or secular, collective or individual.

If we apply these ideas to the construction of heritage, we will see that in Western society (although not in others, unless through mechanisms of diffusion and acculturation), since the beginning of modern times the notion has arisen of a collective heritage that should be maintained as such. Of course, this is not the collective inheritance that is passed on from generation to generation, and which generally has a utilitarian function. The idea is not to preserve the past intact (nor, indeed, would this be possible), but rather to conserve certain referents to the past. But what are these referents, and on what basis are they selected?

When attempting to establish why certain referents go on to form part of our cultural heritage, the factors of shortage and obsolescence are often mentioned, but these account for only a part of the process. Shortage and obsolescence (often closely related) can act as contributory or related factors, accelerating the conservation of certain referents before they disappear completely, but they are not in themselves necessary or sufficient conditions that can be considered fundamental constituents of the construction of heritage, or what can be termed 'patrimonialization'. There are numerous castles in Europe, and this does not prevent them being classified as objects of national heritage, yet an enthusiast could leave behind an unrepeatable collection of models that not even his relatives are interested in conserving. Similarly, most Gothic cathedrals still maintain their original purpose, and are also classified as heritage sites, yet we find it difficult to accommodate our old computers, incompatible with new digital technology. These are all useful examples, but they do not clearly define the issue.

So what elements determine what it is that we decide to conserve, beyond practical considerations of usefulness? What are the main factors behind the construction of heritage? Evidently the past is of vital importance, but it is not the only factor; cultural heritage is not the past itself, nor is it simply a collection of relics, although it is true that these are important elements.[4] And what, then, are the other constituents of cultural heritage? For me, genius (principally of the creative kind) and art. But art as a manifestation of the past? To a certain extent, yes, but also contemporary art. Would anyone really deny, for example, that the Guggenheim Museum in Bilbao forms part of our heritage? Or indeed the cinema of Ingmar Bergman? When we refer to the work of Velazquez, Michelangelo, Mozart or Shakespeare, do we consider it part of our heritage for its antiquity, or because of its genius, and to what extent do we value these considerations?

77

Cultural heritage also includes nature. This may seem a contradiction in terms, but in reality it is no more than a paradox: it is a type of heritage that is culturally defined, in which two phases can be identified (the same could be said for artistic heritage). At first, natural heritage was defined according to a romantic paradigm, hence the tendency to conserve spectacular, exceptional landscapes, of the type that man cannot hope to conquer: rainforests, deserts, mountains and other singular geographical accidents. Later, in the latter half of the past century, an ecological paradigm came to the fore, and we turned to conserving ecosystems threatened by anthropic action and biodiversity. Ironically, we now strive to recover the wetlands that we had previously spent centuries trying to dry out.

What, then, are the fundaments of heritage conservation? The past, art and nature, with the input of the aforementioned factors of scarcity and obsolescence? This is more or less the case, but I believe that a more systematic explanation can be found.

At this point we should ask ourselves what the past, art and nature have in common. The answer, at least to a certain extent, is cultural externality: in other words, the fact that they cannot be easily domesticated, that they lie out of the reach of most mortals. It would be wise, though, to redefine these terms a little. We live in a highly familiar, domesticated world in which culture is constantly explained and regulated, but there remain certain phenomena that we cannot control. As many writers have noted, from as far back as Durkheim, all cultures coexist with these two realities – the controllable and the uncontrollable – that are defined by their context. From this impossibility of controlling everything that surrounds us, of recognizing forces that are beyond the reach of our culture, stem all the religions of the world and our belief in magic, which act as a cultural device for explaining and supposedly mediating with these forces and worlds.[5] A similar pattern emerges in the case of heritage, where referents that recall areas of cultural externality become sacralized. The past, then, is not sacralized as the past per se, but as a sort of 'time outside time', in the same way as the future (for which, naturally, we have no referents that can be converted into relics). Similarly, nature is sacralized as a space outside space: remote and unconquered, free from the domesticating influence of culture (and to violate such a space is necessarily an act of sacrilege).[6] Art is the fruit of genius, the epitome of cultural exceptionality in the face of normality, thus genius and exceptionality often move beyond the confines of art and are found in science and other activities (not necessarily as a force for good). Why do we continue to treat Ground Zero in Manhattan as sacred ground? Why do we keep the portraits and possessions of kings and tyrants? Why do we make respectful visits to the concentration camp at Auschwitz? Simply to acknowledge the past in the hope that such events will not be repeated?

Cultural heritage (including so-called natural heritage) exists as a type of lay religion, whose relics are derived from the constituents of the past (as time outside time), *nature*, and *genius* or *exceptionality* (principally, though not exclusively, creative). This means that any referent that maintains a metonymic relationship with at least one of these elements can potentially be converted into an element of heritage, whereas referents without this relationship cannot (Figure 5.1).

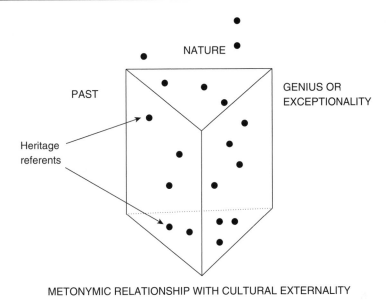

Figure 5.1 Social construction of heritage. Constituent elements.

Moreover, not all potential constituents of heritage actually undergo the trans-formation. Heritage exists in what could be described as a virtual museum that, even if it gathered together all the museums, collections, monuments, conserva-tion areas and other heritage sites from around the world, would never quite become material. Heritage is clearly an abstract construction, which numerous initiatives seek to make into reality, always starting from the basic elements that I have enumerated above.[7] I have called these processes *heritage activations* (the form they take – museums, collections, walks, etc. – is unimportant, and will be addressed later).[8] In any case, these heritage activations generate discourse, which is established through a series of clearly defined steps: selection, organization and interpretation. First, the referents are selected (the words of the discourse), they are then coherently organized with the content of the discourse (the sentences) and, finally, they are interpreted (through text, audio-visual materials, lights, window displays, etc.), so as to restrict the polysemy of the referents and leave the discourse clearly defined (and sacralized, of course, by the appropriate relics). Let us imagine that we are referring to a museum or exhibition, but equally we could be referring to a guided walk, a heritage activation plan at local level, a chain of natural parks, the heritage activation policy of a ministry or department of culture, or even to the UNESCO World Heritage List (with a number of con-ditions, but applying the same basic principles).

A further question we should ask is who could be interested in the activation of heritage, and to what end? In theory, the aim is power; in practice, without power there is no heritage (all types of power but, fundamentally, political power at all levels,[9] particularly national). One must not forget that the notion of heritage,

79

and the activation of heritage, arose during the Industrial Revolution, the bourgeois revolutions and, consequently, the emergence of nationalism that used heritage (and other means) to fuel a romantic conception of nation and nationhood, imbuing it with an ideology in line with the interests of the ruling classes.[10] In this sense, heritage understood as a lay religion operates in the same way as other religions. If we adopt the model suggested some years ago by Clifford Geertz (1973), we could say that heritage activation proposes a *world view* (or national view in this case), which is linked to the creation of an ethos (the national character). This coherence is emotively and artificially expressed through symbols (heritage referents) that reaffirm and sacralize the system, and aim to generate support. Obviously the independent variable is the ethos, which in practice becomes what we could term a catechism of the good patriot, inspired by the interests of the ruling classes. This same mechanism exists at many other levels, from the local to the colonial; citizens of London who have had the chance to visit the British Museum,[11] particularly since the nineteenth century, feel as if they are at the very centre of the world – part of the empire and a superior civilization that has ultimately been capable of subjugating so many nations, bringing the spoils of its conquests to the temple of imperial heritage.

Heritage has been, and continues to be, closely linked to the concept of identity. However, in the wake of World War II, a phenomenon emerged that would have a profound effect first on developed societies and later on the developing world, and which was to alter, or at least diversify, the aims of heritage activation. This phenomenon was the global spread of television and tourism, which transformed the world into a giant stage upon which a *society of spectacle*, or what Verdú (2003) called the *capitalism of fiction* could be consolidated – the latest expression of consumerism. From this point on, heritage undergoes a process of commercialization, in which the effectiveness of heritage activations, even those with more overtly political aims, is measured according to the number of visitors. These heritage activations (not without opposition in some cases) aim to make their discourse more appealing to the public, and they often choose to simplify this discourse and renew their content with temporary exhibitions. Marketing and merchandising become key, and exhibitions and heritage sites tend to expand into other leisure activities such as gastronomy and shopping, which are now carefully developed features of large museums and other heritage sites.

However, these new considerations do not alter the basic principles of heritage construction: we continue to talk of relics. Although there are such things as exhibitions unrelated to heritage or the *ex novo* reconstruction of cultural sites without affecting their tourism appeal, the effectiveness of a symbol is only achieved through the presence of relics that sacralize the discourse. Hence the extraordinary interest aroused by the monographic exhibitions of certain artists, obviously based on their original work, or the unparalleled appeal of authentic places.

Heritage activations can be grouped together in very different ways. Undoubtedly, though, the supreme example is the museum. The International Council of Museums (ICOM) has progressively broadened its definition of what is considered a museum in response to the ever-widening field in which it operates, so as to include natural heritage, as well as immaterial and intangible heritage, and the increasingly diverse forms of exhibit. I do not consider this a wise path to follow since this broader definition often extends the concept of the object so far that it becomes unmanageable. I propose that we consider three main constituents of heritage activation that cut through the specious argumentation currently surrounding the matter, based on three clearly distinguishable elements: the *object*, the *site* and the *manifestation*. The object transports any location – whether indoor or open air, but always clearly demarcated by a perimeter – that contains any type of materials pertinent to heritage, to the world of museums and collections. The site refers us to the world of monuments and archaeological sites, of ecosystems and expanses of nature in general. It is a complex in its own right – a unit of culture that should be considered as a whole. The manifestation refers to those referents of heritage that must be performed or produced in order to exist, and could be variously the music of Mozart, the plays of Shakespeare, a festival, gastronomy or even oral tradition. The key is not whether this kind of heritage is tangible or intangible, but rather that it only exists through the concurrence of production and consumption (indeed, it is sometimes a very material type of heritage, changeable perhaps, but nonetheless material, as is the case of gastronomy and certain festivals). One could consider heritage consisting solely of objects and places linked to Mozart, but this is not his principal legacy. Similarly, one could consider heritage consisting of antique scientific instruments, but science museums conserve above all scientific knowledge that has to be experienced. Unlike other relics, the objects in this case are merely a vehicle for the knowledge they represent: not only *can* they be touched, but they *need* to be touched in order to release the information they contain. Obviously these three main constituents can also interrelate. There are sites that contain collections of objects, but that also present themselves as objects, creating external perimeters in the form of networks or suggested itineraries. The chateaux along the Loire are a good example of this. Many manifestations of heritage take place in heritage sites themselves and use patrimonial objects, which increases the interest they generate and their general effectiveness. I believe that analysing heritage from a perspective of objects, sites and manifestations can help to unravel certain difficulties.

Science and heritage

Is this really human heritage? In truth, the answer is both yes and no. It is a social construct, based on the mechanisms we have seen, which has demonstrated extraordinary vitality, effectiveness and adaptability. Obviously, from a scientific point of view, we can only state the existence of this construction and attempt to explain it, but we are not in a position to endorse it. Indeed, on what basis could we hope to do so? Speaking in strictly scientific terms, we would have to remember that humans are a bio-cultural species, and that as such we have a biological heritage, formed by the human genome in its infinite manifestations, and a cultural heritage, comprising the totality of human cultural diversity that since the origins of the species has allowed us to evolve and transform the world.

There is also our natural heritage, the planet as a whole, which though not altogether ours to claim, has been placed under the management of humans. The entirety of this heritage, and particularly the various cultural adaptations the species has undergone, cannot be preserved, partly because it is systematically destroyed as the species continually develops to ensure its survival and, more fundamentally, because an exhaustive knowledge of the subject is clearly impossible. Furthermore, it has no political value, does not sacralize discourses, and is of no use to commerce or tourism unless it is a product of the past, exceptional genius or untamed nature. This brings us back to the beginning of the debate . . .

However, the social construction of heritage does turn to science, because although it is relatively easy to recognize the abstract criteria, the case of concrete referents is more complicated. Who determines whether something belongs to the past or is simply old? After all, the past has no predefined limits and is not the same for everyone. Likewise, who determines the relative interest of an area of natural beauty, or the importance of a work of art? In these cases, there is only one universally acknowledged authority in current Western society: science. This leads us to a new construction of heritage, a disciplinary construction, since science is structured according to various disciplines, and these in turn are organized according to the particular hierarchies of academia (universities, departments, scientific bodies, etc).[12] Scientific disciplines possess both the authority and the instruments required to certify relics and explore new referents, to speculate on the limits of those criteria that both constitute and relate to the construction of heritage and other relevant factors. But this authority is also dependent on the consensus of opinion, both inside and outside the scientific community; a consensus that can never be absolute, but that should be sufficient nonetheless. Scientific authority establishes its internal consensus through debate and the inherent hierarchy of academia, and social consensus can appear unimportant alongside scientific authority. But as we will see, the importance of scientific consensus is inversely proportional to the relevance of referents and the size of the social collective concerned.

Heritage according to scale

Let us look at what happens in the case of local heritage. For the purposes of analysis, we will distinguish between two types: genuine local heritage and what we will term localized heritage. Obviously all heritage activation can be seen as *localized*, but I use the term here, in contrast to local, to refer to local activations whose interest in tourism or establishing an identity goes beyond the limits of the location in which they take place, and I reserve the term local heritage for those activations, or referents, with a strictly local focus. I refer principally to clearly delineated towns, communities or villages – worlds in which everything and everyone is familiar and interconnected, leaving little room for anonymity. The concept can also be applied to some, though not all, neighbourhoods of large and medium-sized cities. *Localized* heritage activations correspond to the general criteria that I have previously referred to, both in terms of the mechanisms of social construction and the strategies of commercialization. Local heritage, on the other hand, seems to be influenced by other parameters. Even the local experience of localized heritage has no reason to coincide with its external valuation and interpretation, although this will obviously have some effect and generate feedback.

Local heritage, including the internal side of localized heritage, is affected by various local forces: local government; individual and collective local cultural agents, interested to a greater or lesser extent in heritage; the general population; and in particular, the tourist sector and related areas. Also involved are experts in heritage management, if required by the local government or local cultural agents, and higher level authorities when required by the local administration, often related to a specific project.

Local heritage activation can be carried out, or at least planned, for different reasons: as a means of attracting tourism, as a sign of distinction and pride in one's identity, a retreat into local identity as a reaction to rapid growth and change,[13] to revive and restructure local economy and identity following sudden processes of restructuring, simply because it exists, and no doubt for numerous other motives. The result of these activations will necessarily depend on various factors. The effect on tourism will depend on factors from within tourism (if it depended on the power of a certain heritage activation or referent, we would be dealing with localized heritage, and not local). These factors will include whether or not the area is located among tourist destinations consolidated by other types of shopping; the existence of infrastructure for the hotel and restaurant industries; the proximity to markets that generate a high number of day visitors, such as major cities; the effect of seasonal variation; and a combination of these, and other, influences. This is not to say, however, that the probable unfeasibility of many tourism-motivated local heritage projects will prevent them being carried out, either partially or in their entirety.

This situation is a result of the particular (and sometimes conflicting) logic of the forces involved. Local governments are motivated by short-term electoral concerns: they seek broad consensus and follow clientelist dynamics. Consequently, tourism-motivated heritage projects frequently feature as grand promises in electoral campaigns, and on occasions even lead to ambitious initiatives that can generate short-term income for networks of clients (in the form of orders or job opportunities) and gain general approval if there is a sense of local benefit (improved image or short-term economic increase) at low cost, thanks to the attraction of subsidies from higher level authorities. The activation itself, the job position or positions it generates, can be seen as a public asset, even though this is ultimately generated from public funds in the first place. The argument in favour would be that the public prefers to see this money invested rather than think that it disappears altogether. Obviously, higher level authorities will be more willing to contribute to a project if it matches their policies, but the potential returns are a more decisive factor, as are short-term electoral concerns, which lead to inaugurations and increased media coverage. It is also clear that the opposition, particularly on a local level, can use the scarcity or absence of profitability of a given activation to attack the local government and contest votes, but in order to do this, there must be widespread disapproval of the project (or the opposition must be capable of creating this disapproval).

The experts called in to draw up studies and projects also have their own methods and requirements. These projects are generally assigned to groups and consultancies who, rather than offer a specialized assessment that in many cases would advise against carrying out the activation, often decide to protect their own interests and carry out the planning in full. On occasions (depending on various parameters such as the aim of the project, the availability of qualified local personnel, and their own interests) these experts take on a more comprehensive role, and are responsible for carrying out and maintaining the project. In any case, if the activation goes ahead, the experts involved in maintaining it (whether these are the original planners or others contracted at a later stage) will be the first to justify its validity and economic viability, which stem from various activities and services designed to involve the local public in the use of the activation, as well as repeated efforts to attract school parties and senior citizens.

The role of the local population in this process is not always the same. If there is potential for generating tourism (because of location, shopping, etc.), local businesses and tourism enterprises generally give their approval to the project, as long as it is complimented by the services they offer and promises an upturn in business,[14] although it is unusual for them to actively participate in maintaining the project. Local cultural agents can react to such initiatives in very different ways, depending on factors such as their interest in local heritage, their relationship with experts from outside the area,[15] or their links with local government. Those sectors of the population not directly involved in the activation can adopt different stances according to factors that are again diverse, such as their possible association with figures behind or against the project (through friendships or family ties), or their general attitude towards the current local authorities. Indifference is certainly not common in these situations.

There are, however, other basic tendencies among the local population that are highly relevant, but which can only be identified through a patient and extended observation of the field in question. According to the definition we have assigned it, in contrast to localized heritage, we could say that local heritage is the heritage of locations with no heritage. But this absence (or near absence) of heritage, as it would be viewed from outside the area, is not seen in the same way by local residents. The population, or at least a part of it, needs to construct an identifying local discourse. I have already mentioned the flow of internal migration, which occurs at different rates (country to city, which is characteristic of less developed areas, or city to country, which is typical of the conurbations of rich nations). In these cases, we should not rule out the effect of cultural uprooting, and a certain lack of local patriotism, but there is also room to consider the creation of reactionary identities and dynamics of exclusion that accompany the eventual formation of new identities. In any case, the formulation and re-formulation of local identifying discourses will always resort to the notion of heritage as the principal source of inspiration, and for want of grander heritage referents that can be validated by scientific authority and broad social consensus, there is a tendency to reassess the value of existing local heritage referents (Figure 5.2).

At this point, a new factor comes into play, a factor that in theory can only exert influence at local level: memory. I do not refer to collective memory, which is a

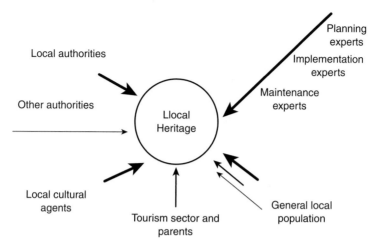

Figure 5.2 Local heritage. The forces involved and how they are structured. Distance and level of involvement.

theory that I am unable to grasp from a scientific perspective, but rather what we might call shared memory, which would create diverse, consensual, hierarchical, partly overlapping and evidently changing discourses. These discourses give meaning to heritage referents (such as the *lieux de mémoire* of Pierre Nora),[16] that have been selected – somewhat curiously – according to the basic criteria that inspire any process of heritage creation (even exaggerating and forcing them to some extent) and legitimize activations. We could say, then, that meaning becomes the fourth basic constituent of the social construction of heritage.

I would like to end this study by posing two questions. First, I have observed this process in various locations in Spain (in Catalonia, to be more precise), but essentially within the same social and geographical context. Does the same occur – with the corresponding adaptations – in other social and geographical areas? Second, are the forces and dynamics that surround the social construction of heritage in a local context noticeably different – as it would appear – to those that apply to wider contexts, for example, at national level? Or is it simply the case that the forces are more visible and manageable at local level? In other words, does scale create qualitative differences in heritage construction, or is it simply a means of observing processes that we can then apply to other levels?

Notes

1 This article forms part of research project SEJ2005-07389/GEOG, *Tourism and Sustainable development in the Catalan interior: Innovative strategies for the use of natural and cultural heritage*, jointly funded by the State Research Office and the Ministry of Education and Science.
2 The general considerations I present here have already been developed in other works I have had published in Spain, France and Latin America. See particularly my book

Anthropology and Heritage (1997) (2nd edition, 2004), the basic theoretical proposals of which can be found in abridged form in *The Concept of Cultural Heritage* (1998) (republished in Argentina in 2000). Later considerations of the specific nature (or otherwise) of local heritage are partially addressed in several other articles, particularly Prats (2003) and Prats (2005), as well as certain works awaiting publication. In the present article, I introduce the theoretical–methodological connection between the dynamic of local heritage and the social construction of heritage as a whole. I am currently developing these areas and the other points covered here in greater depth in a new book, which can be considered a substantially extended, revised edition of *Anthropology and Heritage*.

3   To my knowledge, the considerations, debates and research on heritage generally stem from heritage itself: its scope, how it can be broken down, its gradual development, its social applications, etc. (see, for example, García 1998). I am not sufficiently versed to comment on relevant works produced in England, Germany and other countries, but certainly in Spain and Latin America, in such thought-provoking studies as those of García Canclini (1999), Kingman (2004), Lacarrieu, Rotman and so many others, the debate rarely goes into any depth regarding the actual nature of heritage. The same can be said of France and other Francophone countries that have produced a number of interesting debates and conferences (see, for example, Jeudy 1990), and which have brought important new scientific contributions to the field, on issues such as ethnological heritage, eco-museums, of museums of society (for example, the debate over this last point between Duclos and Cuisenier, or the ongoing contributions of Davallon and other authors from the University of Lyon, not to mention the stimulating work emitted from Neuchâtel, principally from the work expounded by Jacques Hainard). In Italy, considerations stemming from the work of Gramsci and De Martino, dealing with the culture of the lower classes from a Marxist perspective, by various authors including Alberto Cirese and Luigi Lombardi, have brought little to the understanding of heritage as a cultural phenomenon, and the same could be said of the interpretations of those authors that have offered a more postmodern view, such as Clemente, Paglione and others, who have published interesting studies on the reading of heritage in journals like *Ossimori o Antropologia Museale* (see, for example, Clemente 1996). There is a wealth of material from the authors mentioned above and a number of others, but the suggestion seems to be that the nature (socially constructed, of course) of heritage is merely a theoretical issue, in the sense that it does not influence social practice, whereas I understand (and hope to have elucidated) that this is not the case, and that the two elements are interdependent. In September 2005, the Tenth Spanish Anthropology Conference was held in Seville, featuring brief presentations by Portuguese and Latin American anthropologists. Two symposia of differing focus were devoted to heritage (Santana and Prats 2005 and Sierra and Pereiro 2005). Practically all of the 30 or so papers covered by the two symposia deal with issues relevant to social dynamics and heritage management, prompting much debate about the scope of ethnological heritage (Jiménez 2005) or the handling of non-material heritage (Sánchez 2005); issues that I believe can be more easily resolved within the appropriate, global theoretical context.

4   In an interesting article with the sub-heading, 'Theorising heritage', Barbara Kirshenblatt-Gimblett (2001) directly associates heritage with the past and obsolescence. This is a common view, but a simple glance at the Museum of Modern Art or the Metropolitan Opera House in New York is enough to prove the inadequacy of such a theory.

5   I suppose that everyone has their own preferred sources in this area. In my own case, starting from Durkheim, I have long found the relevant work of Jean Cazeneuve (1971) and Edmund Leach (1976) particularly useful.

6   On occasions, the humanized landscape is also sacralized, but in these cases, the sacralization stems more from the past than from nature itself. Nature, unlike other elements in the sacralization of heritage, is not easily linked to other types of heritage referents (principally artistic), and is most influential when considered on its own. This explains the

discussions that inevitably arise from projects of artistic intervention in nature, such as the work of Eduardo Chillida on Mount Tindaya in Fuerteventura (Canary Islands).

7 There are other, equally relevant aspects and nuances that, for the sake of concision, I am unable to develop here. I refer interested readers to the various publications mentioned in note 2.

8 The terms *valuation* and *assessment of value* are often used in reference to processes of 'patrimonialization'. However, this is not correct terminology. First of all, these terms derive from an understanding of heritage as an existing commodity that simply needs to be assigned a value. While this can be accepted to a certain extent if it is understood *why* the commodity exists, this is rarely the case. Furthermore, I believe that the valuation, or assessment of value, or indeed whatever term one chooses to adopt, identifies another process: determining the *cultural value* of the different referents, which is also changeable depending on the context, and which can often be expressed in monetary terms. This should not, however, be confused with the *activation* of heritage, which is a far more complex (and, to some extent, more fundamental) process.

9 Economic power generally appears to have an altruistic interest in heritage, which helps to boost its image through subsidizing foundations and events, research programs, etc.

10 Various systems of symbols including – though not exclusively – heritage are usually referred to in these processes (unless we extend the notion of heritage to unmanageable proportions). It is impossible not to mention here the extraordinary work by Hobsbawm and Ranger (1983). In this regard, and contrary to what was said about social construction of heritage, we do now possess a number of studies of processes of national construction (which acknowledge, logically, the importance of heritage). To cite one example, see Fabre (1996). I wrote my doctoral thesis on the subject, and later returned to the main points in a book written along the same lines (Prats 1988). Comparative studies are consequently now possible, which was not the case some years ago.

11 The British Museum opened its doors in 1759, but it did not acquire its popular, colonial character until the nineteenth century.

12 This disciplinary construction results from a recourse to the science behind the social construction of heritage – as inevitable as it is somewhat undesirable. That said, in one respect it does allow us to broaden our notion of heritage, stretching the limits of its main constituents without at any point breaking them, and even to reflect upon the process itself and propose new ways of approaching the numerous phenomena that are gathered together by the notion of cultural heritage. Second, and more immediately, it leads to a division of socially constructed heritage (and claims to exclusive rights over the various segments) that does not fully encapsulate the real life situation and its holistic character, for all that expressions such as *integral heritage* try to make up for the deficit (the use of the word ´integral` implies prior acknowledgment of the various constituents). It is one thing to view heritage (even socially constructed heritage) from a disciplinary perspective, but quite another to construct and maintain these disciplines.

13 This is a process that, through the musealization of restructured industrial installations, aims to retain the sense of the local structure that surrounds them, at the same time as creating an alternative source of income, often with little success. In the sense that an attempt is made to overcome a collective frustration by resorting to heritage activation, I have frequently referred to this process as the *musealization of frustration*.

14 It can also be viewed with a certain indifference, if it cannot be reconciled with their business strategy, for example, in terms of seasonal variation and the capacity of their establishments (Jiménez 2003), or even with hostility, if it risks compromising investment in more intensive activities.

15 It is also possible for some local cultural agents to be involved in planning, carrying out and maintaining the activations, in which case their personal interests would be added to by the general motives mentioned previously.

16 I do not intend to go into so broad and complex an area as *collective* or *shared* memory, its construction and its social uses. It is both too large and not entirely relevant. Furthermore, there are ample bibliographical resources that, unlike the case of heritage, often approach the subject from its very roots. I shall simply cite one work of which I am particularly fond, which is the combined investigation carried out in Minot by Tina Jolas, Marie-Claude Pingaud, Yvonne Verdier and Françoise Zonabend, and more specifically within this project, the book written by Françoise Zonabend, *La mémoire longue* (1980). Elsa Peralta is about to publish a doctoral thesis that connects memory and heritage, and which will no doubt be very interesting. Until we see it in published form, we can guess at some of its contributions to the field from her recent articles. See, for example, Peralta (2003).

Bibliography

Cazeneuve, J. (1971) *Sociologie du rite*, Paris: Presses Universitaires de France.

Clemente, P. (1996) *Graffiti di museografia antropologica italiana*, Siena: Protagon Editori Toscani.

Debord, G. (1976) *La sociedad del espectáculo*, Madrid: Castellote Editor.

Durkheim, E. (1987) [1912] *Les formes elementals de la vida religiosa*, Barcelona: Edicions 62.

Fabre, D. (ed.) (1996) *L'Europe entre cultures et nations*, Paris: Éditions de la Maison des Sciences de L'homme.

García, J.L. (1998) 'De la cultura como patrimonio al patrimonio cultural', *Política y Sociedad*, 27: 9–20.

García Canclini, N. (1999) 'Los usos sociales del Patrimonio Cultural', in E. Aguilar (ed.) *Patrimonio Etnológico. Nuevas perspectivas de estudio*, Granada: Consejería de Cultura de la Junta de Andalucía, 16–33.

Geertz, C. (1973) *The Interpretation of Cultures*, New York: Basic Books.

Hobsbawm, E. and Ranger, T. (1983) *The Invention of Tradition*, London, Cambridge University Press.

Jeudy, H.P. (ed.) (1990) *Patrimoines en Folie*, Paris: Éditions de la Maison des Sciences de L'homme.

Jiménez, S. (2003) 'El turisme a muntanya: de la mentalitat a la racionalitat. El cas del Pallars Sobirà', *Revista d'Etnologia de Catalunya*, 22: 54–67.

Jiménez, C. (2005) 'Patrimonio etnológico e instrumentalización política', in X.C. Sierra and X. Pereiro (eds) *Patrimonio cultural: politizaciones y mercantilizaciones*, Actas del X Congreso de Antropología, Sevilla: Fundación El Monte, 25–36.

Kingman, E. (2004) 'Patrimonio, políticas de la memoria e institucionalización de la cultura', *Iconos*, 20: 26–34.

Kirshenblatt-Gimblett, B. (2001) 'La cultura de les destinacions: teoritzar el patrimoni', *Revista d'Etnologia de Catalunya*, 19: 44–61.

Leach, E. (1976) *Culture and Communication. The Logic by which Symbols Are Connected*, London: Cambridge University Press.

Nora, P. (1993) *Les lieux de mémoire*, Paris: Gallimard.

Peralta, E. (2003) 'O mar por tradição: O património e a construção das imagens do turismo', *Horizontes Antropológicos*, 20: 83–96.

Prats, L. (1988) *El mite de la tradició popular*, Barcelona: Edicions 62.

Prats, L. (1997) *Antropología y patrimonio*, Barcelona: Ariel.

Prats, L. (1998) 'El concepto de patrimonio cultural', *Política y Sociedad*, 27: 63–76.

Prats, L. (2003) '¿Patrimonio + turismo = desarrollo?', *Pasos. Revista de turismo y patrimonio cultural*, I(2): 127–36.

Prats, L. (2005) 'Concepto y gestión del patrimonio local', *Cuadernos de Antropología Social*, 21: 17–35.

Sánchez, C. (2005) 'Sobre el patrimonio inmaterial de la humanidad y la lucha por visibilizar lo africano en la República Dominicana', in X.C. Sierra and X. Pereiro (eds) *Patrimonio cultural: politizaciones y mercantilizaciones*, Actas del X Congreso de Antropología, Sevilla: Fundación El Monte, 147–63.

Santana, A. and Prats, L. (eds) (2005) *El encuentro del turismo con el patrimonio cultural: concepciones teóricas y modelos de aplicación*, Actas del X Congreso de Antropología, Sevilla: Fundación El Monte.

Sierra, X.C. and Pereiro, X. (eds) (2005) *Patrimonio cultural: politizaciones y mercantilizaciones*, Actas del X Congreso de Antropología, Sevilla: Fundación El Monte.

Verdú, V. (2003) *El estilo del mundo. La vida en el capitalismo de ficción*, Barcelona: Anagrama.

Zonabend, F. (1980) *La mémoire longue. Temps et histoires au village*, Paris: Presses Universitaires de France.

Part II

Remembering and forgetting

Unsettling memories: Intervention and controversy over difficult public heritage

Sharon Macdonald

Through heritage, selected memories are inscribed into public space. Heritage indexes places with histories that are, in part at least, their own, drawing on and further supporting a particular complex of ways of conceiving culture as 'property' and as a manifestation of 'identity'. Usually, the memories that heritage inscribes and the histories that it indexes are integral parts of what is presented as a shared public narrative, bolstering senses of identity and legitimacy. Increasingly, however, these have come to be accompanied in many, though by no means all, countries by unsettling, competing or contested, memories, narratives and heritage. Part of a wider 'heritage epidemic' (Bodeman 2002: 24) or 'heritage inflation' (Hoelscher 2006: 201), this is, in part, a consequence of an identity politics or politics of recognition in which diverse groups seek public recognition, crafting self-narratives and claiming legitimacy through memory inscribed as heritage. In addition, however, if more sporadically, it may be a result of majorities or state agencies not simply *allowing* minorities to create their own heritage niches as part of a more multivocal public sphere but also incorporating at least some such voices into the mainstream. Moreover, this may even extend to majorities themselves engaging in critical self-reflection about the past and seeking to incorporate accounts, and even 'dirty washing', that have previously been excluded from 'official' heritage.

The incorporation of previously excluded memories into the public sphere does not, however, simply expand the remit of what is included and increase the number of 'voices' represented, but it may also unsettle and disrupt existing accounts of the past. New memories do not necessarily just jostle alongside existing ones, like new products on a supermarket shelf, but may expose previous silences, raising questions about their motives or the power dynamics of which they were part. Or they may threaten to eclipse other memories, edging them out of public space or undermining their own achieved settlement as accepted heritage. For, usually, heritage is perceived as *settled* – as a sedimented, publicly established and valued distillation of history. Memory inflation, then, may not only challenge specific existing memories but may also unsettle the traditional view of heritage itself, making it more likely to be regarded as contestable and contingent. This in turn can prompt further questioning, making heritage increasingly the object of critical interrogation rather than acceptance. The expansion of heritage studies – and the production of volumes such as this one – is in part a consequence of this unsettlement. So too is the marked increase in numbers of controversies over heritage and public accounts of the past that there have been over the past 20 years or so. Heritage has indeed become a contested field – even a battlefield – sometimes, at least.

Heritage controversies

Looking at controversies over heritage provides a lens into some of the motives, lines of fission, players and implications of memory unsettlement. Public controversies are concentrated episodes during which alternative positions that at other times may be relatively unarticulated come into often noisy conflict. Like the 'social dramas' that were the focus of the Manchester School of Anthropology, especially in the work of Victor Turner, these episodes provide a window into wider concerns and power dynamics. As Turner wrote of social dramas, '[c]onflict seems to bring fundamental aspects of society, normally overlaid by the customs and habits of daily intercourse, into frightening prominence. People have to take sides in terms of deeply entrenched moral imperatives and constraints' (1974: 35). However, conflicts do not necessarily only mobilize existing positions and principles. Rather, they are moments of heightened friction which may also create new alignments of people and interests, and even change the parameters in which future actions and judgements are made (Tsing 2005). Controversies are not simply a reflection of the disjunctive status quo, then, but are also productive interventions into a labile and changing public sphere. By 'productive', I should note, I do not mean that the outcome of controversies are necessarily 'successful', however that might be judged. Rather, my point is that they make some kind of difference, derailing or unsettling what had seemed to be the likely course of an ongoing process, though not necessarily in ways that those making the intervention might have wished. Indeed, one feature of conflict, controversy and friction is that the outcome is indeterminate, even if it might sometimes seem predictable, especially in retrospect. Sometimes, there may even be an apparent return to continuing as before. For example, curators may take a more conservative and cautious approach to exhibitions in the wake of controversy, as occurred following the eruption of controversy over the display of the *Enola Gay*, the aircraft that dropped the atomic bomb on Japan in World War II, at the National Air and Space Museum, Washington, DC (Zolberg 1996). However, even in these cases such as these, the intervention has produced some kind of change, if only in the awareness of the difficulties that unsettlement may face.

In this chapter, I look at two heritage controversies. Both concern 'memory interventions' that attempted to remind of uncomfortable histories that seemed to be being eclipsed by particular plans. Both, that is, entail challenges to perceived forgetting in the public sphere. Neither are particularly well-known controversies, and while both received media coverage at the time, this was not extensive beyond the localities in which they occurred. And while the memory interventions were successful to some extent in both cases – that is, they helped to prevent what the memory interventionists perceived as an eclipsing of difficult history – they did not directly result in a major revisioning of public memory. Nevertheless, I suggest that they deserve attention partly because small-scale and relatively local-ized interventions of this kind are both individually and cumulatively significant in producing subtle but nevertheless significant shifts in the memory landscape. This is not to say that they are thoroughly 'bottom-up' developments. On the contrary, as we will see, local interventions can draw inspiration and also support from outside, and, equally, they may contribute to altering the ways in which non-local organizations act. Local and beyond local are thoroughly mutually entangled. Nevertheless, the 'locatedness' of the particular heritage site – what I here call 'heritage sitedness' – remains important in heritage controversies, partly because of the fact that heritage imbues place with such identity significance. Moreover, as the examples also highlight, local memory – of previous events, forgetting or injustice – is mobilized within the controversy, contributing to the specificity of the course and outcome of the dispute.

The cases that I describe below are temporally and geographically distant from each other. The first – a controversy over a proposal to turn a major Nazi build-ing into a shopping and leisure centre – occurred in the mid-1980s in Nuremberg, Germany. This was at a time that was widely regarded by German historians and other intellectuals as one of a new wave of memory unsettlement, in which ques-tions of Nazi perpetration and how the past should be addressed had received new levels of public recognition (Niven 2002). This was demonstrated by the *Historikerstreit*, the Historians' Conflict – a dispute, widely aired in newspapers, over the uniqueness of Nazi crimes, the extent to which the nation should continue to feel responsible for them and the forms that commemoration should take (Maier 1997). Events such as a visit in 1985, as part of the 40-years since the end of World War II anniversary commemoration, by President Reagan and German Chancellor Helmut Kohl to lay a wreath at a cemetery containing the graves of members of the SS as well as other soldiers had provoked concern from some com-mentators over whether the Nazi past was being 'normalized' and perceived as just another conflict. And proposals for a new 'national' war memorial and a new national museum of German history fuelled public debate about the nature of the German past and how it should be remembered. While never invoked in the Historians' Conflict, the controversy in Nuremberg shows how many of the same kinds of concerns and positionings were being negotiated at local level too – though with specific local dimensions that related, not least, to the materiality of the heritage involved.

The second case, likewise, can be seen as a localized controversy that arose at a time of wider attempts to interject an unsettling memory into public space – in this case, that of transatlantic slavery in the United States. While there have been many fairly small-scale or localized attempts to commemorate transatlantic slavery underway for many years now, with, for example, tourism to sites such as plantations, it is only in recent years that there has been a more concerted drive to do so, especially in official or well-funded ways (Dann and Seaton 2002). Thus, the establishment of municipally funded museums and heritage sites of slavery has for the most part taken place since the 1990s. This includes examples such as the National Underground Railroad Freedom Center in Cincinnati, opened in 2004 to present information about, and to commemorate, the routes taken by slaves in the United

States (http://www.freedomcenter.org/; accessed 19.10.2007). Sites whose existence and wealth was predicated on slavery have only recently begun to acknowledge this – if at all. At Monticello, home of Thomas Jefferson (US President between 1801 and 1809), for example, mention of slavery, and especially of the possible relationship that Jefferson had had with mulatto slave Sally Hemings, was not included until the 1990s (Gable 2006 and Chapter 10, this volume); Colonial Williamsburg only introduced a permanent section on slavery in 1999. There is still no state-funded national museum of slavery in the United States, though a privately funded National Museum of Slavery is due to open in the near future (http://www.usnationalslaverymuseum.org/museum_why.asp; accessed 24.09.2008). In addition, also in the making and this time federally funded, though not due to open for at least another decade, is the National Museum of African History and Culture, part of the Smithsonian complex, which will include some coverage of the subject of slavery (Smithsonian Institution: National Museum for African American History and Culture; http://nmaahc.si.edu/, accessed 15.10.2007).

Like the Nuremberg example, the second case that I look at – that of a controversy in 2006–2007 over how artefacts from a shipwreck should be exhibited – has not been much invoked in wider debates about remembering transatlantic slavery. Nevertheless, it too is at the same time clearly part of a wider move to incorporate more 'difficult' memory into public space, albeit if sometimes reluctantly so by many authorities. Furthermore, as in the Nuremberg case, the disputes were heated and altered existing plans. In my following short accounts of the controversies, I seek to outline some of the key touchstones and understandings of the nature of heritage and memory as they were mobilized in the disputes, as well as the course that the events took.

Unsettlement one: Consumer paradise in Nazi heritage[1]

Not far outside the scenic Old Town of the City of Nuremberg is a large area of former marching grounds and various completed, semi-completed or ruined massive monumental buildings that were constructed by the National Socialists in the late 1930s in order to stage the mass spectacles known as the Nuremberg Rallies. Since 1945 the City has adopted various approaches to the buildings, including ignoring or destroying some of them; restoring some areas subsequent to them being listed as official heritage in 1974; and, in the mid-1980s, making the first concerted, though still small-scale, attempts to comment on the history of the site, especially a temporary exhibition opened in the Zeppelin Building in 1984. All of these memory interventions had been largely driven by a fairly small group of leftist history activists in the City, some of whom also held City Council positions. Just how marginal such interventions were, however, is in some ways demonstrated by the controversy that I want to look at, though it could also be argued that its outcome provided some evidence of the growing strength of the drive to avoid papering over the City's awkward Nazi past.

In 1987, a local private company – Congress & Partner – produced proposals to convert the vast horseshoe-shaped Nazi building, which had been intended as a

Congress Hall, into a shopping and leisure centre.[2] 'Property with Personality' and 'The World's Money to Nuremberg' were the two slogans that the company used to promote the 500 million DM project. And it presented detailed plans for using the extensive space of the Congress Hall building for high-class shops, restaurants, luxury flats, cinemas, discos, a wide-range of sports facilities including swimming pools, tennis courts, squash courts, gyms and golf-driving ranges, and an older people's home.

Since 1945, various rooms in the listed Nazi building had been rented out to a variety of local organizations, mainly to be used as storage space. However, although the Council gained rent, it also sometimes faced expending considerable sums on repairs to the building, especially to prevent roof leaks which would jeopardize the capacity to rent the rooms for storage and which might also contravene the heritage protection legislation. There were many Council debates over the years during which fears about the demands that the building might in future make – fears that were, perhaps, symbolic as much as practical – were repeatedly aired. This, then, was part of the backdrop to the social democratic (SPD) Council working with Congress & Partner to help produce the proposals and why they were initially welcomed by most Council members. The Council Treasurer was particularly positive about the plans, expressing pleasure that not only would the Council gain an income generator in future years that should easily outstrip any future necessary repairs, but also that the development would 'bring life into the building', in what he called 'the spirit of demythification'. The City's Heritage Protection Office was also on board, requiring only that the external shell of the building was maintained. Indeed, the only initial concerns voiced were to do with details of financing the project, potential traffic problems and the impact on local retailers.

Although the plan to develop this unique fascist building in this way came to be declaimed by some as an astonishing and disturbing instance of forgetting and even repressing an unsettling memory, as I describe further below, the Treasurer's use of the term 'demythification' (a term that was also bandied around in a later Council debate on the proposals) indicates that he had not forgotten the building's history and resonance. On the contrary, what he was mobilizing here was a discourse that had been developed locally precisely to address the awkward presence of the monumental Nazi buildings in the City – a discourse of attempting to 'counter' their potential symbolic power by variously neglecting them or using them for banal uses (see Macdonald 2006a,b). This discourse, which had been developed by the well-known SPD councillor, historian and public intellectual Hermann Glaser, drawing on ideas from theorists such as Hannah Arendt, was part of the existing local heritage complex, available as a resource in negotiations such as this.

It did not, however, cut much ice with some members of the public who variously sent letters opposing the plans to the local newspaper and participated in a 'citizen's initiative' (*Bürgerinitiativ*) to try to prevent it. The latter is a legal right of German citizens to mount a challenge to decisions being made in their name. The initiative charged that since the war the City authorities had failed to recognize the importance of the Congress Hall for public remembrance but had instead 'hushed up, repressed and concealed' the City's past. Letter writers also characterized the plans as evidence of a forgetting or even repressing of the Nazi past. One writer, for example, sarcastically commented:

> Congratulations on this extraordinary idea. Not only will Nuremberg's inner-city ... become a treasure chest again, no, even as unlovable relic from the great days of the Nazi Rallies will become the finest shopping paradise in Franken. There's no better way, 42 years later, to repress misery and atrocity.

And another reasoned that consumerism was always predicated upon forgetting – for example, of Third World poverty and hunger that are produced in service of assisting the wealth of the West – then Nuremberg was the obvious place to build a 'shopping paradise'. This argument, voiced by several letter writers, that consumerism per se was implicated in forgetting – either as a technique or as a symptom – was also one that had gained wider currency in Germany, with the generation known as '68ers' seeing Germany's post-war consumer boom as a symptom of an unhealthy repression of the awkward past by their parents' generation.

Remembrance was posited as an antidote to this sickness and moral turpitude. The buildings should act, argued the citizens' initiative, as a *Mahnmal*. This term, sometimes translated as 'memorial', carries a connotation not only of being a 'reminder' of the past but, as it contains the roots of the word for 'to admonish', also as a kind of warning for the future (e.g. Neumann 2000: 10). The chief conservator of the Bavarian Conservation Department – taking a different line from the City's own heritage officials – also argued that the building should act in this way, rather than being developed into a shopping centre. The building was, he explained, 'one of the most important witnesses (*Zeugnisse)* of the gigantomania of National Socialism'. In other words, the building itself held a capacity to tell of the past – to unsettle forgetting – but only if it was not somehow suppressed by the opposing forces of consumerism. To fulfil this task, the citizens' initiative proposed subjecting the building to 'planned demise', erecting a barbed wire fence across its inner courtyard in order to symbolize the idea of 'barring National Socialism from our lives', and mounting exhibitions within it to help actively and publicly recall its history.

Following a vociferous and closely fought Council debate, the proposals were narrowly rejected; though simultaneously Congress & Partner withdrew them, recognizing that they were proving considerably more problematic than they had anticipated. The memory intervention seemed, then, to have effectively seen off the threatened forgetting that the activists, the conservator and various other members of the public saw in the plans. However, the alternative proposal by the citizens' initiative did not materialize either – there was no erection of symbolic barbed wire, no exhibitions in the building, and its demise was no more planned than it had been earlier. Nevertheless, the controversy came widely to be seen in Nuremberg as a turning point, as a moment when it became no longer possible to simply forget the past. That is, this controversy itself lodged in public memory as a moment at which history could have taken a very different turn. Moreover, the resistance to the shopping centre became cast as a key precursor to the Congress Hall coming in 2001 to at last house a permanent exhibition about the history of Nazism and the Party Rally Grounds. It did so partly because had things gone otherwise in the narrow vote, the building would no longer have been available to be used in this way – or at least not to the same effect – but also because controversies, like other kinds of social dramas, themselves become especially available to public memory as 'condensing narratives', as moments of special significance. The shopping centre controversy, while it did not entirely inoculate the Nazi site against any kind of future commercial activity, certainly seemed to feed into later debates, especially those leading to the incorporation of more unsettling memory amidst the Nazi architecture.

Unsettlement two: Piracy and slave heritage[3]

How far the second example to which I now turn will remain in public memory is hard to say, as it is considerably more recent, though, as will be evident in the account below, its course was itself partly shaped by a previous controversy over a similar matter within the locality. This was part of a local 'heritage sitedness' that was also evident in the Nuremberg example, though in different ways.

The example concerns the public display of maritime heritage – items found on the wreck of a ship called the *Whydah*. Excavated off Cape Cod in the mid-1980s, the *Whydah* was first launched from London in 1715. It was used to transport items such as liquor and tools from England to West Africa, where these were traded for slaves. Up to 700 slaves were then carried on the perilous three- to four-week journey to the Caribbean where they were exchanged for precious metals, indigo and sugar, which were then taken back to England. In February 1717, however, the ship was captured by pirates on what was only its second voyage, as it travelled from West Africa to the Caribbean. Then, only a few months later, it was wrecked in a storm.

Artefacts from the *Whydah* have been displayed at the Expedition *Whydah* Sea-Lab and Learning Center Museum in Provincetown, MA (http://whydah.com/pages/pirate_hunters_pages/cap_bellamy.html; accessed 19.10.2007). But to try to bring them to wider public attention, the ship's excavator, Barry Clifford, successfully negotiated a collaboration between the exhibition-making company Arts and Exhibitions International – responsible for some major exhibitions such as *King Tut* and *Princess Diana* – and the Museum of Science and Industry (MOSI), Tampa, Florida. The plan, publicly announced in 2006, was to exhibit what was described as an 'unparalleled' hoard of 'pirate treasure' in an exhibition to be called *Pirates*. However, African-American activists protested against the plans, complaining that they marginalized African-American heritage – the history of transatlantic slavery. The fact that the plans sought to attract new audiences to the museum by drawing on a popular fascination with pirates, evident in the then recent film, *Pirates of the Caribbean*, was seen as trivializing the history of slavery and, just as slavery had done, putting commercial interests above ethics. Making this argument, James Ransom, a member of the Coalition of African American Organizations and spokesperson of an *ad hoc* group of the black activists called Citizens who Support Preserving African and African-American History, said that this insensitivity risked opening up a 'cavernous wound', insulting many of Tampa's black residents whose ancestors originally came to America as slaves. To display the *Whydah* as a pirate ship, he argued, would be an 'exploitation' of this history and, as such, a continuation of a history of exploitation that black people have suffered (quoted in Allen 2006, see note 3).

This was a controversy, then, about whose memories should be prioritized within public space. Memory was not, however, only an object of contested representation. In a sense, it was the memory of having suffered exploitation – the memory of slavery itself – that shaped the perception of the exhibition as a form of exploitation. Memory also inspired the protest itself – in this case, the recollection of a highly similar controversy and course of events 13 years earlier. At that time, there had been African-American protests against a planned private museum of piracy in Tampa, which was also to have included the *Whydah* wreck as well as other Tampa pirate links. Kevin Yelvington, Neill Goslin and Wendy Arriaga have provided an insightful analysis of this, tackling it both ethnographically and historiographically, and seeking to understand the power differentials and kinds of arguments, and understandings about history itself, that were mobilized during the dispute. They present a context of fraught and sometimes violent racial tensions in which, as they put it, 'pirate politics are more than symbolic' (2002: 356). According to 1993 Census figures, they explain, 'Tampa's black poverty rates were surpassed only by the poverty rates of blacks in New Orleans and Detroit and ... Blacks have continuously been marginalized in the political and economic arenas' (2002: 357). As they argue, the African-American response to the marginalization of their heritage was undeniably bound up with these other forms of marginalization. At the same time, however, they also point out that although the controversy became cast as one of black versus white interests, it was in fact more complicated. In particular, there were some African-Americans who supported the project, partly because of the jobs that it promised to create.

In 2006 there was some attempt by MOSI to draw on the memory of the 1993 failure in order to ensure that history would not be repeated. Some members of the African-American community were consulted early on in its plans. Despite this, however, once the objections were voiced by James Ransom, none of those involved came out in support of the exhibition. Memory of the volatile atmosphere of 1993, and the vilification of those African-Americans who had tried to support the planned museum, may have played a part here. In response to the objections, MOSI initially tried to point out that it would not ignore slavery. Barry Clifford intervened with an argument that an account of pirate life could be a positive one for race-relations as any slaves captured by a pirate ship would have been freed and would have held equal status with other crew members, including an equal share of any loot. This was not, however, an argument that appealed to the opponents of the exhibition. Being invited to share in the admiration of a piratical approach was perhaps not the best pitch with which to appeal against arguments about lack of sensitivity.

Rather than risk a repeat of the angry protests of 1993, MOSI and Arts and Exhibitions International swiftly decided to cancel the exhibition, in Tampa at least. While some judged the museum's cancelling of the exhibition to be the only responsible course of action, others regarded it as caving in to excess political correctness.[4] When I raised this with John Norman, Director of Arts and Exhibitions International, he told me that in his view it 'was not a fight worth fighting'. Those who objected to *Pirates* did so, he believed, without proper knowledge about the exhibition content and then felt unable to back-down. He thus remained confident about being able to find new venues to show the exhibition. And he also said that he was not worried about the activists' threat to protest against the exhibition in any possible new location, because 'I don't know who would object to true history'.

His optimism seems to have been well founded. In June 2007, *Real Pirates: The untold story of the Whydah from slave ship to pirate ship* opened 900 miles North, and thoroughly inland, at the Cincinnati Museum Center – to no reported protests. This was surely not only because nobody 'object[s] to true history' as Norman had trusted. The factual veracity of the pirate account had never been at issue among the exhibition opponents. The objections were to the emphasis and approach. As is clear from the sub-title of the new exhibition, *Real Pirates* does not ignore slavery – though piracy remains the central focus, as is clear from the main title. Furthermore, the exhibition is the kind of impressive multimedia show that is a hallmark of Arts and Exhibitions International productions. It includes not only carefully displayed artefacts recovered from the *Whydah* but also a virtual ship journey. So was just the slight modification to include a little more reference to slavery enough to assuage the sense of offence generated by the earlier plans? While surely partly responsible, also crucial was the disconnection from Tampa, and its existing heritage and memory politics. Not only was there the memory of a similar prior dispute in Tampa, the City had also focused its heritage image on piracy, especially the annual Gasparilla pirate festival (http://www.gasparillapi ratefest.com/; accessed 19.10.2007; Yelvington *et al.* 2002). Disconnection from the locality was also achieved by replacing a local source of scientific authority (MOSI) by a national one: National Geographic. Much was made of this collaboration in the publicity for the new exhibition. Although Cincinnati, like Tampa, is a City with a high proportion of African-American citizens (just over 40 per cent), and although it has some history of racial tensions, its 'heritage complex', unlike that of Tampa, is not centred on piracy. Moreover, and possibly of critical importance, it already included some important public memories of slavery, such as the National Underground Railroad Freedom Center, mentioned above. In its new location, then, piracy was subsumed under a wider emphasis on remembering slavery rather than the other way around.

Discussion

Memory interventions of the kind that I have outlined here are far from unusual and, indeed, are surely increasing in frequency as more and more groups demand a public space in which diverse interests and an addressing of uncomfortable aspects of the past are included. In both of the examples, the interventionists came initially and primarily from outside official governmental organizations, though in both they gathered support within official organizations as the controversy developed; in both cases officially sanctioned accounts that incorporated the awkward memory followed, if not immediately. Such a course of events – intervention from a minority prompting revision and at least partial incorporation into the official and public sphere – is surely rather frequent, though I would not want to elevate it to a universal structure of the sort that Turner attempted to outline for social dramas. Nevertheless, Jennifer Jordan's argument that moves towards memorialization typically follow a trajectory in which 'the calls of memorial entrepreneurs' find broader public 'resonance', some gaining wider publicity until 'the campaign seems to reach a point of no return, a moment at which any alternative use of the land becomes unthinkable, and it becomes politically difficult *not* to support a given memorial project' (2006: 12), seems to characterize the process well. Of course, this does not mean that all interventions necessarily find such resonance, neither that, even if they do, memorialization always follows, or at least not immediately or completely – the Nuremberg example shows a considerable time delay and the Tampa example shows an only partial shift towards the demands of the interventionists. All the same, it is clear that such interventions can make a difference, even if they are not acknowledged as part of the official story later.

While we can detect a frequent pattern or trajectory in memory interventions of this sort, I have in the account here also sought to point out how the specificity of 'heritage sitedness' and local memory, of, for example, earlier disputes, can inflect upon it. So, for example, the Nuremberg controversy was framed partly in terms of what interventionists claimed to be a long history of the City forgetting and repressing the past, and, materially, failing to treat Nazi building appropriately. Or, in the slavery example, what was at issue was partly the specific Tampa history, and we saw how what was another instance of marginalization in one context might transmute into being part of a wider heritage offer in another context in which difficult history was already on the agenda.

The move towards incorporating more unsettling memory in public contexts itself deserves further comment. In the introduction, I outlined some of the shifts with which this has been involved – in particular, the attempt by groups whose memories have been excluded to be publicly remembered. This is illustrated here by the slavery example in particular. However, this does not adequately explain all cases, including that of Nuremberg, where calls for remembrance came from Germans, many of them local people, for whom the awkward memories were ones capable of unsettling their sense of self. In other words, they were not simply seeking to have 'their' account added to the mix but to admit a fuller and more disturbing version of a past that they recognized as their own. This is part of a much wider move, seen in other parts of Germany and elsewhere. While shortcomings in some of the self-critical attention have been identified, the ire invoked among those who feel such self-criticism to be somehow shaming and displaying a lack of proper patriotism, as in the *Enola Gay* case or in protests about an exhibition at Britain's National Maritime Museum showing how the country profited from slavery (Duncan 2003), shows clearly how unsettling such accounts can be for some at least.

Nevertheless, there clearly is such a move underway in many parts of the world; as Robert Shannon Peckham observes, 'memories of trauma are taking the place of an increasingly discredited heritage' (2003: 207). Nervousness over heroic accounts of the past has contributed to a wider unsettling of a conceptualization of heritage as necessarily settled and laudable. But far from depleting the significance of heritage in the public realm, this unsettlement has made heritage all the more available as an ethical space – as one in which values can be explored and debated.

One feature of both of the cases that have been discussed was that intervention, rescuing from forgetting, was couched partly in terms of a countering of crass consumerism or commercialism. This, I suggest, is evidence of an attempt to secure heritage as an ethical space, capable not only of affirming certain identities but of prompting more complex, often humanistic and cosmopolitan, reflection on matters such as the relationship between past, present and future, and on the nature of heritage itself.

Acknowledgements

The research on which this is based was funded partly by an AHRC special leave award and by the Alexander von Humboldt foundation. I am also grateful to the Nuremberg Stadtarchiv for assistance with the material relating to the Nuremberg example. Elsa Peralta and Marta Anico deserve thanks for stimulating the chapter and forbearance in waiting for its various revisions.

Notes

1 This case is taken from Macdonald (2009), where it is covered in more detail, together with further contextualization.
2 The following account is based on original documents in the Nuremberg Stadtarchiv, especially Pressemappe Congress & Partner, and newspaper articles from the *Nuremberg Nachrichten*. An account can also be found in Dietzfelbinger and Liedtke 2004. I have translated from the original German.
3 I have discussed this case elsewhere, briefly in an opinion piece, 'Stormy Waters', in *Museums Journal*, May 2007, and also in Macdonald 2007. The account is based on interviews with John Norman, Director of Arts and Heritage International and in news articles, including the following: Greg Allen, 'Museum cancels pirate exhibit over slavery issues', 18 December 2006, *National Public Radio* (http://www.npr.org/templates/story/story.php?storyId=6640303&ft=1&f=1001; accessed 29.04.2007); Kevin Graham, 'MOSI drops plans to display artefacts from slave ship', 5 December 2006, *St Petersburg Times* (http://www.sptimes.com/2006/12/05/Tampabay/MOSI_drops_plans_to_d.shtml; accessed 20.04.2007); Justin George, Bill Varian and Janet Zink, 'Tampa slavery ship exhibit sparks controversy', 9 November 2006 (http://www.flcourier.com/index2.php?option=com_content&do_pdf=1&id=446; accessed 29.04.2007); Larry Rother, 'A Tempest in Tampa over an ex-slave ship', *New York Times* 12 February 1993 (http://query.nytimes.com/gst/fullpage.html?sec=travel&res=9F0CE6DD1738F931A25751C0A965958260; accessed 29.04.2007).
4 See, for example *Tampa Pirate*, 'Civil Rights Activist diminish blacks yet again' (http://tampapirate.com/?p=277; accessed 20.04.2007).

Bibliography

Bodeman, M.Y. (2002) *In den Wogen der Erinnerung*, Munich: dtv.

Dann, G.M.S. and Seaton, A.V. (eds) (2002) *Slavery, Contested Heritage and Thanatourism*, New York: Haworth Press.

Dietzfelbinger, E. and Liedtke, G. (2004) *Nürnberg – Ort der Massen. Das Reichsparteitagsgelände. Vorgeschichte und schwieriges Erbe*, Berlin: Ch. Links.

Dubin, S.C. (2006) 'Incivilities in civil(-ized) places: "culture wars" in comparative perspective', in S. Macdonald (ed.), *Companion to Museum Studies*, Oxford: Blackwell, 477–93.

Duncan, J. (2003) 'Representing empire at the National Maritime Museum', in R.S. Peckham (ed.), *Rethinking Heritage. Cultures and Politics in Europe*, London: I.B. Tauris, 17–28.

Gable, E. (2006) 'How we study history museums: Or cultural studies at Monticello', in J. Marstine (ed.), *New Museum Theory and Practice*, Oxford: Blackwell, 109–28.

Hoelscher, S. (2006) 'Heritage', in S. Macdonald (ed.), *Companion to Museum Studies*, Oxford: Blackwell, 198–218.

Jordan, J.A. (2006) *Structures of Memory*, Palo Alto, CA: Stanford University Press.

Macdonald, S. (2006a) 'Undesirable heritage: Fascist material culture and historical consciousness in Nuremberg', *International Journal of Heritage Studies*, 12(1): 9–28.

—— (2006b) 'Words in stone? Agency and identity in a Nazi landscape', *Journal of Material Culture*, 11(1/2): 105–126.

—— (2007) 'Schwierige Geschichte – umstrittene Ausstellungen', *Museumskunde*, 72, 1/07: 75–84.

—— (2009) *Difficult Heritage. Negotiating the Past in Nuremberg and Beyond*, London: Routledge.

Maier, C.S. (1997) *The Unmasterable Past. History, Holocaust, and German National Identity*, 2nd edn, Cambridge, MA: Harvard University Press.

Neumann, K. (2000) *Shifting Memories. The Nazi Past in the New Germany*, Ann Arbor, MI: University of Michigan Press.

Niven, B. (2002) *Facing the Nazi Past. United Germany and the Legacy of the Third Reich*, London: Routledge.

Peckham, R.S. (2003) 'Mourning heritage: Memory, trauma and restitution', in R.S. Peckham, *Rethinking Heritage: Cultures and Politics in Europe*, London: I.B.Tauris, 205–14.

Tsing, A.L. (2005) *Friction*, Princeton, NJ: Princeton University Press.

Turner, V. (1974) *Dramas, Fields, and Metaphors*, Ithaca, NY: Cornell University Press.

Yelvington, K.A., Goslin, N.G. and Arriaga, W. (2002) 'Whose history? Museum-making and struggles over ethnicity and representation in the Sunbelt', *Critique of Anthropology*, 22(3): 343–79.

Zolberg, V. (1996) 'Museums as contested sites of remembrance: The Enola Gay affair', in S. Macdonald and G. Fyfe (eds), *Theorizing Museums*, Oxford: Blackwell, 69–82.

Public silences, private voices: Memory games in a maritime heritage complex

Elsa Peralta

No one has ever paid much attention to Nietzsche when, accounting for an expensive surplus of history for life, he stated that it is "completely impossible to live without forgetting" (1874). This argument seems to be completely at odds with the general value that is assigned to remembering, instead of forgetting, in modern and contemporary times. In a recent seminal paper, Paul Connerton (2008) precisely notes that forgetting is often seen as a failure whereas remembering is seen as a virtue. No one is proud of having forgotten people, names, facts, events. This is usually considered a fault, the lack of a faculty or a kind of malfunction that generally fails to convey our sense of historically laden individual or collective self.

Furthermore, the infatuation with history experienced from early modernity and up to the present gives evidence to the importance of remembering, not forgetting. Nations, ethnic communities, peoples, cultures are all constituted historically, that is, by reference to a certain – more-or-less stable – past. This assumption has led to all sort of studies devoted both to the way the past shapes our sense of self and identity and to the way our present values, perceptions and aspirations constantly shape that past. The growth of a field of inquiry that can be labeled "Memory Studies" is a consequence of these concerns.

But memory involves forgetting as much as remembering. In order to remember some things properly we have to forget others. This is as true for individuals as it is for groups and communities. Memory is not the same as the past events as they did in fact take place in the past. Rather, it is the way we represent the past – or a part of it – in the present, removing from it all those issues that do not convey our sense of self. As such, memory is not just the past as we remember it; it is also the past as we have forgotten it. That is probably why Nietzsche also stated that "forgetting belongs to all action" (1874) because for someone to carry on in life he must discard those events that are either disruptive to their existence or simply fail to convey the cultural fabric in which they are placed. If we are not to turn the present into a graveyard of the past, we need to forget as much as we need to remember. In this sense, remembering and forgetting are both productive, that is, both are meaningful activities.

With some exceptions, this assumption has not, however, kept up with much of the academic debate on cultural memory. Most academic work on memory focuses more on remembering and celebration and much less on forgetting. Moreover, in memory studies forgetting is usually seen in repressive terms. In this sense, forgetting is ideologically engendered for communities to experience a sense of past that conveys the interests of certain groups. According to this approach to memory, social remembering and social forgetting are both products of the manipulation of social elites and powers that publicly assert their own versions of history and identity. As such, they are mediums of social control and ways of legitimating power. This approach to memory cannot be discarded as there is enough empirical evidence to show that we cannot study memory without considering power relations – whether it implicates open conflict and contestation or not. What is at stake is not just the repressive or manipulative nature of both remembering and forgetting but also their meaningful nature. It is my view, then, that we should be equally aware of how societies forget, acknowledging the social significance of forgetting in the constitution of a sense of collective identity and communality.

I am as concerned with the dynamic relationship between remembering and forgetting as I am with the dynamics between public and private views of the past. Putting the public and the private at the core of the analysis of the representations of the past is a way to unfold remembering and forgetting. Through this I try to see if what is commemorated – and silenced – in the public sphere coincides with what is rememorized in private circles. When I say "silenced" I do not by any means take these silences as being just the result of an ideological effacement. I also see them as the result of the community's ongoing consensus about its own past and, as such, about its own sense of identity. Furthermore, I do not mean to say that all the private voices contradict the representation that is made in the public sphere. Some private voices are heard in the public arena and some are not. The purpose of this chapter is therefore to explore the processes by which some private voices become public while others do not. By interconnecting remembering and forgetting and public and private in this manner, I hope to stress the relational dynamics – or the memory games – that are central to memory practices.

In this chapter, I want to address these issues by looking at a local maritime heritage complex. More specifically, I shall look at the memory games involved in the representation of a maritime past in the public sphere. These games relate to the actual processes by which certain versions of the past are provisionally constituted and stabilized. In these processes, some private voices are transformed into public culture (Flores 1995), while others are discarded. Nevertheless, I suggest that this disposal deserves attention because it opens up a wider discussion about the meaningful nature of both remembering and forgetting with respect to establishing a sense of community and identity.

As I will explain in greater detail below, this heritage complex is roughly constituted by the legacy of one specific fishing activity – the cod fisheries – as it was practiced in the golden years of Salazar's regime, the dictatorship that governed Portugal for 40 years until finally toppled in April 1974. Even though these fisheries were national in scope, as they were a state-sponsored activity, its foreground representation can only be found at local level, in Ílhavo, a coastal locality in northern Portugal where I undertook a three-year field research. I take the fact that this is a localized heritage – rather than being treated as a national legacy – as very significant, because it allows me to understand better how the local and the national are mutually intertwined to build a memory complex that goes far beyond local. In Portugal, when the case is about maritime legacies, the intersection between local and national is even deeper, as the imagined nation is built up upon a whole complex of myths related to Portuguese maritime history.

A maritime heritage complex

My case study concerns a local maritime heritage as represented in Ílhavo, a coastal town in northern Portugal. This maritime complex is mainly constituted by the legacy of a specific fishing activity – the cod fisheries. It should be said that the cod fishing is not *just* a fishing activity; it is also, or even primarily, a naval enterprise. In fact, the men involved in this kind of fishing are not seen as fisherman but as sailors or seafarers. This is an activity filled with epic images taken from a repertoire of national myths associated with the maritime discoveries in which Portugal was involved, since cod fishing first began to be developed at the same time as the earliest of the major discoveries, in the fifteenth and sixteenth centuries.

Until the end of the sixteenth century, the Portuguese, together with the Basques, dominated these fisheries, but from then until the early twentieth century, the cod trade was controlled by the English and French. In this period, Portugal was a huge importer, as cod had become well-established as an important, if not crucial, part of the national diet and culinary traditions. Indeed, cod is "the" national dish of Portugal and a potent symbol of national identity. With such a large consumption, and as Portugal was mainly an importer in a very protectionist and unstable market, from time to time there was a crisis in supplies entailing serious political consequences. The problems with the supply of this and other basic food products created an enduring political instability which, with other factors, later led to the establishment of the dictatorship and the concomitant corporatist regime – the *Estado Novo* (New State) – that lasted from 1933 to 1974 (Garrido 2003).

Salazar's authoritarian rule created public policies in order to develop the Portuguese cod fishing fleet and free Portugal's economy from the foreign monopoly of cod supplies. The state intervened directly in the fleet and in the industry as a whole, dictating what kind of ships investors could buy, how big and what their capacity should be, how the cod should be commercialized and at what price. In return, the state would offer private national entrepreneurs the guarantee of a constant demand market. In order to be sustainable, the fishing had to be practiced at a very low cost. Because of this the fleet mainly comprised white sailing boats during this period, known as the Portuguese *White Fleet*, which despite its legendary status, was far less effective than the modern motor boats other European fleets were adopting. And while others privileged large catches with industrial fishing nets, Portuguese ship-owners largely adopted cod line-fishing with *dories*, small boats that would fan out into the ocean around the main ship. In these small boats, a solitary fisherman would try to catch as many cod as possible, using just a hand-held fishing line and homespun devices. He would fish for hours, completely alone in the freezing waters, miles away from the main ship and from any help, and in the harshest weather conditions.

These fishermen were recruited in poor coastal fishing communities throughout littoral Portugal. Facing severe living conditions they saw cod fishing as an opportunity to have a more stable income, at least for the six months a campaign usually lasted, from April to October each year. During these six months, they were either catching cod in their small boats or processing the fish on the main ship. There were just enough pauses to eat and sleep by shifts. Everything was controlled and watched over by the captain, who was the authority on board. The captain ran the ship, decided where to fish and when to fish, organized the crew, took note of how much fish each man caught, and made sure that there was no troubles or disputes during the campaign. He was definitely the man in charge. His authority was sometimes considered despotic, but it did not just derive from the power invested in him by the fish-owner or by the corporatist regime. It also involved the social gap between the captain and the fishermen. One of the ways this gap was made clear was in the conditions captains enjoyed on board, quite different from the inhumane conditions the fishermen experienced. This is not to say that captains were comfortable, but they were certainly much better off than the fishermen. And they earned much more too.

In contrast with the roughness and primitive conditions of the cod fishing, the state was very much more interested in conferring an epic aura on the enterprise. There was a powerful ideological investment in cod fishing as part of a larger narrative aimed at representing the *Estado Novo* as the guardian of the national maritime legacy and as the natural restorer of the imperial regime. The fishermen were symbolically converted into sailors and navigators and the cod fisheries poetically named *Faina Maior* (literally, harder work). There were major celebrations and rituals associated with cod fishing in which the entire nation was included, from the heads of the corporatist organization to the representatives of the local fishing communities. So, despite being on a national scale, these celebrations had also a localized dimension. This was in fact an inclusive narrative, embracing the national and the local.

This activity, and the celebrations surrounding it, were practiced until 1974. When the *Estado Novo* fell, the cod line-fishing definitively came to an end. The business continued with motorized fishing boats, but the fact is that the sector had been experiencing a severe decline since the early 1970s, and was collapsing. The changes in the international law of the sea made it possible for countries like Canada to restrict fishing in their national waters, imposing strict operating limitations on the Portuguese. Moreover, the cod stocks were collapsing due to overfishing. These factors, together with the adjustments Portugal had to make in the fishing sector in order to prepare its entry into the European Economic Community in 1986, sent cod fishing into an irreversible decline.

Portugal, however, is still the largest *per capita* cod consumer, and cod remains the principal symbol of Portuguese culinary tradition. Despite the cultural, symbolic and historical prominence of cod in the nation's fabric, it has not been subjected to a national representation since the end of the *Estado Novo*. Only at a more local level does the memory of cod fishing seem to persist, especially in those coastal communities which used to play a major role in the enterprise. One in particular has been very active in the public representation of this past: Ílhavo, the case study which is presented and analyzed here.

Ílhavo used to be deeply involved in these fisheries and a large proportion of its population participated in it. Contrary to other localities, Ílhavo had two special features: first there was an important port structure in the area and a lot of shipping companies were from the region; second, a large proportion of the ships' masters were from Ílhavo. Probably because of this, Ílhavo has for some years now been staking its claim as the capital of cod. These claims first emerged in the early 1980s when cod entered the local public sphere, with the setting of some small exhibitions about cod fishing in the local museum. Before then, the local museum focused on the representation and celebration of the "local people" and their environment. Although it already displayed objects related to maritime activities, this was by no means a maritime museum, as it represented various aspects of the locality and the region. The local museum just started to accommodate and replicate a master narrative about cod in the early 1980s. Over the years, this narrative broadened and in 2001, after the museum was almost completely rebuilt to become a masterpiece of public architecture, it reopened definitely as a maritime museum, with cod line-fishing as its main display.

It is no coincidence that the representation of this past in the public sphere started at a time of social and economic changes. The cod line-fishing and its enveloping ideological apparatus had disappeared in 1974 and by the mid-1980s the whole fishing industry was collapsing. At the same time, Ílhavo was experiencing great changes. Employment patterns changed dramatically with the decline of fishing and with the growth of employment in industry and in the service and administrative sectors. Tourism also expanded substantially. Ílhavo also grew considerably in demographic terms. With approximately 37,000 inhabitants today, every year the town attracts new residents and this has dramatically altered the physical and social landscape of the locality. Change and diversity help to explain why cod has become so prominent in the representations of local identity. The disappearance or decline of certain types of occupations and activities has had important social and cultural implications, generating a sense of loss. At first this was felt most by those who had previously had a high symbolic status in the locality, namely the fishing vessels' captains. Not only had their employment suddenly declined but their hierarchical status was upset. They were the first to be seriously engaged in making cod a pervasive major local symbol.

Others were to follow. One of them was Ribau Esteves, the present mayor of Ílhavo. Soon he noted the high degree of consensus generated in the community by seafaring in general and cod fishing in particular. Even before he was first elected in 1997 he had started to associate himself with the captains' and shipowners' agenda. For the new council, the historical and symbolic importance of the sea, and cod fishing in particular, became a key element in the development of the town's image. In order to raise the profile of this symbol, thereby gaining political dividends, and to capitalize on it, the mayor decided to promote a new image for the locality with the marketing slogan *Ílhavo: The Sea by Tradition*. The most important element of this scheme involved the renovation of the museum building, an enterprise that was called for by captains and ship-owners but that was made possible by the mayor. This led to a certain amount of conflict between the two as both aspired to be identified as the main proprietors of this memory. If the captains and ship-owners were mainly interested in the perpetuation and affirmation of their own class identities and privileges, the mayor was more concerned in enhancing his own political reputation and that of the locality within a wider context. This means that the daily practices by which local identity is constructed are neither fixed nor rigid, but subjected, rather, to variable and conflicting interests (Macdonald 1997).

Public silences

Let me now turn to the way cod fishing is represented today in the local public sphere. I will focus mainly on the way it is displayed in the local museum, even though other sites and occasions exist at local level in which this past is celebrated. Reopened in 2001, the new museum is exclusively a maritime museum giving full prominence to cod line-fishing. That's why the exhibit devoted to this was first named *Faina Maior*, and later *Captain Francisco Correia Marques*, in homage to someone who was then a true living symbol of an epic nostalgic memory, a former ship's master who was strongly implicated in the invention of this tradition. The display combines a realistic style with an aesthetization of the exhibition space, recreating a mythical, involving and mournful environment, and it is mainly composed of a replica of a classic sailing ship used in cod line-fishing. This is a huge replica, perhaps even too big for the available space, set at the center of the room and leaving just narrow side spaces for contextual objects. Visitors can climb aboard and walk around the deck of the ship. There they can see what "life" was like on board, how the space was arranged and how work was done. The purpose was to reproduce the physical and material environment of this type of fishing, the dories and the tools and devices used in the preparation of the fish once caught. What is represented here is work, not worldviews, practices, or even difficulties. When I asked Captain Francisco Marques why work has been made the focus, he just said to me, "that's the only way to represent the life we had. It was only work, always on the deck working day in and day out. There was nothing else".

What "else" there was considered worthy of being represented is displayed along the right and left sides of the central replica. On the right there are some old photos showing the fleet sailing over from Lisbon during *Estado Novo* rituals, along with some rather incomprehensible fishing instruments. On the left is the display of the cabins that were below decks which could not be reproduced in the replica. First, there are the officers' quarters and the captain's cabin. Then the hold of the ship where the cod was salted and processed. Only afterward do we find the fishermen's accommodations, the sleeping berths, the quarters and the galley. As represented in the exhibition, the officers' world is set apart from the fisherman's world, reproducing the hierarchies found on board. At the end of the display there is a black and white motion picture, produced in the golden days of line-fishing, documenting the lonely fishermen in their dories, happily landing their catch on the main ship. Nowhere does the display mention the severe conditions under which the fishermen operated. By the same token, there is a total absence of historical information which certainly would contribute to a better understanding of both the upsurge and the decline of this activity. Moreover, the strong links between cod fishing and Salazar´s regime are almost completely ignored.

Focused as it is on the material dimensions of cod line-fishing, the poetics of the display naturalize its ideological content. Therefore, the social, economic and political context in which it was practiced is never mentioned. Instead, by emphasizing the object and the materiality of this past, the exhibit crystallizes the previous power relations, perpetuating its symbolic hierarchies. *Faina Maior* makes this rather clear: by giving centrality to the ship, it perpetuates the symbolic power of the ship-owner and of the captain, while the lonely doryman is clearly left aside. In stark contrast with the monumentality of the captain's domain, the ship, the fisherman's domain, his *dory*, is represented while on the deck, inactive. As a consequence, the visitor cannot truly comprehend its real importance on the practice of cod fishing or even understand how the cod was actually fished. In this sense, the prevailing symbolic hierarchies are kept invisible. By emphasizing the tools and the activities involved in the preparation of the fish on the deck, the cod is elected to be the main protagonist, not the ship's master or the fisherman. These characters are represented harmoniously, as both were actively engaged in the whole fishing. Work comes out as a unifying viewpoint, as there is no doubt that captains and fishermen had all to work equally hard during the campaign.

In this sense, the past which is represented articulates cultural and social differences on the basis of a common, highly depoliticized, standpoint: that of a common life style (Dicks 2003). Tensions, class conflicts or the deep social abyss that lay between fishermen and captains are all silenced by an ethos of common suffering, hard work and heroism. By forging an egalitarian representation of the community's past, the display also fashions the contours of a horizontal community. Local memory is thus drained of its previous ideological content and as such, the social tensions and frictions that were experienced in the past are erased from daily experience. This has not been without criticism, as some people have shown they are uncomfortable with the fact that the exhibition does not give due prominence to the "lower" strata of cod fishing's hierarchies. As noted by Bodnar (1992), collective memory is always a controversial public domain. But the truth is that the exhibition does generate a great amount of consensus as it favors a sense of belonging or even a sense of familiarity with this past. The exhibition is directed to the entire community, which is represented as if an organic whole was still participating in a singular and unique past that has now been reactivated and cleansed of its murky details. Cod was in fact a very important part of the community's life in the past, and no one questions that. It is this previous social valorization that provides a support for the general consensus about the exhibition and about the silences it engenders (Prats 2004).

These consented silences express a will to rehabilitate the community's past, which is then represented in a glorious and uncritical manner. In this regard, they are imposing a taboo. While in the field, I in fact sensed that people felt quite uncomfortable when asked to talk openly about the less honorable facets of the cod fishing campaigns, as if it was something unnatural or shameful that disrupts the idealist self-image that the community has built up for this past. Facing a sense of loss, because of the abrupt disintegration of these activities, and also experiencing an unspoken humiliation as it is sensed that bigger powers controlled the "natural" and historical privileges that were formerly the preserve of the Portuguese fishing fleets, local civil society has engaged in the heroic representation of the community's past. There is also some embarrassment due to the implications of local cod fishing with the Salazar's dictatorship, which even today is a tricky subject at national level. Through an ideal representation of itself the community is rehabilitating its sense of historic continuity, glossing over the wounds, the discomforts and the tensions that this past has left behind. In this respect, these silences, although a form of covering up the past, also express the establishment of a community consensus about those aspects of the past that are consigned to a gloomier world. These consensual silences can then be understood as a way of constructing a new identity for the community, enabling it to cope with the demands of a new present and a new future. As Connerton has written about such silences, "while they are a form of repression, they can at the same time be a form of survival, and the desire to forget may be an essential ingredient in that process of survival" (2008: 68).

I take the whole rebuilding of the museum in 2001 as quite illustrative of this desire to rehabilitate the community's past and to refashion it for the future. What used to be an ethnographic local museum has now became an exclusively maritime museum, housed in a building with a bold, cosmopolitan impressive architecture, which received several awards in Portugal and abroad. With this new aesthetics, the museum publicly asserts the historical and symbolic distinctiveness of the sea, and of cod fishing in particular, as a key element of the local identity, in a time of great change and uncertainty regarding the future. In this manner, the local community affirms its difference, negotiating a favorable position in both national and global cultural arenas. As Marta Anico and I have noted before, "regarded as public assets of matchless value these museums contribute to the creation of an image of vitality and modernization which, while being rooted in the past, nonetheless allows the negotiation of change positioning the local in the global context" (Anico and Peralta 2007: 196). In the process, the less convenient or interesting facets of this past are put aside. As such, the maritime museum can be taken as a major symbol not only of public remembering but also of public silence.

Private voices

Over the years I conducted my field research in Ílhavo, I became quite aware of the incoherencies left by this publicly blanked-out version of the past. These were better distinguished when looking at the way this past was recalled in the private sphere. This is not to say that the private versions are at odds with the official representations or that they provide a bottom-up alternative representation. There are a lot of voices that can be heard privately. Some of them find resonance in the public sphere. Others do not. As pointed out by Anne Gotman, different visions of the same past, and the strategies implicated in its transmission, vary with the social trajectories of each individual (1990). As a matter of fact, the whole invention of *Faina Maior* as a great local tradition was the result of private actions and influences. To get a sense of this, I will first look at two examples of private actors playing in the local cultural field.

Cod was not a site of public culture when it was actually being fished. It was not until the mid-1980s when cod fishing suffered a critical slump that some individuals collaborated to preserve the legacy of *Faina Maior*. One of its main supporters was Captain Francisco Marques. He belongs to a family traditionally involved in naval and fishing activities and following in his ancestors' footsteps he went to sea, becoming a captain at the age of 23. He was a proud captain, who above all wanted to bring his vessel home laden with cod after the six-month campaign. He was attentive to the ship-owner and the corporate organization of fisheries. Although already an old man when the fishing industry collapsed, he was the main proponent of bringing *Faina Maior* to the local museum, greatly influencing the way this past is now publicly represented. The replica of the ship that is displayed in the museum's exhibition was made with his own bare hands with the help of a naval shipbuilder. When I asked him what motivated his engagement in this, he told me that was "to leave at least a bit of this past for the future," as he feels "a great sorrow, a frustration, for the disappearance of cod fishing, because the upcoming generations won't be able to do what we did." Thus, cod fishing was something great and it was that greatness that was the bit of the past he wanted to pass on. In fact, his private view of this past is full of epic and apologetic images and never once did he mention or even seem to recall the tensions, the conflicts, the asymmetries or even the primitivism of the activity. Take this quote as an example,

> A mariner, a sailor, is a person with a special character. He doesn't fear the sea, although he respects it. This is how we were, naturally, it was our way of living. That's why there never were any problems. We all worked together, and we worked hard, for the same purpose. . . . Everyone knew that was hard, that we were going to face bad weather, but we had to earn our living. We were in God's hands. [But] it was a fascination.

Aníbal Paião shares with Francisco Marques this view of this past. A much younger man, he is a ship-owner, a business man, and a proud member of an ancient local family of several generations of captains, naval officers, and ship proprietors. He continues to battle for the increase of Portuguese cod fishing possibilities in the North Sea and uses historical and symbolic arguments in his claims. In 1994 he became the president of the Friends of the Museum of Ílhavo, an association that existed for some decades, but then gained a new configuration, with Aníbal Paião recruiting people involved mainly in maritime activities. No different from the

113

outlook of Francisco Marques, Aníbal Paião's view of the cod fishing past is one of heroism and harmony, derived from a common way of life in which everyone, regardless of their status or rank, could identify with. In this way, the "people" are represented as having a natural or essential maritime identity. Through this egalitarian representation, the frictions derived from past experiences are naturalized and consensualized. But this is a class-biased representation as it is shaped by the action of certain individuals or groups that seek to prevent abrupt transformations from upsetting certain previously dominant class identities. By being strongly involved in the museum representations, they seek to regain their symbolic status and privileges within the local community and beyond, which they lost when the activity collapsed. These anxieties have made their private voices became public.

In both cases, these are private voices that find resonance in the public sphere. There are others that do not. Those that became public involved a considerable amount of emotional investment and the development of careful strategies of transmission. Those that were kept private are contained within the feeble limits of oral memory, and will fade away with time. Nevertheless they provide evidence that public silences do not necessarily mean forgetting, as those blank spots that are left behind in the official representations are recalled privately. Here is just one example of a dissonant memory of this past. It is kept by one cod line-fisherman, Manuel Pinto. He started to fish in a dory at the age of 16. He went through 40 cod campaigns. He loved it, despite its roughness: "It was a hard life. It couldn't have been harder. But we loved it. We were singing all the time, together, when we were gutting the fish on the deck. But we worked so hard there wasn't even time to sleep."

In spite of everything, this is a positive and socially integrated representation of this past, so once again the value of hard work appears as the main social and symbolic articulator, naturalizing the hardness of the activity. Any blame was laid on the backs of the captains, the visible and direct authority, for the cruel conditions they imposed: "the captains were all mean people who treated us all like slaves." "That's why I don't go to the museum. That's why I like to tell things as they were. . . . It was slavery. It is true. I'm not inventing it." Instead of viewing this past in a harmonious way, the memory held by Manuel Pinto disrupts the conventional public memory, as it highlights the social gulf that existed between the two classes of the same industry. Even so, he does not discuss the ideological and political foundations of it, and he does engage this past through the taboo of the common standpoint of "hard work." Breaking this taboo would be far too disruptive to the community's integrity.

Vanishing voices, perennial silences

Looking at the processes by which certain versions of the past go public – engendering silences that nevertheless do not obliterate dissident private voices – it is clear that heritage is always controversial, contested and transitory. As the Birmingham Centre for Contemporary Cultural Studies has shown, marginal versions of the past can exist side by side with established history. This also reveals the power dynamics that lie beneath any heritage site. Heritage is always about "culture wars", wars between different worldviews that compete in order to establish – albeit provisionally – what culture is or should be. Inevitably, remembering and forgetting are at the core of these wars, as legitimacy rests upon the prescription of an appropriate memory and on the eradication of a disturbing one.

But silences about the past do not always assume a repressive form. As a matter of fact, they are not even always driven by formalized political institutions. As noted again by Paul Connerton (2008), the establishment of a set of tacitly shared silences may be the result of the construction of a new identity. In this sense, the silencing of the past may be a productive process, enabling people and communities to move on, discarding those memories that just do not fit present practical purposes. This is quite evident in Ílhavo. On one hand, there are the power relations and political interests that contribute to the silencing of an important part of the cod fishing past; on the other, the whole community seems to consent to these silences, not because they have forgotten what is being publicly silenced, but just because they do not talk about it or claim it publicly.

This raises important moral issues about the social significance of forgetting (Misztal, Chapter 8 in this volume). Can it be possible for a society to be just and democratic and live together peacefully if the "truth" about the past is not publicity restored? Should a mature community not assume its "debt" toward the ones that have been excluded in the past and continue to be excluded today? There will be no simple answers to these questions if we relate them not to the idea of "debt" but rather with the idea of "loss," as proposed by Pierre Nora (2002). What is at stake here is the rehabilitation of a community's sense of identity when its ties with its past are abruptly cut off. Since memory holds the key to identity, an all-encompassing uncritical memory helps the community to deal with loss.

Public silences are then a way of symbolically inscribing an identity when paradoxically the society as a whole is experiencing great transformations and cleavages. In this sense, the local heritage complex functions as a "zero institution" (Lévi-Strauss 1974), a neutral reference point that congregates all differences and enables all members of the community to represent themselves as such (see Zyzek 2004). This implies shared, unspoken silences about the community's past. These silences do not necessarily mean forgetting. There are voices that can be heard privately which are against the consensual public memory. But these are vanishing voices, held within the limits of oral memory, and ultimately they will disappear in time if they do not join the local heritage games and find a way of mobilizing citizenship to a more inclusive view of the past.

Acknowledgments

I am very much obliged to Marta Anico, Sharon Macdonald, and Eric Gable for their constant inspiration. I am also grateful to Tânia Ganito for her comments on this chapter. Bruno de Góis deserves thanks for stimulating debate over the moral issues of remembering and forgetting.

Bibliography

Anico, M. and Peralta, E. (2007) "Political and social influences affecting the sense of place in municipal museums in Portugal," in S.J. Knell, S. MacLeod, and S. Watson (eds) *Museum Revolutions. Twenty-First century museum studies*, London: Routledge, 189–97.

Bodnar, J. (1992) *Remaking America: public memory, commemoration and patriotism in the twentieth century*, Princeton, NJ: Princeton University Press.

Connerton, P. (2008) "Seven types of forgetting," *Memory Studies*, 1(1): 59–71.

Dicks, B. (2003) *Culture on Display: the production of contemporary visibility*, London: Open University Press.

Flores, R. (1995) "Private visions, public culture: the making of the Alamo," *Cultural Anthropology*, 10(1): 99–115.

Garrido, A. (2003) *O Estado Novo e a Campanha do Bacalhau*, Lisbon: Círculo de Leitores.

Gotman, A. (1990) "Le présent de l'heritage," in H.P. Jeudy (ed.) *Patrimoines en Folies*, Paris: Éditions de la Maison des Sciences de l'Homme, 109–25.

Lévi-Strauss, C. (1974) *Anthropologie Structural*, Paris: Plon.

Macdonald, S. (1997) *Reimagining Culture: histories, identities and the Gaelic renaissance*, Oxford: Berg.

Nietzsche, F. (1997 [1873–1876]) *The Untimely Meditations*, trans. R.J. Hollingdale, Cambridge: Cambridge University Press.

Nora, P. (2002) "The reasons for the current upsurge in memory," in *Tr@nsit-Virtuelles Forum*. Available online at http://www.iwm.at/t-22txt3.htm (accessed April 21 2004).

Prats, L., 2004, "Activações turístico-patrimoniais de carácter local," in E. Peralta and M. Anico (eds), *Patrimónios e Identidades: Ficções Contemporâneas*, Oeiras: Celta, 191–200.

Zyzek, S. (2004) *A Subjectividade por Vir: Ensaios Críticos Sobre a voz Obscena*, Lisbon: Relógio D'agua.

The banalization and the contestation of memory in postcommunist Poland

Barbara A. Misztal

While postwar Europe was built upon deliberate forgetting, since the end of the Cold war, Europe, and especially Eastern Europe, has been constructed "upon a compensatory surplus of memory; institutionalized public remembering as the very foundation of collective identity" (Judt 2005: 16). Poland's communist period (1945–1989) provides proof that the first type of order, that is, the system based on the politics of forgetting, is unsustainable. The transformation from communism to postcommunism has been accompanied by discoveries of many "blank spots" and attempts to settle wrongs that were committed during the communist era by the state and its agents. Yet, according to Judt (2005), this second type of order – one based on remembering – is also not without its own problems because some amount of forgetting is the necessary condition for civic health. Difficulties of such politics of memory are already visible in Poland's attempts today to deal with the communist past and to challenge the old taboo on any serious discussion of Polish–Jewish relations.

The Polish battles to correct the national memory are rooted in two different concepts of national identity. These different images of the national distinctiveness have fuelled search for a new balance between remembering and forgetting. It is the aim of this chapter, by identifying difficulties of reordering of memory of the communist past and incorporating the destruction of the Jews into the Polish contemporary memory, to follow up this search for equilibrium. Before presenting the Polish case, I will summarize the main theoretical perspectives on the importance of social functions of both remembering and forgetting.

To start with the role of social remembering, following Olick and Levy (1997: 921) we can define collective memory as an ongoing process of negotiation through time. Understood in this way, collective memory is not just historical knowledge, as it is the experience mediated by representation of the past that enacts and gives substance to the group's identity. Memory helps in the construction of collective identities and boundaries, whether these are national, cultural, ethnic, or religious (Misztal 2003). It provides legitimization to the nation, characterized by "the possession in common of a rich legacy of memories" (Renan 1990: 11) and ensures the reproduction and cohesion of its social and political order (Hobsbawm and Ranger 1983). Yet, memory can also be seen as the guardian of difference because it allows for recollection and preservation of our different selves which we acquire and accumulate through our unique lives (Wolin 1989: 40). Remembering, the central medium through which meanings and identities are constituted thus is seen as the essential condition of a meaningful and plural civil society.

Furthermore, remembering is seen as being important for democratic community because collective memory is the condition of justice and freedom of democratic order (Misztal 2005). This argument is based on the assumption that every democratic nation in order to live together as a just and free community must first deal with past pathologies and crimes. Among many reasons why we should remember crimes against humanity, the most important are desires to not repeat the past crimes and not to allow the past to be rewritten. According to this perspective, the truth about the past is an essential human right because it ensures that the victims and past injustice are not forgotten. In other words, this way of conceptualizing the relationship between memory and justice is rooted in the belief that democracy's health depends upon social remembering of the past (Adorno 1986; Margalit 2002).

The positive and strong links between memory and democracy, justice and civil society are rejected by the perspective which asserts that our societies' nature is better grasped by the notion of forgetting, understood as the opposite social activity of collective remembering. Forgetting is seen in various ways: as the disappearance of frameworks of recollection or as an instance where memory is undone, erased, or as part of the transformation of memory, or as the substitution of one memory for another. Social forgetting is explained as an outcome of society's need to eliminate segments of its social memory which are interfering with the society's present functions. Defined in sociological terms, forgetting is seen as performing several functions. First, forgetting is essential for the construction and maintenance of national solidarity and identity. This role of forgetting was famously noticed by Ernst Renan in his 1882 lecture in which he argued that in order to ensure national cohesion there is the need for forgetting about the violence and threatening unity events, but remembering heroes and glory days. He insisted that forgetting is an essential element in the creation and reproduction of a nation since to remember everything could bring a threat to national cohesion and self-image. The essence of a nation is not only that its members have many things in common, but also "that they have forgotten some things" (Renan 1990: 11).

The discussed approach calls for forgetting because memories can "do more harm than good," the more we remember our past, the less likely we will be able to endorse equality for all. To accomplish political and legal equality, through contract or covenant, the individual has to forget past injustices and social categories that were the marks of inequality (Wolin 1989: 38). For example, Gupta (2005) rejects memory because the more we remember our past, the less likely we will be able to endorse equality between people. "So we must first learn to forget our prejudices and our petty memories if we are to be equal to the task that modernity has set for us" (Gupta 2005: 48). Gupta endorses forgetting as a solution to ethnic, religious and other conflicts because only forgetting can make the fate of all citizens more equal. He argues that the fascination with memory acts as an obstacle to a global civil society and democracy in general because focusing such group memories on narrow ethnicity results in groups competing for the recognition of suffering, and thus undermining the democratic spirit of cooperation.

So far, our examination has established the importance of social functions of both remembering and forgetting and that the value of neither memory nor forgetting can be taken for granted. It is clear now that the first view correctly insists on the value of memory, yet it tends to overlook the nature and unintended consequences of the game of memory. Since whose vision of the past is recognized and celebrated could be a result of power, we need always to study both mechanisms of constructing the past and we should remember that the value of the past relates to the uses we make of it and the manner in which we reminisce. How to reconcile memory and forgetting on the normative level has been recently suggested by the ethics of memory perspective which focuses on relations between forgetting and forgiving and offers compromise to the clash between memory and forgetting on the normative level. This perspective formulates the relationships between remembering and forgetting from the point of view of the public good and the importance of the relations between memory and justice. Ricoeur, Todorov, and Margalit – all assert that the value of memory needs to be evaluated in terms of its capacity to benefit others. They argue that memory is neither good nor bad in itself, and that the value of the past relates to the uses we make of the past and the manner in which we reminisce. For example, Todorov (2003) argues that memory of the past can be useful for us if it enhances the cause of justice. According to Ricoeur (1999), it is justice that turns memory into a project and it is the same project of justice that gives the form to the future and the imperative duty of memory. Ricoeur's ideas of the duty of memory as the imperative of justice resembles Margalit's (2002) idea that obligations to remember are generated by the type of relationships we have with others. In short, any search for possible resolutions to the dialectical relationship between remembering and forgetting should be taken in the interest of cultivating a relationship with the past that enhances societal well-being in the present.

If we agree, following the ethics of memory, that moral values can only be attached to memories that benefit others and that modernity is best served when both equality and plurality are endorsed, our task should be to search for a relationship between memory and forgetting which improves equality, while at the same time promoting diversity and intergroup cooperation. Since groups' cooperative attitudes toward others are the results of their ability to critically evaluate their own respective pasts in such a way that secures tolerance and removes barriers to mutual understanding, only an open, critical and reflective memory represents the morally important value. On the other hand, a closed, fixed memory of the event, which offers only the single authorized version of it, can cause moral damage to civil society by conflating political and ethnic or cultural boundaries. Hence memory, when used to close boundaries of ethnic, national or other identities, and memory, which accepts some versions of the past to be "the true," can aggravate conflict. However, when memory is open-ended, it can be an important lubricant of cooperation. Such reasoning leads us to judge the value of the process of the restoration of Polish national memory after 1989 in terms of the new memory's capacity to shape postnationalist solidaristic political communities.

In communist Poland, as in all Soviet bloc countries in Eastern Europe, the forced forgetting was highly organized and strategic, as memory was constructed and implemented to justify the communist order. The majority of communist countries "went into great lengths to create new myths and to instill these in society through the types of political socialization mechanisms" (Cohen 1999: 27). Without any other solution to the conflict over memory other than only manipulation, memory was not only controlled and constructed from above but also any potential challenges threatening the official version of the past were eliminated. These politically and culturally oppressive states treated memory and commemoration as a source of support for the exercise of their power and as instruments of manipulation to control society, in other words, as an ideology. Poland used official ceremonies, education and socialization to create and foster a single, national, class-based interpretation of national history.

The communist regimes imposed forgetting by rewriting national history and the destruction of places of memory. There were various consequences of these undemocratic systems' tendency to freeze memories and not to permit pluralistic debates. On the one hand, the undemocratic system's tendency to freeze memories increased the likelihood of such unscrutinized memories becoming sources of old grievances, prejudices and xenophobia. On the other hand, when people's memories conflicted with the official version of history, the memory often played an important role as a source of truth. When people understood that "the struggle against power is the struggle against forgetting" (Kundera 1980: 3), the preservation of unofficial memory became a way of sustaining collective identities and preserving suppressed narratives. As in all cases, where political power heavily censors national history and where oppressed nations have a profound deficit of truth, Poles living under the communist regime looked toward their private memories for authentic stories about their past. Oppositional memories, or unofficial memories, despite the techniques and practices of the communist power, did – to some degree – exist in communist Poland and they provided an alternative version of the past, although none of the alternative versions of the past really entered the public official space. Thus, the official memory remained stable, unchallenged, and unexplored, sustaining old stereotypes and taboos.

Looking at the Polish communist history of WWII we can see these two consequences of the policy of imposing a singular reading of the national past and the strategy to construct memory from above. The official vision of WWII was marked by a lack of the recognition of the Jewish suffering and by "blank spots" in the narratives of Polish–Russian relations – as illustrated by the suppression of the 1940 Katyn Forest Massacre of Polish officers by the Soviet secret police, the NKVD. Jewish experience was bracketed off and removed from consideration when the story of "Polish society under the German occupation" was narrated (Gross 2006: 185). The communist propaganda assumed that anti-Semitism belonged to the capitalist past and presented the Holocaust as purely connected with Nazi Germany's crimes. It eliminated the Jewish stranger from the narrative, while focusing on the Poles' heroism and victimhood and presenting Auschwitz as a symbol of Polish martyrdom. "The Polish national narratives, based on the romantic myth of sacrificial love for the fatherland, together with aberrations of communist rule in postwar Poland, thus cumulated in a particular skewed story of World War II" (Glowacka and Zylinska 2007: 5). The consequences of such a vision of WWII and of the use of anti-Semitism as an ideological weapon became visible in the next period of Polish history. In the representative survey in 2003, the majority of Poles who were asked pointed to WWII as the most proud event in Polish history and practically none saw anything shameful about this period (Szacka 2006: 184).

The postcommunist Polish strategies for dealing with the complex past illustrate the complexity of links between memory and justice in the context of a fragile democracy. The issue of anti-Semitism was left as a taboo through the first decade of newly democratized Poland, although attempts to rediscover the truth about the communist past have become one of the main feature of Polish political culture from 1989. After the downfall of communism, with the formation of democratic structures, with the opening to Europe and with the elimination of censorship, the first and the most natural reaction to the former "refusal of memory" was the "restoration of memory" of the so far hidden elements of the communist past. The replacement of many old monuments – which legitimized the previous political order – by new ones – which celebrate the new order – and numerous changes of street names, have been accompanied by the re-emergence in the public arena of the long-lasting self definition of Poles as "a martyr of nations." The image of Poland as occupied, humiliated and oppressed by aggressive imperial powers has reinforced the feeling of the constitution and the stability of national identity. This model of Polishness, which has been adopted since the eighteenth century and which is rooted in a messianic image of the Polish nation and based on the romantic vision of Poland as the "Christ of nations," is still the main base for self-definition of Poles.

> This vision of history was close to the popular national imagination and included also some mythical icons of the past and present, epitomized by such themes as "Polish heroism and patriotism," "unpunished communist crimes against the Nation," "opposition to Communism."
>
> (Ziolkowski 2002: 22)

At the end of the twentieth century 78 percent of surveyed Poles still believed that the Polish nation had historically been the victim of injustice more frequently than other nations (Krzeminski 2002: 48).

To reinforce this image of national identity has been one of the main goals of the policies dealing with the communist past. Among such policies, which Poland – like many other postcommunist countries – tried to implement, the most common was the policy of lustration. This policy of screening the past of candidates for important positions aims primarily at eliminating from crucial public offices those people who worked in or collaborated with the communist security forces (Misztal 1999). Poland's long and protracted history of legislative attempts to introduce lustration law started with the first Polish postcommunist government trying to "let bygones be bygones" in the name of reconciliation and transformation. By adopting the idea of compromise, forgiving rather than revenge, the Solidarity government expanded the scope of freedom in the use of the past to construct new postcommunist identities (Misztal 1999).

121

However, this forward-looking approach, which aimed to smooth and stabilize the transformation process, very quickly attracted criticism for preserving intact the identity of the former communists. In 1999, ten years after the collapse the old regime, Poland, due to continuous calls for addressing the past, passed a lustration law which imposed a forced compromise – only top officials were vetted – and the importance of which was already reduced by conflicts over previous misfired lustration bills. Yet, as the debate over who should have control over the secret policy files continued to politicize the issue of the communist past, the main conservative and nationalist groups became very vocal in expressing their dissatisfaction with the compromised measure of "purification." In March 2007, two years after these groups' electoral victory, a new lustration law was introduced which required all Poles born before August 1972 and occupying professional jobs in the public and private sectors to declare in writing within two months whether or not they had collaborated with former communist security services. Those who refused or gave false information could be banned from practicing their professions or holding public office for ten years. The new law was presented as vital to Poland's clean break from its communist past and as central to the "moral revolution" promised by the Law and Justice Party, the ruling party of the day. "We have to come to terms with the past to build the foundations of a strong state" – a Polish MP, quoted in *The Guardian*, July 20, 2006. While the Law and Justice Party was using the lustration to legitimate its own vision of Poland and to base national identity on the history of heroic struggle against the communist regime, the opposition protested against this law claiming that it could open the way for a witch hunt against former communists. The growing active opposition of intellectuals, academics, and liberal groups in general led to a legal challenge to the lustration policy. As a result, on May 11, 2007, only several months after its declaration, Poland's Constitutional Court declared many of the new lustration procedures as being unconstitutional. Its presiding judge ruled that "[l]ustration cannot be used to punish people as a form of revenge" (Michnik 2007: 25). This decision was met with relief by the majority of Poles who do not want lustration, with only 46 percent seeing any need for such a policy, and only 31 percent declaring some importance for its implementation, while 52 percent asserted that lustration would worsen the political climate of the country (Pacewicz 2005: 1). For the majority of people with liberal views and the majority of the younger generation, the idea of lustration is a shameful matter in which only the political elites were really interested (Pacewicz 2005: 1).

The reliance on the credentials of "noncollaboration" with the communist establishment to construct new identities, as the ruling coalition was proposing, was not an acceptable solution for society for several reasons. Poles did not show too much interest in the reevaluation of the communist past because of the complexity of the problem, more specifically because of a lack of acceptable criteria to evaluate the communist past. A common belief that any dealing with the communist past involves too many ambiguities and generates too many conflictual interpretations, together with the use of the past by main political parties as an instrument in the political battle, further explains the lack of interest in the communist past. Even more importantly, in one way or another everybody was involved, although people tend to forget their own participation. Yet, although the memory of the communist past does not engage the emotions and interests of the poles, they still refuse to "discard or negate their past; they want to have a sense of continuity" (Ziolkowski 2002: 20). These two tendencies, the first, the attempt to forget and, the second, the attempt to preserve a sense of continuity, have been responsible for a visible "depoliticization" of popular memory of the communist past (Ziolkowski 2002: 20). In other words, while the rival political parties upheld their respective versions of the past and their respective ways of dealing with it – thus, ensuring that the question of lustration became politicized – people lost their interest in the past – especially in narratives of the communist period – and decided to return to history transmitted directly within groups (Szmeja 2007). Between 1988 and 2003 the percentage of highly educated Poles – a group that always shows the highest passion for history – not interested in the past increased from 5.7 to 23.3 (Szacka 2006: 219).

So, in spite of the present political elite's attempts to introduce the issue of communist wrongdoings into the political arena, the memory of the communist past is seen as presenting a threat to society's continuity and therefore to societal self-respect, and, on the other hand, as a rather banal and lacking in any social significance issue. This devalorization of the policies dealing with wrongdoings of the communist past is reflected in people's positive evaluation of the condition of work and an absence of unemployment under communism, with 42.4 percent surveyed in 2003 positively evaluating the communist period in these terms (Szacka 2006: 217).

Despite this declining support for the use of the past to revitalize national identity and bonds, the ruling Law and Justice Party and its supporters continue to use the past in an instrumental way under the label of "historical politics." This perspective, which has been declared an official cultural program of the government of the day, aims to use history as a political instrument. Recognizing the role of history in ensuring national continuity and shaping national identity, this approach condemns any critical revision of national myths and taboos as a potential threat to solidarity and cohesion of the nations. Its attempts to construct the Polish identity are focused around such national values as religion and tradition as well as the memory of the struggle against the communist regime. It discourages politics of forgiveness or collective guilt as totally unpatriotic, naïve actions, and political mistakes. Stressing the importance of national ties and pointing out that it is impossible to distance oneself from the national community, this strategy of using the past for political and ideological reasons rejects liberal views that national identity is a matters of choice (Krasnodebski 2001).

In the last decade, this continuous attempt to limit the definition of national identity to the national struggle against communism has been gradually challenged by the growing awareness that "history is more complex than a black and white pattern poising the false communist version as the only one and the only true but partially mythical popular presentations of Polish history" (Ziolkowski 2002: 22). This shift from pursuing memory solely against the official communist propaganda, to the more open, and dealing with the fate of minorities memory has been helped by Jan Tomasz Gross's book *Neighbors* – published in Polish in 2000 and then in English in 2001 – which asks important questions about Polish national identity and about Poles' attitudes to others. Gross describes events of June 11, 1941, when, following a period of Soviet occupation and immediately after the German re-invasion – the region had been briefly under German control in 1939 – the Polish community of a small town, in the north-eastern part of today's Poland, murdered nearly its entire Polish Jewish population. *Neighbors*, by disclosing the events from Polish history that do not fit into the Polish ethos of suffering and heroism, stimulated one of the most significant debates about Polish national identity since WWII. The book has undermined the traditional Polish national consciousness based on Romantic visions, and the self-presentation of Poles as being solely the victims of Nazi executioners and Poland as the "Christ of nations." By dismantling the existing images of Polish attitudes and behavior under the German occupation, it catalyzed discussions of Polish–Jewish relations and rethinking the Polish war experience.

The story of the Jedwabne massacre had an impressive media coverage; all the leading newspapers and journals entered the debate. The issue of how Catholic Poles of Jedwabne assumed the role of willing voluntary executioners of their Jewish neighbors was discussed on radio and television, and many features, reports and documentaries about Jedwabne were produced. Such a wide coverage was possible because of postcommunist Poland's advances in the process of democratization and its integration with the wider world and also because of the impact of examples of various other countries confronting the dark pages of their history. Because of the importance of this debate for the constitution of political culture, the Jedwabne controversy was often compared with the Dreyfus Affair (Kazmierska 2002; Leder 2001; Tornquist-Plewa 2003). "It was claimed that just as in France a hundred years earlier, a confrontation had occurred in Poland between the forces of nationalism and traditionalism on the one hand, and the forces of modern enlightened liberalism on the other" (Tornquist-Plewa 2003: 165). The battle in Poland, as in nineteenth-century France, was over the vision of the nation and its identity, with various political orientations adopting different stands and using the memory of Jedwabne for their own purposes (Frenztel-Zagorska 2002; Paczkowski 2001; Tornquist-Plewa 2003). In short, the ultra-Catholic, populist and nationalist groups, such as the League of Polish Families, "accused its ideological opponents, the liberal and the left, of using Jedwabne to knock down such national values as religion and tradition that allegedly make Poles provincial, anti-Semitic, racist and intolerant" (Tornquist-Plewa 2003: 166). Liberals hoped that the Jedwabne debate, by providing Poles with an opportunity to re-form their identity, would help to transform Poland into a modern, democratic, open, and tolerant society (Tornquist-Plewa 2003: 166). The political groups in power, worried about what the world would say about the Poles, pragmatically accepted that Poles played a significant role in the crime. A special research institute, the Institute of National Remembrance, originally created to organize public access to communist secret files, was asked to investigate the Jedwabne case. The results of its investigation led the Institute to conclude that not 1,600 but probably 400 Jews were killed by their non-Jewish neighbors without interference from the Germans (*Gazeta Wyborcza*, 19.12. 2001: 1).

At the ceremonies held at Jedwabne on the sixtieth anniversary of the killings, a monument with a newly changed inscription was revealed. While the old inscription attributed the massacre to Gestapo and Nazi soldiers, new words read as follows: "To the memory of the Jews of Jedwabne and its vicinity, men, women and children, co-hostess of this region, killed, burned alive on this spot on 10 July 1941" (Deak 2001: 52–3). This compromised message was also repeated in President Kwasniewski's conditional apologies. Aiming to defend the Polish honor, he apologized in the name of the Poles whose "consciousness is struck by this mass murder." By stressing that it was not the Polish state that violated the law but Poles who "committed crimes against Poland" and its history and "great tradition," the President managed to externalize the Polish perpetrators and to place them "outside the Polish tradition," which thus "could remain sacred" (Tornquist-Plewa 2003: 158).

Yet, in a comparison with ordinary Poles, the political elite was "much more willing to admit the Poles' role in the crime and completely unwilling to put all the blame on the Germans" (Frenztel-Zagorska 2002: 135). The defensive attitudes of rank and file Poles manifested themselves in many ways; for example, only 30 percent of Poles who were surveyed agreed that Poles should apologize to the nation for the crime in Jedwabne and 28 percent of asked Poles believed that Germans killed the Jews in Jedwabne, and only eight percent said that the Poles were wholly responsible (Trend Reports 2002: 123). These statistics, together with some recent cases of anti-Semitism, suggest that Poland still has a lot of work to do in order to address the legacy of anti-Semitism.

Gross's book has demonstrated that Polish and Jewish memories of the war remain in conflict and that Polish unrevised memories of the Holocaust were responsible for Polish anti-Semitism after Auschwitz – for example, such as the pogrom in Kielce in 1946. *Neighbors* and the discussion that followed have documented that Polish anti-Semitism was a result of societal unwillingness to confront the truth about the attitudes and actions of some poles toward Jews during the Nazi occupation. While in the Polish vision of WWII there was a certain acknowledgment of some Polish collaboration with the Nazi occupiers, it tended to be followed by a standard commentary that "[t]here is scum in every society," which rendered "the story banal and uninteresting" (Gross 2006: 190). On the other hand, such crimes as the killing of Jews by their neighbors have never made it "into the historical consciousness of the epoch at all" (Gross 2006: 190).

Nonetheless, the Jedwabne massacre, despite the compromised attitudes of the political elite and the resistance of more nationalist groups to address it, has imposed itself on the collective memory because it touches on central symbols in the collective past and collectivity's relationship to the past. It needs to be disputed and negotiated in the interest of redefining the nation's present day identity. Gross's book, by shedding the memory of total innocence, violated the taboo of the Polish role in the Holocaust (Bikont 2004). Because "taboos help set terms of discourse and boundaries of identity" (Olick and Levy 1997: 924), the debate started an unprecedented soul-searching process and caused a reshaping of the collective memory of the Holocaust. It focused public attention on the issue of collective guilt and shame and, by challenging the main taboo in Polish collective memory of the Holocaust, has caused an identity crisis in Polish society, which can only be addressed through dealing with the heritage of anti-Semitism. Thus, it can be said that the issue of Polish–Jewish relations, not the communist past, has been the subject of political contestation in Poland since 2000.

The Jedwabne controversy has demonstrated that the existence of this taboo is troubling, that is a source of fears and, without addressing it, it will be a constant moral challenge which will cause Poles to be always "glancing over their shoulders, trying to guess what others think about what they are doing. They will keep diverting attention from shameful episodes buried in the past and go on defending Poland's good name, no matter what" (Gross 2001: 169). Yet, Poland is not an exception in this respect and it, like other nations, in order to reclaim its past, "will have to tell itself anew" (Gross 2001: 169).

Conclusion

With the growing process of democratization and European integration, Poles have been undertaking the task of facing the old national myths and taboos. Postcommunist Poland's policy of lustration and controversies surrounding the publication of Gross's book *Neighbors* illustrate that the politics of memory in Poland are now divided between those who propagated the use of memory of the communist past for the nation's self-definition and those who believe Poles need to critically work through their collective memory if they want to become a modern, tolerant, and open society. If we assume that the value of the past relates to the uses we make of the past and the manner in which we reminisce, the history of Polish lustration, which demonstrates that "justice is more political in transitional situations than under normal circumstances" (Elster 1998: 16), forces us to question the social value of the type of remembering imposed by the state's policy of dealing with communist wrongdoings. The lustration strategy, which aimed to use the past to construct new postcommunist identities, due to the politicization of dealing with past injustice, and the ambiguities and multiplicities of interpretations of the communist past, did not help the process of formation of citizenship and collective identities in the newly democratized Poland and subsequently it lost social support and significance.

On the other hand, the debate on Jedwabne was significant because it was concerned with the status of the Holocaust as a taboo in Polish memory. It posed a powerful antidote to the self-righteousness of the "political history" approach. The Jedwabne controversy encouraged Poles to confront the facts but at the same time provided "a way to do so that does not damn the guilty party forever" (Olick 2003: 117). If the social meaning of the past is a function of the way in which we interpret the past vis-à-vis other events within the interactive process, the new Polish–Jewish past can be seen as constructed from the standpoint of the new problems faced by a society undergoing the process of political, social and cultural transformation. Although, it is impossible, as Tornquist-Plewa (2003: 169) noted, to discuss the Holocaust in today's Poland without taking the events in Jedwabne into account, Poland's failure to confront adequately the memory of the Holocaust and particularly its failure to acknowledge Poles' attitudes to the fate of the Jews during WWII still constitutes one of the main challenge faced by Poland today. The challenge is to maintain "the productive impulse in this acknowledgment rather than to let ourselves slip into the conclusion that because we are all guilty, we need not to worry about it too much" (Olick 2003: 117).

Bibliography

Adorno, T.W. (1986) "What does coming to terms with the past mean" trans. T. Bahti and G. Hartman, in G. Hartaman (ed.) *Bitburg in Moral and Political Perspective*, Bloomington, IN: Indiana University Press.

Bikont, A. (2004) *My z Jedwabnego* (We Are From Jedwabne), Warsaw: Wydawnictwo Proszynski and S-ka.

Cohen, S.J. (1999) *Politics without Past*, Durham, NC: Duke University Press.

Deak, I. (2001) "Heroes and victims," *New York Review of Books*, 31 (May): 51–6.

Elster, J. (1998) "Coming to terms with the past," *European Journal of Sociology*, XXXIX(1): 7–48.

Frenztel-Zagorska, J. (2002) "Leading politicians on Jedwabne," *Polish Sociological Review*, 1(137): 129–36.

Glowacka, D. and Zylinska, J. (2007) "Introduction," in D. Glowacka and J. Zylinska (eds) *Imaginary Neighbors. Mediating Polish–Jewish Relations after the Holocaust*, Lincoln, NE: University of Nebraska Press, 2–18.

Gross, J.T. (2000) "Themes for a social history of war experience," in I. Deak, J.T. Gross and T. Judt (eds) *The Politics of Retribution in Europe*, Princeton, NJ: Princeton University Press: 15–37.

—— (2001) *Neighbors. A Destruction of the Jewish Community in Jedwabne, Poland*, Princeton, NJ: Princeton University Press.

—— (2006) *Fear: Anti-Semitism in Poland after Auschwitz. An Essay in Historical Interpretation*, Princeton, NJ: Princeton University Press.

Gross, J.T. and Judt T. (eds) *The Politics of Retribution in Europe*, Princeton, NJ: Princeton University Press.

Gupta, D. (2005) *Learning to Forget. The Anti-Memoirs of Modernity*, Oxford: Oxford University Press.

Hobsbawm, E. and Ranger, T. (eds) (1983) *The Invention of Tradition*, New York: Cambridge University Press.

Judt, T. (2005) "From the house of the dead. On modern European memory," *New York Review of Books*, 6 (October): 12–16.

Kazmierska, K. (2002) "Memory and oblivion," *Polish Sociological Review*, 1(137): 106–12.

Krasnodebski, Z. (2001) "Czern w Jedwabnem" (The Mob in Jedwabne), *Znak*, 549 (February): 11–121.

Krzeminski, I. (2002) "Polish–Jewish relations, anti-Semitism and national identity," *Polish Sociological Review*, 1(137): 25–49.

Kundera, M. (1980) *The Book of Laughter and Forgetting*, New York: King Penguin.

Leder, A. (2001) "Jedwabne-polska sprawa Dreyfusa," *Res Publica*, 17: 67.

Margalit, A. (2002) *The Ethics of Memory*, Cambridge, MA: Harvard University Press.

Michnik, A. (2007) "The Polish witch-hunt," *New York Review of Books*, 28 (June): 25–6.

Misztal, B.A (1999) "How not to deal with the past: Lustration in Poland," *European Journal of Sociology*, XL(1): 63–87.

—— (2003) *Social Theories of Remembering*, Maidenhead: Open University Press.

—— (2005) "Memory and democracy," *American Behavioral Scientists*, 48(10): 1320–39.

Olick, J.K. (2003) "The guilt of nations?" *Ethics and International Affairs*, 17(2): 109–17.

Olick, J.K. and Levy, D. (1997) "Collective memory and cultural constraint: Holocaust myth and rationality in German politics," *American Sociological Review*, 62: 921–36.

Pacewicz, P. (2005) "Polak o lustracji: nie chce, ale musze," *Gazeta Wyborcza*, 7 February: 1.

Paczkowski, A. (2001) *Droga do 'Mniejszego Zla': Strategia i Taktyka Obozu Wladzy*, Krakow: Wydawnictwo Literackie.

Renan, E. (1990 [1882]) "What is a nation?" in H.K. Bhabha (ed.) *Nation and Narration*, London: Routledge, 7–19.

Ricoeur, P. (1999). "Memory and forgetting," in R. Kearney and M. Dooley (eds) *Questioning Ethics*, London: Routledge, 5–12.

Szacka, B. (2006) *Czas Przeszly, Pamiec, Mit*, Warsaw: Wydawnictwo Naukowe Scholar.

Szmeja, M. (2007) "Why do the Poles remember history in different way?" paper presented at the European Sociological Association conference, Glasgow, 3–6 (September).

Todorov, T. (2003) *Hope and Memory. Reflections on the Twentieth Century*, London: Atlantic Books.

Tornquist-Plewa, B (2003) "The Jedwabne Killings – a challenge for Polish collective memory," in K.G. Karlsson and U. Zander (eds) *Echoes of the Holocaust*, Riga: Nordic Academic Press, 141–76.

Trend Reports (2002) "Poles' opinions about the crime in Jedwabne," *Polish Sociological Review*, 1(137): 117–28.

Wolin, S.S. (1989) *The Presence of the Past*, Baltimore: Johns Hopkins University Press.

Ziolkowski, M. (2002) "Memory and forgetting after communism," *Polish Sociological Review*, 1(137): 6–24.

A landscape of memories: Layers of meaning in a Dublin park

Kate Moles

> [M]emory, so far from being merely a passive receptacle or storage system, an image bank of the past, is rather an active shaping force, that is dynamic – what it contrives . . . to forget is as important as what it remembers . . . memory is historically conditioned . . . so far from being handed down in the timeless form of tradition it is progressively altered from generation to generation . . .. Like history, memory is inherently revisionist and never more chameleon than when it appears to stay the same.
>
> (Samuel 1994: x)

Introduction

The quote above is invoked at the onset to allow us to consider what memory is about. Remembering and forgetting are not opposites; instead they are both constitutive parts of what comes together to mean memory. Through remembering and forgetting, we privilege, we construct and we assign meaning. Certain things are retained, others detained, meanings are ascribed and meanings are learnt. The one consistent is that, as Samuel (1994) reminds us, change is abundant and inherent, and that time and space conflate to produce constantly shifting meanings, understandings and memories.

The chapter will begin by considering issues of national identity and heritage. The key ideas running through this consideration are about whose heritage it is, what is being remembered and why, and how does it become the accepted version of history that constitutes the national space. The chapter then moves on to consider a landscape of memory. By this I mean the different topological, cultural and material monuments, events, people, words, stories and meanings that come together to construct a particular place, all of which are grounded in shared and personal memories of the space. This will then move on to address these issues with two 'grounded' examples from a Dublin park that were gathered during a three-year ethnography of the space. This chapter thinks about the position of the park in the Irish imaginary, as a space of collective memories and shared understanding, as a place where what it means to be Irish is demonstrated *writ large*. The interpretation and presentation of the history of the park plays a large role in this construction, and the different ways in which this infuses individual narratives is discussed.

National identity and heritage

Heritage often fulfils several opposing uses and carries conflicting meaning simultaneously. As Graham *et al.* (2000: 2) argue, 'if people in the present are the creators of heritage, and not merely passive receivers or transmitters of it, then the present creates the heritage it requires and manages it for a range of contemporary purposes'. So what is the meaning of particular heritage; why do people create it in a certain way? As Lefebvre (1991) posits, space is not an independent given, but a mutable and ever-changing product of economic, social, cultural and political processes. And this also is how the landscape of heritage can be understood in this chapter; something that is formed through the intertwining threads of economy, society, culture and politics, reformed and reconstituted continually through the shifting interactions of these constitutive parts.

This heritage is the construction of the past that has been selected in the present for contemporary purposes. The worth attributed to the various material and cultural artefacts that are included rests less in their intrinsic worth – if such a thing exists – than in a complex array of contemporary values, demands and even moralities. Heritage helps define the meaning of culture and power and is a political resource, and as such it possesses a crucial socio-political function. Consequently, it is accompanied by an often bewildering array of identifications and potential conflicts, not least when heritage, places and artefacts are involved in processes of legitimation and authentication.

As part of this chapter, it is argued that all heritage holds with it a process of legitimation and authenticating. Only one narrative of history can be displayed in processes of heritage, and this is always going to be based on a sole way of remembering events, places and people. However, as this chapter will present, there are multiple, overlapping, conflicting and often unrelated understandings of particular events, material and cultural artefacts that constitute places of heritage. It becomes particularly interesting when these material and cultural artefacts are understood as constitutive of a particular national identity; when the material artefacts hold a cultural presence in the nation's history.

National identity exists through particular understandings of a linear, teleological history that positions events as contributory to an end point that is the nation. The storyline must be clear. It requires 'nothing less than the abolition of all contradiction in the name of a national culture' and 'projects a unity that overrides social and political contradictions' (Bommes and Wright 1982: 264). Indeed through the construction, and rejection, of the 'other', the 'self' is ratified, enabled to exist. As such, heritage that contributes to a particular national history is constructed to fit into this particular national narrative. The empirical examples in this chapter will demonstrate how particular narratives, uncovered through interviews with visitors and residents, have been silenced in the official discourse as they do not fit the particular story the park wants put across. The remembering and forgetting of particular facets of events, people and places are part of the construction of a narrative and imagination of a particular Irish national identity.

A landscape of memory: Phoenix Park, Dublin

Landscapes are made up of events, acts, times, places and people that have passed by and through them. These things leave traces (Anderson, forthcoming) behind them, which can be both material – for example 'things' such as buildings, signs, statues, graffiti – and non-material – for example, activities, events, performances or emotions. The ways in which memory and landscape intertwine produce different experiences of place and different meanings associated with the place. Landscape is the hybrid product of biography and location(s), constructed into a narrative that makes sense. However, when people begin to think about 'national spaces' or places that hold national significance the individual meanings and meaning making that goes on becomes much more complicated. When spaces are allocated significance according to one understanding, they can be important markers of versions of identity, inclusive and affording of a sense of belonging, but at the same time they become exclusionary and closed to alternative readings and understandings associated with the place. This process incorporates ideas of othering that help define and demarcate the self. This chapter uncovers and untwines different narratives that make up, and pull apart, a national space.

Phoenix Park is in the north-west of Dublin, along the quays. It is located very centrally; a walk from the very centre of the city, and a stone's throw from the Guinness Brewery. It was developed initially as a Royal Deer Park during which time the Viceroy of Ireland lived in the park. It was opened to the Irish public in 1745 by Lord Chesterfield, after whom the main avenue is named. The Dublin Zoo is located within the walls. Áras an Uachtarain, the President of Ireland's official residence and the American Ambassador's official residence are both inside the park, as are the Garda Síochána – Irish police – Headquarters, Irish Army Headquarters and Farmleigh, the house where visiting dignities are hosted.

The park forms an important part of Dublin's cultural and material topography, especially amongst the capital's residents. For those who grew up in the vicinity, the park as a playground comprises an important part of their early childhood memories, informing and changing the way they now remember and think about the space. As people grew older, the park was a place associated with 'courting', and many Dublin couples took their first walks there. These memories, images, imaginaries and conceptualizations of the park are likely to be different for people who are from Dublin and for those who are visiting. In this way the park can also be variously a natural place, a historical place, a magical place and a place where key events, both personal and national occur.

As such, it can be understood to be the location of a number of key monuments of a particular Irish identity, different things that are located in the national narrative found in the park. This chapter is going to focus on two important dates in the park's history, the Phoenix Park Murders and the Papal Visit. These are key events in the park's history; however how they are portrayed within the narratives of the park differs greatly. The Papal Visit, is positioned within the official narrative readily; the Phoenix Park Murders are much more contested and do not figure as prominently. One is remembered very actively, the other is as actively forgotten about. These two events have undoubtedly left cultural marks on the landscape, and they have also both left material marks on the ground – though of a very different scale. Using these material artefacts, the cultural and social marks are also uncovered, developing an idea of how these events and monuments are incorporated into the authorized park's narrative, and how this impinges on the idea of national space developed, and by implication the idea of nationality associated with it.

The cross on the mound – The Papal Visit, 1979

In 1979, Pope John Paul II visited Ireland for the first time in the nation's history. It was, for an overwhelmingly Roman Catholic country, a very important event. Over 1.25 million people, about a third of the Irish population at the time, attended the main meeting on 29 September, which took place in Phoenix Park. This visit had important social and political timing; the Pope in his speech warned against turning away from faith as a way of organizing your life, and his speech was underpinned by an idea of 'oneness', one Roman Catholic Church uniting its followers across the world and, in Ireland's case particularly, across borders. The message from the Pope was a warning to the Irish people about the negativity associated with the breakdown of a united society, and the necessity to remain true to their faith. The Pope also visited Galway, Drogheda – which had important spatial significance, as it was the closest the Pope could be to the North of Ireland, without crossing the border – the Knock Shrine and Limerick, where almost all of the other two-thirds of the Irish population attended.

At 11.00 am on the September Saturday morning, the Pope's plane, an Aer Lingus plane called *St Patrick*, which had been specifically designed for the Pope, flew over the Phoenix Park on its way to Dublin airport. The crowd cheered and waved flags, and the Pope is reported to have risen out of his seat in the plane and blessed the assembling crowd (Nolan 2006). Following his landing at Dublin airport, the Pope was taken by helicopter to the park, where he addressed the masses. The event was a clear demonstration of what was a cohesive society; that level of attendance and the good behaviour that characterized the day could not be reproduced in today's Ireland. However, this outward cohesion masked coercion and social pressure to attend. For one participant in the research, volunteering at the local hospital was the only legitimate way to avoid the stigma of not attending. The social and political power of the Roman Catholic Church was being demonstrated and reinforced through this visit.

For the Pope's visit a large, white 40-tonne cross had been constructed behind the 12-metre high platform that the Pope used to address the crowd. It was meant to be removed after the visit, but a petition was lodged with the Office of Public

Works, the governmental body in charge of the park, asking for its preservation and so it has remained until today. The area around it has been redeveloped, with a car park and tree-lined path guiding visitors to the base of the mound and steps leading up to the cross. From the summit, the view across the Forty Acres and the usual presence of deer makes it a very attractive spot, meaning the car park is often full with tourists and day-trippers visiting the park. However, at night time the car park has also been taken over by joy-riders, which poses a particular problem for the limited Garda presence in the park. This adds to the layers of meaning that make up this particular monument, and also the park itself, as the 'dark side' of the nightlife[1] continually impinges on daytime understandings and uses.

The Visitor Centre that is located in the Park, which provides the official commentary on the park's historical and contemporary position, presents the idea of a unified nation through the narration of the event. The display says, 'We Irish people did all of that – and did it in eight weeks – and did it magnificently. If we can all do that – then we, as a nation, are truly capable of great things. It was indeed a beautiful, beautiful day'. This puts forward a very strong sense of a united group, achieving something important – as indeed it was; it was the Irish people positioning themselves on a world stage. Though on a more local level, the awareness of this or the interest that most people would have regarding it was probably usurped by the social and cultural pressure to conform and 'walk the line' of attending. It was first and foremost a statement of conformity and unification by the Roman Catholic Church, and the unification that the Visitor Centre highlights was an effort to pull together the unravelling strands of Irish society and bound them tightly into a unity Roman Catholic coil.

The sense of optimism espoused by the Visitor Centre display, 'if we can do that . . . we, as a nation, are capable of great things', was unsustainable in relation to the Roman Catholic Church in Ireland. While the visit prompted a rise in vocational applications for that year, the first time since the 1960s, it dropped again the following year. The metaphorical 'patch' that the visit put on the problems facing the Roman Catholic Church in Ireland was only temporary; the cracks began appearing soon after the Pope left. The entertainment of the young people in the Galway mass before the Pope's arrival was by the charismatic Bishop Eamon Casey and the 'singing priest' Father Michael Cleary. Their presence was severely overshadowed in retrospect following the discovery that the Bishop was the father of a 17-year-old boy with an American mother, and that the Father had conducted an affair with his housekeeper that produced two children, the first of which had been put up for adoption. Following these, there was an avalanche of allegations and emerging stories surrounding the physical and sexual abuse of children and the Magdalene laundry scandals. Casey and Cleary are clerical bookends on either side of the Ireland of the 1980s; they embodied the optimism, captured in the display in the Visitor Centre, of 1979 and they precipitated its final crisis in 1992.

Different memories were uncovered about the Papal visit in the interviews I conducted during the research on the park. The interview extract used below took place at the base of the cross; two older men were standing there, talking. I approached them, outlined briefly what I was doing in the park and used the location as a prompt. I asked them if they remembered the Pope's visit, and one of them had been at the event in the park:

KM: What about the Pope?

V1: Oh yea I was there.

V2: He was there.

KM: That must have been a good day?

V1: *Well I suppose it was, I suppose it was. Em, again, it's I'm not a totally religious person and I wasn't just that impressed. Especially when two of the priests on the altar have had kids and knocked off money, ya know it doesn't impress you.* But yea it was an amazing day in that a million people all came with the one thing in mind. And eh they were up-lifted I presume you know. Yea it was an amazing day.

(Visitors 14 and 15, Papal Cross, 3 March 2006, emphasis added)

This extract summarizes an important position adopted by many people interviewed; the day itself was 'an amazing day', echoing the Visitor Centre display that describes it as 'a beautiful, beautiful day'. There was a real sense of unity that transcends the religious in its meaning – as the account above shows the visitor is 'not a totally religious person', but states twice that it was 'an amazing day'. However, there is a distancing evident – 'the people all came with one thing in mind'; it is as if he is distancing himself from this unity because of the events that later distorted the meaning of the event in relation to its religious meaning, as discussed above. The personal and the official memories have intertwined, perhaps as a remnant of the official coercion at the time.

This example demonstrates the different layers of meaning that exist around one space and one time within that space. There are multiple memories and multiple narratives of the event. Some of these enable unification between people who were there and relate to the dominant, official discourse, whilst others unpack and pull apart the meanings 'officially' associated with the day. By associating the breakdown of the Roman Catholic Church with this event, the two visitors are undermining the very meaning that the visit supposedly portrays: that of the strength of the Roman Catholic Church in Ireland. The dominant discourse, of a 'beautiful, beautiful day', conceals other discourses through its pre-eminence and the social forces which maintain the dominance, one of which is the official park narrative. As the park is a part of a national space, and there are specific ideas of Irish identity related to it, the space and its material artefacts conceal the mundane realities of Irish people's experiences of the Pope's visit. There is a desire to perpetuate a particular narrative around the day, and it is only chipped away at by uncovering personal memories that offer different perspectives and additions to the overriding narrative. The landscapes of memory around this cross are politically and socially informed, and personal memories are infused with contemporary retrospect.

The cross in the ground – The Phoenix Park murders

The next account looks at an event that has a more problematic position in Irish history, the landscape of the park and the cultural and material artefacts it has left behind. This historical importance of this event is as great as the Pope's visit, and is as much a part of the history of the park. However, this event is problematic and fits uncomfortably into the official landscape of the park. It is not a time of celebration for the park, but instead a time of commiseration and negative press. The way that this event is positioned in the park's official understanding and the different ways memories have been intertwined with the events provide an alternative understanding of the landscape of the park, and different positions on alternative landscapes of memory.

On the 6 May 1882, the Invincibles, a Fenian splinter group, stabbed to death the Chief Secretary Lord Cavendish and his Undersecretary Thomas Burke with surgical knives. This happened within sight of what is now Áras an Uachtaráin, and was then the Viceregal Lodge. Lord Cavendish had been viceroy in Ireland for less than 48 hours at the time of his murder. The Visitor Centre describes it as a 'tragic murder', and takes the accounts from the newspapers at the time, to avoid making a political comment on it. The murders were linked to a fight for independence from the Fenians, and so were regarded sympathetically by those people who would go on to fight in the 1922 War of Independence. In an interview with the Chief Superintendent, he was able to discuss this in relation to Park Rangers' opinions, and link it to how the Visitor Centre display was put together, as can be seen in the extract below.

> CS: And when we were doing the layout [the displays in the Visitor Centre] some of the old rangers here were in the Troubles in 1922, they used to call them the Cavendish assassinations, they wouldn't call them murders you know, and eh so, when we came to do the video here, so the guy [name], who was a forester but became an environmentalist and there was a Professor from Galway was the consultant. And he said we'll see what the papers of the day were saying, and that's what we went with and the kids were shouting stop press stop press murder in the park, it's more acceptable when you're quoting. So it was reporting on what was said back then.

> KM: Was that the thinking for the displays?

> CS: It's always a tricky one for a state body, but you know having said that eh the video that's done in Kilmainham, they're after getting an award in England, but before that the place also won a prize because it was so fantastic, but it got all Irish history in about half an hour, but I used to joke with my brother that you'd need counselling after it because some of the stuff was so horrific. People thrown into jail, kids for a loaf of bread, but there's sensitivity with dealing with different populations, different backgrounds, different experiences.
> (Chief Superintendent, 13 December 2005)

135

According to the Chief Superintendent, the park has a responsibility to the visitors to not be overly explicit about historical events. Visitors to Kilmainham Jail may expect some sort of insight into unpleasant conditions given they are visiting a jail, but visitors to the park would not have those expectations. People come to the park for a nice day out, and so to be confronted with murders could prove unprofitable; they might not want to return. In addition, as alluded to by the Chief Superintendent when he mentions the Park Rangers not calling it a murder but an assassination, the political levels of this murder have powerful poignancy in the history of Ireland. In the Visitor Centre, there is a purposeful avoidance of engaging with the political and social ramifications by relating only what the newspapers reported at the time.

The political ramifications for the murders could have been far greater than they were; the Irish public were appalled rather than inspired, and the battles that followed were fought in the political arena rather than the social one. This does not mean that they did not mark the landscapes of meaning that people associate with the park; the murders are the most commonly invoked event that occurred in the park when you ask people about it; it has made an indelible impression. In 2006, *Today with Pat Kenny*, an Irish radio show, ran a segment about Phoenix Park, and the murders were described as being one of the most influential occurrences in Irish political history, and were 'very powerful'. However, the mark it has physically made on the landscape of the park is less impressive.

The only official testimony to the murders and to Lord Cavendish is in St Margaret's Church in Westminster. In Phoenix Park, there are no official statues or memorials to any of those killed: Burke, Cavendish or the eight men who were executed for the murder. There is, however, an unofficial memorial to the murdered men in Phoenix Park, and it is not entirely clear which murdered men are being remembered. The thing of folklore, and something which was dismissed by many of the officials in the park as a myth, there is a small cross, about 75 cm long and 50 cm wide, cut into the bank of grass opposite Áras an Uachtarain where the murders occurred. The secretary of the head office in the park along with many gardeners and grounds men felt that it was put there by a taxi driver in an attempt to increase business through tourism.

The Chief Superintendent had his own version of why the cross was there, which added another layer to the story. Every year, on 6 May, somebody would come and place a bunch of flowers to commemorate Cavendish and Burke. The Chief Superintendent had worked in the park for almost 15 years before being enlightened as to who placed the bouquet there, and it was only through recounting this tale to the Old Dublin Society about the history of the park that he found the answer. At the end of the talk, a man came up to him and told him it had been his family doing it since the murder occurred. As the Chief Superintendent recounted,

> CS: Now I was giving a talk at the Old Dublin Society, this guy that was actually chairing the meeting, he said I beg your pardon, and I said we suspect it's a taxi man to boost the trade, and he said I beg your pardon, it's been my relatives that have done it for three generations, and

now my grandkids are doing it. And I said that's amazing stuff, and I said how did that start? And his great-grandfather was on the three-wheel bicycle [who found the bodies], and having witnessed what happened, he undertook to commemorate it some way.

[. . .]

So your man, a nice guy, Carrey from Fishamble St, and I was coming through the Park a few years ago on 6 May and I see another guy putting flowers on it, and so anyway, I said that's not the guy and he was an old guy as well, and picked him up [in his car]. I said what are you doing? He said I'm commemorating the murders, and I said isn't that fantastic. And I said but you're not the guy, and he said it was his brother. And I went to the house, I live in the Park there, and I took a photo of the guy and we'd a cup of tea and a sandwich.

(Chief Superintendent, 13 December 2005)

The importance of the event for the men who placed the flowers and the Chief Superintendent is evident in the above quote. The Chief Superintendent feels that there should be a memorial there, though he recognizes the sensitivity of the event. In addition, he said there are problems with putting 'contentious' things up on display, many of which are vandalized or taken away. As he describes,

CS: Now, we put a little timber surround on it [the cross], and we might put a second one there, something I suppose a bit off the record but eh there's a block of stone there and it has been damaged, and we think that's because someone thinks that's the marker, but it's only a marker for traffic. . . . And the self-guiding heritage trail, some of them have been stolen and now we've knocked some of them down ourselves moving timber but some of the more sensitive ones have been stolen. And we haven't got around replacing them.

(Chief Superintendent, 13 December 2005)

The people who were hanged for the murders were widely regarded as criminals whose actions were unreasonable and a disgrace to Irish society at the time, and this view predominantly continues in contemporary times, though there are alternative accounts. *The Blanket*, a strongly nationalist journal of 'Protest and Dissent,' uses the Phoenix Park murders as a means of condemning the political relationship between the Irish and British at the time, and cites the Irish Republican Brotherhood as saying the people who carried out this 'execution . . . deserve well of their country' (http://lark.phoblacht.net/shadowgunman.html, accessed 2 February 2005). There were some press reports at the time that referred to the Invincibles as anarchists and, allegedly, Frederick Engels called the Invincibles 'Bakunists' (Black 2005). In London, the short-lived German anarchist paper *Freiheit* was shut down as a consequence of publishing an article 'applauding the assassination of Lord Frederick Cavendish by Fenians in Phoenix Park, Dublin, in May 1882' (quoted by Black 2005). Another account explains the cross in a different way, recounting how in 1938 James T. Farrell, the American novelist, came to Dublin to visit Jim Larkin, a prominent trade union and socialist leader in Ireland in the early 1900s. Farrell relates that while there Larkin

> asked me if I wanted to see the monument to the Invincibles . . . I imagined that I was going to see a statue, but this did seem passingly curious. The idea that there would be a monument commemorating the Invincibles in Dublin didn't make sense. We stopped in Phoenix Park, just opposite the Archbishop's palace. . . . We got out. Jim walked along a path, looking down at the grass. I was bewildered. Jim became nervous, and he stared on the ground with some concern. Then he pointed. There it was. I saw a little hole where grass had been torn up. A cross had been scratched in the earth with a stick. I gathered that many Dubliners did not know of this act commemorating the Invincibles. Jim's boys always went out to Phoenix Park, and marked this cross in the earth. No matter how often grass was planted over it, it was torn up. The cross was marked in the earth.
>
> (quoted in Black 2005)

This account provides the alternative viewpoint that this cross is for the Invincibles and not for the murdered men. It would also seem to stand in contrast to the placing of flowers as discussed above. The most recent history of the park also claims that nationalist historians place the cross there each year as a means of commemorating the Fenian martyrs (Nolan 2006).

The landscape is marked by the event, but the meaning behind the mark is contentious, and far from being a simple memorial to murdered men. The mark in the landscapes of the memories of people I encountered in the park held many different meanings, drawing from the different perspectives in the accounts above. Indeed, some visitors had constructed meanings for the cross in the ground that drew on a wide range of, largely fictitious, understandings that bore little resemblance to any account presented here. Their landscapes of memory were not grounded in the narratives of history or official understanding, but were inspired by alternative things, such as childhood memories or imaginaries.

Conclusion

The park represents a landscape of memories. This chapter has drawn on two empirical examples to highlight the many memories, meanings and understandings associated with two important cultural and material artefacts found in the topography of the park. These examples have also brought forward the idea of an official heritage of the park, and shown where this official story stands in contrast to the meaning and memories of visitors and residents of the place. More than a simple legacy from the past, heritage creates or constructs a particular idea of the park, a particular type of national identity, one that cannot accommodate dissident views as they would undermine the singular narrative of the national space.

The first example, the cross on the mound, is allocated an important position in the park. The Pope's cross has been made into one of the most important visitor attractions, facilitated through the development of the area around it to be accommodating to coaches and cars and thus subjecting it to the tourist gaze (Urry 1990). The event is positioned very positively in the park's official story as well; it is regarded as a 'beautiful, beautiful day' in the Visitor Centre. However, the memories of visitors have been marred by contemporary events, and so the event has altered in the meaning they assign to it, and as such the meaning of the large cross that adorns the park's landscape. The coercion to attend the event, developed through the unifying and inclusionary discourse of the visit, meant that falling outside it was to position yourself as an 'other' to the Irish national identity that was being propagated at the time, and is continued in the heritage of the event in the park today.

The second example, the cross in the ground, does not fit as comfortably into the park's official heritage. There is no 'official' memorial of the Phoenix Park Murders and so the landscape of the park could have been void of any material artefact related to it. Though mentioned in the Visitor Centre, the Chief Superintendent describes the perceived problems associated with the event's inclusion in the history of the park. Engaging with the event politically, culturally and socially would necessitate a deeper engagement with what Irish identity is about, and how this particular violent act should be understood. Instead, the displays in the Visitor Centre avoid engaging with these questions, instead using historical newspaper headlines to convey the reactions of the public at the time. Of course, this is the views of some of the public, and some of the newspapers. Divergent views existed about the event, which some of the Irish public and international presses regarded as an act of politically motivated assassination. As well as these divergent views, there exists a continued diversity of meaning associated with the cross in the ground. While the Chief Superintendent was happy to put across the meaning he associated with the cross, as it could be fitted into the official narrative of the park that avoided political association with the event or the cross, other understandings existed and continue to exist in the experiences of visitors and residents of the park.

The park incorporates many landscapes of memories within its walls. As an important national space, there are many monuments to Irishness located within it; some visible, material artefacts but many more cultural and social artefacts that exist in memories, both shared and personal. The construction of the park as a national space facilitates the formation of these shared memories and informs the personal ones, but it also excludes 'others' alternative understandings and meanings that do not endorse the narrative necessary for ideas of nation and national identity. As such, there are not only multiple layers of memory, but multiple layers of meaning, place and identity.

Acknowledgements

The research that informed this chapter was made possible by funding from Cardiff University, the Economic and Social Research Council and the British Association of Irish Studies.

Note

1 Prostitution, particularly male, and drug use are prevalent in the night-time Park.

Bibliography

Anderson, J. (2009) *Understanding Cultural Geography. Traces & places*, London: Routledge.

Black, J. (2005) 'It happened in the Phoenix Park all in the month of May'. Available online at http://www.indymedia.ie/aricle/69521 (accessed 3 January 2005).

Bommes, W. and Wright, P. (1982) 'Charms of residence: The public and the past', in Johnson, R., McLenon, G., Schwartz, W. and Sutton, D. (eds), *Making Histories: Studies in History Writing and Politics*, London: Hutchinson, 253–302.

Dunne, P. (2003) 'The shadow of the gunman' in *The Blanket: A Journal of Protest and Dissent*. Available online at http://lark.phoblacht.net/shadowgunman.html (accessed 2 February 2005).

Graham, B., Ashworth, G.J. and Tunbridge, J.E. (2000) *A Geography of Heritage*, London: Arnold.

Kundera, M. (1996) *Testaments Betrayed*, London: Faber and Faber.

Lefebvre, H. (1991) *The Production of Space*, Oxford: Basil Blackwell.

Nolan, B. (2006) *Phoenix Park: A History and Guidebook*, Dublin: The Liffey Press.

Samuel, R. (1994) *Theatres of Memory; Vol. 1: Past and Present in Contemporary Culture*, London: Verson.

Urry, J. (1990) *The Tourist Gaze: Leisure and Travel in Contemporary Societies*, London: Sage.

Part III

Domination and contestation

Part II.

Domination and contestation

Labor and leisure at Monticello: Or representing race instead of class at an inadvertent white identity shrine

Eric Gable

I want to use Monticello, a place whose caretakers refer to as "the home of Thomas Jefferson," but also Colonial Williamsburg, a reconstructed and restored colonial town, to make some fairly obvious (and therefore perhaps significant) observations about the often paradoxical ways that sites representing the slave era produce national identity in the United States. On the face of it, plantations are not the best places to instill what Benedict Anderson and others stress is the essential fraternity of shared identity in the imagined community of the modern democratic and egalitarian nation-states. They are, after all, places of aristocratic privilege based on the absolute disenfranchisement of one category of people by another. Nowadays you would be hard pressed to find more than a few white Americans, even white Americans whose ancestors may have owned plantations, who want to think of themselves as masters. Instead you would be much more likely to encounter white Americans who express sympathy, even admiration, for slaves. Yet, for over 80 years, plantations in the American South have been, and continue to be, sites of national celebration. This is because they are inadvertent white identity shrines. At these places, and this will hardly surprise anyone, racial identity trumps class identity.

We should be cautious, however, about using the term identity to describe this process at these sites. Identity is perhaps an overused word (Handler 1994). It is a term increasingly ubiquitous in the social sciences and humanities, a term Europeans both among the intelligentsia and on the street use to refer to membership in social groups (e.g. Bourdieu 1984: 479; Evans-Pritchard 1940: 5), but a term without the same traction in the American vernacular. In the United States, a much more common term that acts like identity for Europeans is "culture." Americans assume that people are members of different cultures and they assume that cultures embody mental states. They talk about "youth culture" and "the culture of fear," for example. They refer to corporate culture, and while they assume that corporate culture might differ from the culture of government bureaucracies or entrepreneurial culture, they also expect that even different corporations involved in producing the same kinds of products might have different cultures. For most Americans, culture is at once a product of choice – you pick your subculture, for example, learn its rules and mores – and a product of fate. The culture you are born into molds you, shapes you, shapes especially your moods, your personality, your mind. Moreover, cultures, in the sense of groups of people sharing similar attitudes and feelings, for Americans, in contrast to

American cultural anthropologists, can be compared and evaluated as better or worse, as more creative or free or good or less. Many Americans no longer believe that there are races in the biological sense; far fewer are skeptical about whether there is a black culture that is in some senses different from a white culture. Moreover, many white Americans still assume that black culture, like black race, is intellectually deficient when compared with white culture. Because of their culture, blacks have "Ebonics" – that non-standard way of speaking that keeps them from getting good jobs – or they have peers who make fun of them for trying hard in school, or parents who do not have the cultural capital to pass on to them to give them an edge when they take standardized tests. If identity is about belonging to a group and partaking of something essential about that group, then culture is identity in America.

By contrast, for Americans, at least in my experience, identity is almost always assimilated into something like personality or character in the more individual sense of the term. Thus, Americans can advertise a town in Texas on the outskirts of Dallas as a wonderful tourist destination because its historic main street is lined with stores "each with its own unique identity." Thus too, an Internet hotel company called Joie de Vive is currently trying to distinguish itself from the competition by offering its potential guests a "one-minute psychometric identity test" to pin down a guest's "personality" and therefore their needs and desires. In America, we sometimes speak of "identity politics," and here we assume that personality blurs into the character or attributes of a group, but identity politics is something only "minorities" practice. In this sense identity does slur into culture as a native concept. There is black culture and black identity. But there is, if you are white at least, rarely white culture and white identity. Culture and identity in these senses are what other people have, what minorities have (e.g. Banton 1983).

So, not surprisingly I cannot remember a single instance when I heard the (for the most part, white) staff at Monticello or Williamsburg refer to themselves as producing or representing an identity or, for that matter, a culture during the roughly three years of ethnographic research I undertook at those heritage sites (Gable 2005; Handler and Gable 1997). They did, however, routinely say that they were in the business of reflecting upon what it meant to be American by representing a past that was in a collective sense "our past." And they also assumed that to be American was, among other things, to be actively engaged with the American past.

When I was doing research at Monticello and at Williamsburg, the administrators and staffs of both places wanted the term "American" to include African-Americans. They wanted their sites to reflect America in a demographic sense by attracting African-Americans as well as white Americans. They pursued this demographic goal by trying to make the sites more congenial to African-Americans, and in describing what specific measures they were taking did talk about identity, but as a verb rather than a noun. By and large, they assumed that people visited places they could "identify" with. If a person could see themselves reflected in the site, then that site would be meaningful to them. This should remind us that identity is enacted rather than merely represented. Identity entails *identification* and *dis-identification* (Appiah 2005; Appiah and Gutmann 1998;

Clark 2008; Connolly 1991) as, for example, when tourists and those who work at Monticello or Williamsburg recognize (or refuse to recognize) themselves in the historical personages the site portrays. It is also of some significance that while the enactment of identification at such sites is at times an explicit and self-consciously recognized program, it is also more routinely an implicit, even unintended consequence of the various ways tourists encounter the site and interact with the site's caretakers. As I will show, because of the way identification works at Monticello and Williamsburg, racial differences and class distinctions continue to vex and disturb, even as these sites are more or less effective in producing uncontested arenas of national identification.

Identification and the ethnographer

To get a sense of the routines of identification, consider two conversations I had with visitors to Colonial Williamsburg. The first conversation occurred outside the gates of Williamsburg's Bruton Parish church – famous for being among the oldest continuously operating churches in the United States, and a place whose episcopal liturgy, worn cemetery headstones, and architecture hark back to bucolic England. I am explaining to a middle-aged man that I am doing research for a book on Colonial Williamsburg and want to ask him some questions. Before I say anything more, he tells me how much he loves Williamsburg, and that he is Italian American, that he owns a plumbing business in beautiful Marin County California where he also has a beautiful home, but that if he could, he would want to be buried "right there" he points, "in the church yard." Assuming, I think, that I work for Williamsburg, he then asks if I know how that sort of thing is arranged. Are there spaces in the cemetery? Does the museum solicit donations that might make a plot available?

On another occasion, I am eating lunch at one of the many taverns that are meant to mimic the eighteenth century, and add a bit of life to the generally quiet streets while providing a convenient place to eat for the museum-town's visitors. It is well past lunch time but not near dinner and the only other guest is a young African-American man and his two children. When I tell him I am writing a book and ask him where he is from and why he is there, he sits in silence and smiles before answering: "I am showing them" and gestures toward the children, "his story." I hear him, but at first I miss the point, so he repeats. "His story, you know? His-story. They need to know his story to understand how it all works." I laugh and he does too.

Both conversations reveal identity as a process of identification. In the considerable scholarly literature on national identity, it is usually stressed that national identities do not necessarily come easily. They are neither natural, nor are they inevitable. It takes considerable work on the part of the state to turn, "peasants into Frenchmen" or "Indians into Mexicans" (Frye 1996). Among scholars of such processes, there is tendency to revel in the state's failures to accomplish this feat. Indeed, the general scholarly position is one of critique. Nationalism, after all, like patriotism, is a word most scholars sneer at. Compounding this, of course, is a usually implicit, occasionally overt

Marxian slant to the scholarly discourse. If peasants (or workers!) become Frenchmen, or the Welsh become Britons, then they kill or are killed by other peasants (or workers) who have been likewise turned into Germans. As such, that always out of reach but desirable class consciousness, or its romantic analogue, place consciousness (a form of identification that does seem to have occurred) gives way to (in the Marxian perspective) a form of false consciousness – a kind of ideological legerdemain. If that work of statecraft is successful, then national identity is experienced as natural, inevitable, unremarkable. And this is a bad thing.

I am no different from most of my scholarly colleagues. So, for me, the Italian American from California embodied that kind of troubling if unremarkable inevitability because his love for Williamsburg seemed so out-of-place. Indeed I could not help but see his desire to be buried at Williamsburg as pathetic. Could not he tell that the church, while in Williamsburg, was also independent of it, and did not he realize that you could not just buy a plot in a church like that? Did not he even worry just a little bit that the locals who worshipped there, many of whom cherished their long pedigrees linking them back to Virginia's founders, might look down their noses at him – a plumber! An Italian! I also wondered why he even wanted to get buried there. California, I could not help thinking, seemed to me so much congenial to an Italian American than Virginia with its humid summers and cold winters. Would not a patch of Napa Valley be more in keeping with his heritage and just as American in the bargain?

By the same token I was already expecting (and I am ashamed to admit even hoping for) a response such as the one I received from the African-American man. Thus, the laugh of mutual recognition. I had been strolling the reconstructed city's streets for months by then, watching and listening to visitors. African-American visitors were a rarity, even though there were many blacks who worked at Williamsburg – as maids or waiters, or groundskeepers. That Williamsburg's colonial-era population was comprised of roughly half slaves and half free whites made the visibility of the black workers a sort of indictment. The paucity of black visitors added teeth to the indictment. At the time I was having these conversations, both Colonial Williamsburg and Monticello were making every effort they could conceive of to make "his story" – the history of white masters – into a more collective and inclusive history. That so few blacks visited those places was an embarrassment to them and a pleasure to me. That in a nutshell is how identification works as it is perceived through the jaundiced lens of the scholarship on it.

Making his-story into history

To make his-story into a shared history, both sites offered programs that populated the past with African-Americans. And they felt proud of their efforts. Thus, for example, Daniel Jordan, director of the Thomas Jefferson Foundation, as he listed the ways that the Foundation was making a place for African-Americans, told me that the gift shop was now selling a postcard (the first in a series commemorating the slaves) – the photographic portrait of Isaac Jefferson, the slave blacksmith.

Isaac's portrait was also prominently featured on a new brochure dedicated to the slaves who lived and worked on Mulberry Row. To sum up why these new efforts had been a success, he told me a story about a group of African-American school children from Oklahoma whose faces had lit up when they saw the postcard.

White museum administrators such as Jordan feel that they are doing the right thing when they find and display black history for black audiences. To give them Isaac to identify with is to, by extension, give them a place in history from which they were once excluded. Not articulated because taken for granted is Jordan's assumption that white people's identities are already taken care of at Monticello. If black schoolchildren need a postcard of Isaac to take home with them as a memento of their visit, white children already have Thomas Jefferson.

This, then, is the identity problem. The identity problem is a race problem. Crudely put it is, "I," white person, expect that "you," black person, will identify with the slaves. They are your ancestors. Thomas Jefferson – he is my ancestor. To put it more crudely still, antebellum heritage museums *promote*, if inadvertently, this kind of segregating identification. They do so not only when they try to make a place for the previously excluded in the stories they tell. But they especially do so when they market themselves to the public. Keep in mind that most people who visit such museums are white and "well-above average in education and income" (as in-house marketing surveys are often proud to proclaim). Observe that museums work hard to sell this public products imbued with the aura of the Big House and the luminaries who lived there. To market the simulacra of an ultra-upscale eighteenth-century lifestyle founded in race-based slavery cannot help but reinforce racially motivated identification.

Marketing extends to the way a place is advertised as a tourist "destination." When Colonial Williamsburg represents itself to its public "out there" on America's highways and in America's living rooms, it invariably chooses images such as the photograph of a white couple in a carriage driven by a black man in full livery. The black man in livery is "the other" that makes your foray into the past authentic and elegant. He is your virtual-reality servant.

It is not, however, only the marketplace that implicates the museum in identity segregation. Guides who are taught to "connect" visitors to the site also segregate as they invite "you" to imagine yourself an inhabitant of the colonial past. At the Wythe house at Colonial Williamsburg, for example, you might be standing at the threshold of the parlor or dining room and be told about the slaves in the back rooms. "They" launder, cook, and clean while "you" are invited by your guide to sip sherry or drink tea with your imaginary hosts.

These forms of virtual-reality segregation might disappear as the demographics of the visiting population changes – as it becomes, so the euphemism goes, more "diverse." And, as we all know, a guiding policy concern in heritage museums today is to promote just this kind of "diversity" – occasionally in the name of maintaining market share in a multicultural future, usually in the name of ameliorist morality and democratic principles. So, in the near future, we might see an advertisement featuring a clearly black couple in the colonial-era carriage driven by the older black gentleman in livery.

But to anticipate that identity segregation will disappear once there is a large and thriving black middle-class in America and once a significant number of this middle-class feels the need to visit antebellum heritage sites, is somehow to lose sight of why racism continues to be a problem today. Racism would not be a problem at all if it were simply a matter of you believing that you are better than me because of the racial differences that you believe divide us into separate groups. Racism is only a problem because belief seems to be translated, in a systematic way, into material inequity. To return to the image of Isaac at Monticello: Isaac lived in a shack on Mulberry Row and was a blacksmith because this is where people like Jefferson believed he should be and where people like Jefferson had the power to keep him. Jefferson's power kept him in that position; Jefferson also believed that his own innate superiority justified this exercise in power. For Jefferson, as he so bluntly argued in *Notes on the State of Virginia* (2002[1787]), slaves of African descent were simply less mentally capable than were whites. Thus, for Jefferson, his mental superiority as indicated by the books he read, the music he played, the art he enjoyed, and Isaac's inferiority were a matter of natural fact. Slavery, for Jefferson, may have been wrong or morally dangerous, but it was clearly not unnatural. It merely enshrined as a legal and social system of human difference what biology had already put there. That there continue to be large differences between racial categories in distributions of wealth, income, and in the access to what Pierre Bourdieu calls "cultural capital" is but the echo and ongoing reiteration of this material and cultural fact.

Labor and leisure at Monticello

White identification with Jefferson at Monticello is not direct and that is why it is so pernicious. White visitors I talked to never presumed to speak of themselves as Jefferson's peer or equivalent in any direct way. Indeed, they tended to extol the gap in accomplishments and talents between them and him. Jefferson, they would say, "was a genius." They were not. Some also alluded to his wealth. He "came from money" one said to me, implying that the visitor did not.

Such comments intrigued me because I wanted to see how Americans used such a place of manifest privilege to think about the nature of privilege itself – its morality. Could a statement count as a criticism? Americans, poll after poll demonstrates, do not begrudge the wealthy their riches. But we want to be sure they deserve it – that they have earned the privileges they enjoy.

Monticello might count as a perfect place to think about the morality of privilege. It is a plantation after all. That so many people work so that so few can enjoy life's pleasures might engender class critiques. Yet there are only barely visible signs of the presence of slaves. Mulberry Row was a pathway that ran under an avenue of trees. Along this row had been several slave quarters, a blacksmith's shop and a nailery, a place where young slave boys pounded out nails from long thin bars of iron. The nailery had been quite a success. In Jefferson's day, the plantation usually lost money. But the nailery provided some welcome cash, and

Jefferson paid the boys extra for their work. You learned all this from plaques along Mulberry Row where the structures had once been. There was still the ruin of a chimney at the site of the blacksmith's shop. You could also read about the Row and the 130 or so slaves who lived at Monticello in a brochure, or in signage in an archeological exhibit under the house, or at a nicely compact museum at the Visitor's Center.

Below Mulberry Row was a beautiful garden, and orchard, and beyond that, like an ocean, were the rolling hills of the Piedmont receding like waves into the flat horizon. At the center of the garden stood a newly reconstructed pavilion. It was a beautiful conceit, a wonderfully planned out trifle of a building. Jefferson's bagatelle. Tall and narrow, but majestically proportioned for its size, it harkened to a temple. Palladian windows doing double duty as doors. In it were a few Windsor chairs. Room enough for a couple of people to sit and enjoy the view – of the garden, of the gracefully receding rows of hills. That is about all the room there was. Monticello had decided to build the pavilion at great cost. Jefferson had left architectural drawings and the small structure was quite beautiful. Jefferson himself had written about the pleasures of sitting in that space; he had written about the joys of working in the garden.

Meanwhile Monticello had decided not build slave quarters. They worried about whether such structures could be constructed accurately. No plans existed, although there were sketches of plans, again in Jefferson's hand. Would they look tacky, obviously new, and detract from the aura of the main building? After all, this building, Monticello's then director – a man very much dedicated to making slaves' lives a crucial part of the story the place told – reminded me was "eighty to ninety per cent original" while perhaps "less was more" regarding the slave quarters. To build them might "ruin the view," as the site's architect put it, for most visitors eager to see an original and authentic house and decor. So the slave quarters were not built.

When I began observing Monticello, I wondered whether or not visitors would reflect on the contrast that I imagined should be salient on Mulberry Row: the drudgery of teenaged boys put to work pounding out nail after nail six days a week (but getting paid for it!), so that Jefferson could play his violin, or ride (for exercise) his horses, while also toiling in the garden in the cool of the evening. How would visitors reconcile these twinned traces of the past? It was in trying to answer this question that my research came to be about identity rather than class.

One way they reconciled these traces was by accepting Jefferson's right to enjoy the view he seemed to have fashioned. At Monticello, Jefferson is constantly portrayed as a man of busy leisure. He invents or dabbles in gadgetry. The great clock, the polygraph, the dumbwaiter. He collects Indian artifacts and mastodon bones to make his entry foyer into one of America's first museums. He records the weather every day for decades. He grows grapes for wine and several varieties of peas, which he especially enjoys because he is an epicurean with a taste for the naturally healthful. He plays chess and the violin. He rides horses. But above all he reads and writes. There is his library with his thousands of books – books, we learn, he later donated to the Library of Congress, books written in the six languages he had taught himself to read, for pleasure and for edification. We learn about the twenty thousand letters he wrote, despite his recalcitrant wounded wrist, and using a polygraph machine to make perfect copies of every one, letters that were a constant chore Jefferson dutifully penned from dawn until noon.

His written words are the origin of most of that you learn at the site. Guides quote him, brochures borrow his words to frame what they tell you about gardening, slavery, architecture, pretty much everything. Jefferson's words make him the protagonist of the place. He is the actor, Monticello and its surroundings are the acted upon. "Though an old man I am but a young gardener." "I rise every day with the sun." As actor, he encompasses the actions of others, even the slaves who worked on the plantation. Thus, in the vitrine display at the Visitor's Center of artifacts from the slave quarters along Mulberry Row, Jefferson's words provide the headline, "To be independent for the comforts of life we must manufacture them ourselves," followed by a longer excerpt:

> My opinion has ever been that, until more can be done for them, we should endeavor, with those whom fortune has thrown in our hands, to feed and clothe them well, protect them from ill usage, require such reasonable labor as is performed by freemen, and led by no repugnances to abdicate them, and our duties to them.

Monticello is a kind of biography of Jefferson, a generally celebratory biography. Jefferson's words are used to authorize Monticello to speak for him, to stand for him: "All my wishes end, where I hope my days will end, at Monticello." As an authorized biography, its architecture, the landscape that surrounds it, and the artifacts the house contains serve as vignettes that prompt guides to ventriloquize Jeffersonian sound bites. Jefferson as text is everywhere and in everything. That Jefferson wrote and that he read are central to the site's portrayal of him. His writing inscribes his intelligence. Indeed, it is as if he were intelligence embodied. Man as mind. Moreover, as a writer, he is also America's author. He wrote the Declaration of Independence which authorizes our equal right to pursue happiness as a civic virtue. At Monticello, Jefferson's pursuit of aesthetic pleasures has been portrayed as both a sign of and a reward for his success at living a life according to the civic virtues he authored and also as a tangible symptom of what all those inscriptions and activities make obvious: his intelligence.

Just as Monticello is about Jefferson, the reader and writer, so too is Monticello about race, even if *Notes on the State of Virginia* – that founding text of American scientific racism – is uncanny in its absence. In *Notes*, Jefferson asserted the absolute mental inferiority of blacks to whites. According to Jefferson, when blacks wrote, when they attempted literature, they always produced inferior, derivative work. They were good, however, at copying, replicating. If they equaled whites in any mental ability, it was in the capacity for memory. Blacks, as Jefferson wrote about them, may even outdo whites in memory. About memory they were masters.

Lately, Monticello has been about race on purpose, even if *Notes on the State of Virginia* does not supply its requisite snippets of pungent text. But it also continues to be about race by accident in its pernicious sense. Indeed, I will suggest in what follows that Monticello represents reading and writing as practices that blur the distinction between labor and leisure, while also representing such practices as marking distinctions between kinds of labor and, inadvertently, kinds of people – races, classes – that comprise the nation as a fractured whole. Thomas Jefferson is white. His whiteness goes without saying, but it engenders a contrast. If Jefferson is white, then someone else has to be black. Superiority requires inferiority.

Memory versus history

In the years I observed Monticello closely, few visitors seemed to care that so many slaves had to work so that Jefferson could read and write. Yet, many visitors seemed to enjoy making the guides at Monticello squirm by asking them about Thomas Jefferson's alleged affair with Sally Hemings, a slave. At the time, Monticello followed the lead of many professional historians in dismissing this story as a pernicious rumor generated by Jefferson's political enemies. Members of the visiting public, however, had different ideas. In 1989 and 1990, it sometimes seemed that at least once a day every guide would encounter some visitor who would ask them why they "hadn't talked about Jefferson screwing colored girls." Some visitors were more circumspect but equally subversive. When a guide would talk about Jefferson's daughters and his grandchildren, they would interject "What about Jefferson OTHER children?" An in-house publication instructed the guides how to respond to the question, "What is the truth about Jefferson and the slave Sally Hemings?":

> Sally Hemings, a mulatto slave born in 1773, was a valued household servant at Monticello and served as lady's maid to Jefferson's daughters in France in the 1780s. The allegation that Sally was Jefferson's mistress and bore his children was first published by a vengeful journalist . . . in 1802. Fawn Brodie's biography of Jefferson and a novel by Barbara Chase-Riboud have recently reiterated this claim. Although it is impossible to prove either side of the question, serious Jefferson scholars are unanimous in discounting the truth of such a liaison. In the opinion of Jefferson's biographer, Dumas Malone, it would have been totally out of character and "virtually unthinkable in a man of Jefferson's moral standards and habitual conduct." Two of Jefferson's grandchildren explained that one of Jefferson's nephews was the father of Sally's children.

To have this kind of advice in their back pocket was doubtless a comfort because, for the most part, the guides found the kinds of insinuations visitors made about Sally Hemings and Jeffersons to be impertinent. Bad manners at best. It proved to the guides how so many visitors had crude tastes, or had bought into the standard conspiracy theories about government cover-ups and chicanery in high places, or had succumbed to the wrong literature, confusing a novel with serious scholarship! In thinking about their guests this way, guides also, of course, identified with Jefferson. Like him they too were intelligent and superior in their intelligence.

To guides, such visitors were easy to dismiss in part because they were white. A man who leers at you when he asks you to tell them about Jefferson screwing colored girls sounds like a bigot, and it makes you feel superior not only in intellect but in morality when you refuse to stoop to his level. But Monticello could not so easily dismiss African-Americans making similar accusations. When you stonewall them, then you look like the bigot. In the same years that Monticello was instructing its guides to dismiss the "allegation" of the liaison as a fiction, the museum was quietly making a sort of accommodation to one particularly vociferous African-American group, the Woodson family, about the issue of the Sally Hemings' liaison. The Woodsons claimed descent from Sally Hemings and Thomas Jefferson through a putative first child of Hemings' called "Tom." Tom, they claimed, was born at Monticello, but quickly spirited away so as not to cause scandal. They made this claim first on national television, using Monticello as a convenient backdrop, and they continued to make this claim until, as result of their persistence, there was the eventual DNA testing performed by Dr Foster on Hemings descendents and the descendents of Jefferson's brother. Another result was a long collaboration between Monticello's staff historians and the family to produce a family chronicle. This chronicle became the basis for the "Getting Word" Exhibit at the Visitor's Center.

When the exhibit first went up, it had a temporary, slapdash, amateurish look. It was shoved into an empty space at the back of the permanent exhibits – glass cases that echoed or emphasized what a visitor would learn on a house tour, the same sound bites, the same stress on Jefferson as author, the same stress on his general benevolence as a master. Thus, we are told that Jefferson "provided each family with its own dwelling. He also provided shoes, stockings, and every third year a hat, a blanket, and a hempen roll mattress." This quote, for example, frames a display of coins and fragments of porcelain unearthed from the remains of the slave quarter entitled "In Their Own Time":

> After their working day and on Sundays and Holidays, the Monticello slaves could turn to recreation. Many however devoted their free time to improving the circumstances of their lives. They supplemented the basic provisions of their master – and even earned money by working their vegetable gardens, poultry yards, by fishing, and trapping, and by making furniture and clothing . . . . In 1796 a Monticello slave could earn a dollar – equal to the daily wage of a skilled bricklayer – by selling Jefferson any one of the following: eight chickens, four ducks, 16 dozen eggs, two mink skins, six fish, 50 cabbages.

In the Mulberry Row display, Jefferson comes across as a farsighted and sensitive CEO. His workers, the slaves, are to be admired as well for their work ethic. But their endeavors are conflated with his: "To be independent of the comforts of life we must fabricate them ourselves."

When I last looked at Getting Word in 2006, it was more or less as it had been in the late 1990s. Just as slapdash. Just as pathetic. Yet, there is also something interesting going on in that the stress is on the heroic struggles of slaves, often against Jefferson: "Despite long work days and lack of encouragement from Thomas Jefferson, African Americans living at Monticello strove to learn their letters."

Thus too we are reminded that whatever the slaves achieved for themselves, they had to achieve after providing for the luxuries Jefferson enjoyed:

> Within the confines of slavery, the African-American men and women led double lives. From dawn to dusk they raised Jefferson's crops, planted and tended his gardens, helped build his house and made his furniture; prepared his food and cared for his children; and enhanced his entertainments with their music. On their own time they . . . transmitted skills, talents and values . . . .

Getting Word is a celebration of one extended family's triumph against the impediments of slavery and postbellum prejudice. It gives individual African-Americans individual voices, using a format that echoes the highlighting of Jefferson's words in the Mulberry Row vitrines ("We have contributed as a family to the total fabric of this country." "I have found out what education is and intend to strive hard to get it."). Indeed Getting Word probably works best as complement to the general theme of the exemplary and the heroic that is also a focus of the impact of Jefferson's "words" (as opposed to his deeds) on Americans through history. The trajectory of the family's triumph is one of progress – a collective Horatio Alger story – which starts with slaves:

> Their descendants have been and are farmers and gardeners, carpenters, and architects, chefs, cooks, and caterers, artists, and musicians, nurses, midwives, and physicians, civil servants and soldiers, engineers, attorneys, journalists, teachers, and ministers.

The exhibit is framed by two walls of photographs making up a kind of visual family tree. The Woodson descendants pictured are an American success story which has always swum well within the currents of the mainstream – a family of community leaders, scholars, entrepreneurs, and activists. Their collective success is a measure of the capacity many African-Americans have had to overcome the impediments our nation has placed before them.

In other ways, however, Getting Word has succumbed to an unfortunate capitulation to the very racial dichotomy Jefferson anticipated in *Notes*. As the crucial vitrine in the exhibit proclaims, "The Getting Word Project honors" the African-American "oral tradition as we gather generations-old stories and recollections. The tape-recordings and transcripts will be stored in the Monticello research library where they will become an integral part of the historical record and can be consulted by scholars and researchers." It stresses that "even after becoming literate, African Americans continued to favor oral means of passing along knowledge." Blacks have memory; whites have history.

153

White identity despite itself

In general those who operate Monticello believe that they should not only produce accurate representations of the past as a common heritage, but that they should also make the site attractive to a representative body of the nation's citizens. Heritage sites, they believe, should embody as they represent. To make the site embody the entire nation in all its diversity Monticello (like Williamsburg and other similar sites) endeavors to make the place more congenial to African-Americans, and they do so, by and large, by telling more than they once did about the lives of slaves. As such, they assume, as do most of their audiences as well, that there should be an equivalence between a visitor's racial identity and the identities of the historical personages with whom that visitor will identify.

This consciously recognized effort at identification creates its unconscious obverse. If contemporary African-Americans are the descendents of slaves, then contemporary whites can count Jefferson as their ancestor. Because of this, despite its best efforts Monticello continues to be a white identity shrine. When Monticello invites the Woodsons to the mountaintop and gives them space to mount an exhibit celebrating their progenitors accomplishments it replicates a black/white binary that not only implies difference but distinction – a better and a worse. In the scheme that has been pervasive since Jefferson wrote *Notes on the State of Virginia*, blacks are less original, creative, intelligent, than whites, while also exceeding whites in their capacities for memory and, of course, mimicry. Meanwhile, at Monticello, Jefferson's leisure continues to be justified by his capacity for creative work. He writes and reads; he deserves what he has as a result.

As Americans talk today about "racial reconciliation" in various fora, it is easy for them to reach consensus that "prejudice" is bad, and that "prejudice" – white people thinking that black people are inferior – is a legacy of slavery. More vexing is what to make of the "coincidence" of race-based slavery and current racially marked economic inequities. Monticello, like any antebellum site, could be a perfect place to begin addressing this issue. As one of the members of the African-American advisory board said to me, to see slave poverty juxtaposed to Jefferson's "ostentation," slave labor juxtaposed to Jefferson's "leisure," is to recognize that whatever Jefferson accomplished, he did so because so many others worked for his happiness, not theirs. For her, the slaves' exploitation echoes through history because unequal groups today "didn't get started at the same starting-line." But to convey this message and make it stick, one would have to create a site where white visitors, like black, identified with slaves like Isaac Jefferson and not masters like Thomas Jefferson. This will not happen until we divorce Jefferson's genius from his whiteness. This will not happen until we identify as a class rather than as a race.

Bibliography

Appiah, K.A. (2005) *The Ethics of Identity*, Princeton, NJ: Princeton University Press.
Appiah, K.A. and Gutmann, A. (1998) *Color Conscious: The Political Morality of Race*, Princeton, NJ: Princeton University Press.

Banton, M. (1983) *Racial and Ethnic Competition*, Cambridge: Cambridge University Press.

Bourdieu, P. (1984) *Distinction: The Social Critique of the Judgment of Taste*, Cambridge, MA: Harvard University Press.

Clark, S. (2008) "Culture and identity," in T. Bennett and J. Frow (eds), *The Sage Handbook of Cultural Analysis*, Thousand Oaks, CA: Sage Publications, 510–29.

Connolly, W. (1991) *Identity/Difference: Democratic Negotiations of Political Paradox*, Minneapolis, MN: University of Minnesota Press.

Evans-Pritchard, E.E. (1940) *The Nuer*, Oxford: Oxford University Press.

Frye, D. (1996) *Indians into Mexicans: History and Identity in a Mexican Town*, Austin, TX: University of Texas Press.

Gable, E. (2005) "How we study history museums: Or, cultural studies at Monticello", in J. Marstine (ed.), *New Museum Theory: An Introduction*, Oxford: Blackwell Publishing, 109–25.

Handler, R. (1994) "Is 'identity' a useful cross-cultural concept?" in J.R. Gillis (ed.), *Commemorations: The Politics of National Identity*, Princeton, NJ: Princeton University Press, 27–40.

Handler, R. and Gable, E. (1997) *The New History in an Old Museum: Creating the Past at Colonial Williamsburg*, Durham, NC: Duke University Press.

Jefferson, T. (2002) *Notes on the State of Virginia*, David Waldstreicher (ed.), New York: Palgrave.

155

11

The ancient city walls of Great Benin: Colonialism, urban heritage and cultural identity in contemporary Nigeria

Flora *Edouwaye* S. Kaplan

Introduction

Whereas historic sites are rooted in and attributed to the past, they are to be considered in light of the living contexts that lend them political currency in contemporary society. They legitimize the goals of preservation by providing visibility that serve as 'proofs' of cultural identity. Heritage sites may also be seen as useful units of social and political analysis. The networks that flow from (and to) them link individuals and social groups in the endeavour to preserve sites, and they will reveal and reflect tensions and competition for power that lie beneath the surface in the urban settings of nation-states. A well-defined and drafted study of heritage sites is a valuable tool in large-scale complex societies where group boundaries are difficult to define and identify. The ideas of heritage and cultural identity are intertwined, involving both people and 'things' (tangible and intangible), and they involve degrees of organization and action by groups and the material culture they choose to identify with. Thus, the ideas of heritage, cultural identity and artefacts are to be seen as both 'made' and malleable in society (Anderson 1983; Hobsbawm and Ranger 1983; Kaplan 1982, 1996).

Cooperation and support for preservation of the ancient city walls of Benin among the present population are scant, challenged locally and nationally by the eroding economy. Ordinary men and women – petty traders, small business men and women, professionals, craftsmen and market women, many of whom are also occasional farmers – increasingly struggle to get by each day. For them, in large part, cultural heritage and preservation are not priorities. World religions (mainstream Christian and Muslim) have long played major roles in undermining and changing the perception of local peoples' indigenous systems of belief and values – *from* ethnicity, spiritual belief and shared traditional views of this world and the next – *to* global world views and personal choices of who they are and where they belong in time and place.

From the 1980s on, the national museum system (known of the National Commission for Museums and Monuments (hereafter referred to as NCMM) was expanded to

Figure 11.1 Posters for a Great Gospel Campaign, 2005. These were widely posted in the center of town near the Oba's Palace and around Benin City.

Photo: The author

integrate and represent Nigeria's multitudinous ethnic groups (over 250 or more). At the same time heavily funded foreign missionary and evangelical groups already in Benin City, on approaching the millennium, increased their presence, and undermined earlier federal government efforts at preservation and appreciation of cultural heritage. A plethora of missionaries today come from the United Kingdom, Europe, the United States of America, and other countries. Television, videos and local radio stations abound in different styles of preachers and preaching, sermons and services, instruments and music, and successfully attract large crowds at this time. Home-grown Christian denominations, evangelical and Pentecostal churches and others in the city are simpler, smaller enterprises with local and limited funding. But a few, for example, the Idahosa family-run church is an exception.

Neither the Christian churches, nor the Islamic mosques are interested in urban historic heritage, cultural identity and history, and its preservation. They have even less interest in Benin culture and traditions – if not openly expressed, by implication. Dual loyalties are actively discouraged, and even participation in indigenous court life, festivals and ritual tied to cultural identity at the Oba's Palace are often met with outright disapproval. Benin religion is seen as heathen worship, equated in negative terms with multiple deities and false gods in a belief system that is rejected by Muslims, proselytizing mainstream churches and the new missionaries.

The rising membership of new fellowships and churches are often attracted as much by the medical, educational and social services offered, as by the service and beliefs. Among the proselytizing religions, converts who accept Christ into their hearts and declare themselves 'born again' are welcomed. Converts say they like the sheer joy of expressive, participatory evangelical worship.

A case study: Cultural heritage and identity in Benin

Cultural heritage and identity are associated with places, people and the 'things of culture' that they value and hold dear (tangible and intangible). As ideas they are made and malleable artefacts of culture (Anderson 1983; Hobsbawm and Ranger 1983; Kaplan 1998). The Benin City walls, listed among the 100 Most Endangered Sites by the World Monuments Fund, find them to be a major feat of tropical rainforest engineering in south-west Nigeria. The 'World Heritage Convention' came into force in 1975, and is guided by the UNESCO Committee (UNESCO 1978, 2003–2004, 2007).

Heritage sites offer scholars of anthropology, political, social and cultural history the opportunity to do in-depth studies of identity and change in complex societies. They are nexuses in nation-states where shifting stress lines in society may cross or come together – revealing contending groups that may be submerged in other institutions or are hidden on the dense surface of a sprawling, teeming urban landscape. Heritage sites may be viewed as virtual units of analysis – isolable, observable and self-selecting. Those taking part may have, add or assume a shared ethnic identity with others, and they may choose one ethnicity or the other in order to adopt contemporary leadership, membership, networks and collective decision-making. The strategies employed may be used to construct and/or deconstruct contemporary narratives of 'us', and 'them', the 'other', self, and identity (Kaplan 2006: 153, 167–8).

'Identity' usually is determined in part by birth and/or citizenship in nation-states, but individuals also have and utilize a wide range of options. Individuals and groups come together in a nation, on the basis or a combination of common interests, like ethnicity, ideology and powerfully today, religion. Occasionally, in urban settings, transient groups surface briefly, and just as quickly disappear. I describe them as 'cultural wildings', events in which disparate individuals come together for a purpose, event or a moment in time, and then disperse immediately or soon afterwards. In some cases their presence at an historic site is destructive, in others, merely a diversion. These individuals are without an organization or a hierarchy, informal or otherwise. They also lack continuity in time. Some individuals and groups will act and appear and then sometimes reappear in different combinations, and at other sites and times. Their goals are specific, if short term.

Most groups, however, are organized, analysable (formal and informal), and sustained for an extended period beyond a single event. Therefore, they are traceable in public events. Groups may identify themselves with a place, a monument, an object, a ritual, or an act of expressive culture (and/or some combination of them), and they invest meaning in those things (animate and inanimate, tangible and intangible phenomena). Shared meaning in turn imparts and reinforces shared values and ideas held by the culture bearers of different nations. When invested and deeply felt, heritage sites become focal points of action that serve to unite or divide those groups seeking and competing for visibility and political power in one or more public arenas in society.

There are also today a number of important international arenas, where professional and/or museum organizations can reach consensus across contemporary national borders and around the world and on the Internet (Kaplan 1999; Knowles 1999). ICOM (International Council of Museums) is the most ecumenical and important world organization of museums. Founded soon after World War II, in 1946, it followed that global conflagration in which the threat and danger to irreplaceable works of humankind and nature were recognized globally. ICOM now has more than 140 member countries, 117 national committees and 30 international committees based on special expertise (ICOM 2007). ICOM is associated with UNESCO and together they represent and espouse a broad consensus and collective concerns for diversity in the *cultural* and *natural worlds* that constitute 'heritage' (as they describe and have defined it below). It has been accepted globally (French 1999).

Cultural heritage is defined to include those works classed as 'monuments': architectural works, works of monumental sculpture and paintings, elements or structures of an archaeological nature, inscriptions, cave dwellings, and combinations of features, which are of outstanding universal value from the point of view of history, art or science. It also includes groups of buildings because their architecture, homogeneity or place in the landscape has universal value. So, too, cultural heritage sites are works of man or a combination of nature and of man, and so are archaeological sites of outstanding universal value from historical, aesthetic, ethnological or anthropological points of view. The walls of Benin City clearly belong to this class.

Natural heritage is defined by UNESCO and ICOM to include 'features'. These features consist of physical and biological formations or groups of such formations, which are of outstanding universal value from the aesthetic or scientific point of view. Also included are geological and physiographical formations, and delineated areas that are habitats of threatened species of animals and plants of outstanding universal value from the points of view of science or conservation. Other heritage encompasses natural sites of delineated areas of outstanding universal value from the points of view of science, conservation or natural beauty (UNESCO 1978).

Intangible heritage is the most recently defined in 2003, and was the theme of the last *2004 Triennial Meetings of ICOM's General Assembly*. It includes the learned processes of people, along with their knowledge, skills and creativity, the products they created, and the resources, spaces and other aspects of social and natural context necessary to sustain them. These processes are notable in providing living communities with a sense of continuity with past generations and are important to cultural identity. They safeguard cultural diversity and the creativity of humanity (Pinna 2003).

It is notable that a more active role is being played by ICOM, UNESCO, The World Monument Fund and like organizations that goes beyond what was envisioned after World War II (Vinson 2001). Increasingly, these organizations are called upon to express and represent concerns for world heritage that transcend the shifting national, state and local boundaries. Without enforcement powers these organizations, nonetheless, seek to mediate the potential loss and damage posed by wars, conflicts, neglect as well as natural disasters, and acts of wilful destruction. In this, ICOM and its committees, often in concert with other groups, are emerging as the enlightened conscience of the world. They speak for the broad, long-term, and global interests of human society and the planet – against the more narrow, short-term, and skewed values of the few. In its way, ICOM has assumed a new and quite revolutionary role.

Historical background: Benin and the city walls

When the Portuguese embarked on their 'voyages of the discoveries' in the fifteenth century, they opened new vistas and markets to Europeans along the west coast of Africa (Fage 1980). They wrote of an ancient kingdom and a god-king, an Oba, who ruled from a vast walled Palace, a city within the walled city of Great Benin. Entry to the city was through nine gates with locks and keepers, and closed at nightly curfews (Egharevba 1950). There were well laid out streets and houses of mud architecture, polished until they shone like mirrors and were a marvel to behold! (Ninety miles of city walls were surveyed (1961–1964) in the twentieth century by Graham Connah (1975: 101). Beyond these walls were further monumental earthworks that meandered for a total length estimated at over 9,000 miles (16,000 kilometres) through the surrounding dense tropical rainforest of what is today south-west Nigeria (Darling 1984a: 6). Benin art in copper alloys, leaded brass and ivory from the sixteenth century on are replete with imagery of the Portuguese presence at the royal court (Willett 1985). Most of these works of art repose today in museums and private collections around the world.

Urban architectural heritage fared less well than Benin's mobile works of art, especially after the city came under fierce attack at the end of the nineteenth century. In 1897, a major British military expedition destroyed much of the Oba's Palace and the city walls with ruinous fires and demolition to prevent further resistance by Benin warriors (Bacon 1897). In the aftermath, more than two thousand works of art in bronze, brass, ivory, wood and iron were stripped from the palace shrines, archives and private rooms of the Oba and his chiefs. Their removal resulted in loss of models and memory, especially with cessation of court activity. The objects taken were inventoried, then shipped to England where they were sold to pay the costs of the British military expedition. The reigning Oba *Ovonramwen* (1888–1914) was exiled to Old Calabar in the east, and he was replaced with chiefs chosen by the British colonial administration.

Restoration of the palace began after 1914, with Oba Ovonramwen's passing, and when his son and heir, Oba *Eweka II* (1914–1933), came to the throne. Oba *Eweka II* slowly began to rebuild the main palace structure from the 1920s on,

Figure 11.2 View of remains of Benin City walls, 1984. In the background, a group of homes is visible at the top of the walls. A stream can be seen in the ditch below.

Photo: The author

but not the walls that had encompassed a far larger area. Some of the pre-1897 grounds that were within the palace compound now constitute a large part of the civic centre of the city, including the two and a half acres on which the Benin National Museum is built, the grounds occupied by the Post Office, the Town Hall (Urhokpota Hall); and the city's main roundabout, Ring Road, as well as other buildings and sites (Connah 1972: 27).

In the late twentieth century, the city walls were so thickly overgrown they could scarcely be discerned. In some areas, remaining sections of the deteriorating city walls were used as a source of raw materials with which to repair and build homes of those living in the communities that abutted them. Despite posted wood signs announcing the presence of the city walls, the ditches are frequently used as garbage dumps. Since 1961, the walls were (theoretically) 'protected' by legislation as a national monument.

From 1897 until Nigeria declared its independence in 1960, British colonial administrators and Christian missionaries suppressed expressions of Benin pride, ritual and awareness of their history and culture to lasting effect. The mighty inner city walls or dump ramparts that had once risen vertically, from 52 to virtually 60 feet high (*c.* 18 metres), are believed to have been built by Oba *Oguola, c.* AD 1280. For centuries since, they protected the Oba's Palace and the city's many inhabitants from surprise attacks. They were ignored, if not forgotten, in the colonial and postcolonial era.

Discussion

What now of Benin City and the Benin people's view of their history, culture and heritage? Present-day indigenous inhabitants of *Great Benin* are under siege to become converts of missionaries to world religions. They face internal economic policies that are products of foreign and federal domestic agendas set in the national capital of Abuja by the most populous ethnic groups. Benin City itself and its environs are home to an increasingly diverse population, one that no longer is associated solely with Benin culture. Many are groups who paid tribute to the Oba of Benin in past centuries (Kaplan 2004). Many others maintain their own religious and ethnic identities whose centres of origin are located elsewhere in Nigeria and even abroad. Benin City, once the long-time capital and commercial centre of a mighty kingdom remains a shadow of itself, as the British colonial administration willed it. Now the administrative centre and capital of Edo State, Federal Republic of Nigeria, it is in need of development and renewal. Preservation and restoration of a significant section of its great earthen city walls would be an important first step in revitalizing its indigenous pride and energy through cultural urban heritage.

Most ethnic groups throughout the country express admiration for the Benin who, they say, 'respect themselves', and 'keep their culture', and it is widely acknowledged that 'you cannot buy a chieftainship in Benin'. However, other ethnic groups neighbouring Benin in the south, to the west and east, still fear them for their (former) practice of human sacrifice, oaths and knowledge of 'medicines'. These fears were very much alive in the mid-to-late twentieth century and are even now, especially among those groups who paid tribute to the Oba of Benin in the past. Their dread of Benin, however, had serious consequences after 1897, and contributed to the neglect of Benin City under British colonial rule. It also impeded the city's recovery even after Nigerian independence (Kaplan 2004).

The walls of Great Benin (and a few related sites that had been part of the royal Palace – pre-1897 British conquest) were imperfectly mapped in the 1950s and 1960s, on the cusp of Nigerian independence. The difficulty of doing archaeology in the dense tropical rainforest echoes in Connah's observation about the problems of mapping the city walls in Benin in 1962: 'To do this it was necessary to *machet* [emphasis mine] through many miles of dense vegetation in thorny ditches' (1975:103). He and other early outside archaeologists who worked in the colonial period did so rapidly and as a largely salvage operation just ahead of ongoing new construction in the city in the 1950s and 1960s (Goodwin 1957a,b, 1963; Willett 1964).

The work of Connah and others clearly showed the value of systematic archaeology, using test pits and limited excavations to address problems of chronology, contacts and history. Regrettably, there has been virtually no follow-up to their initial promising results. Darling's surveys begun in the early 1970s are a welcome exception, but he was interrupted by Nigeria's civil war, and the survey has yet to be completed. The walls proved difficult to map and even more confusing to analyse. Nonetheless, archaeologists confirmed Benin's achievements in a natural landscape of great scientific interest, beauty and challenge.

Figure 11.3 Annual Benin community-wide Festival of Ewere, Ewere, 1989. Benin chiefs bring 'the leaves of happiness' identified with Ewere, a sixteenth-century queen, who personifies the virtues and joy a good wife brings to all husbands and families among the Edo people. Oba *Erediauwa* receives the first leaves, then they are given at homes throughout the city. The act ends the traditional year in Benin.

Photo: The author

Darling pointed out that Benin's pre-mechanical construction of earthen forest walls was 'four to five times longer than the Great Wall of China and with over a hundred times as much material moved as the Great Pyramid of Cheops' (1984a: 6). Connah speculated that the innermost Benin City walls could have been erected in a single dry season by 5,000 men, working ten hours a day (1975:103). It is more likely they were built over a longer period, and would have had to be repaired after each rainy season in any case. It appears the walls were probably built and rebuilt in the reigns of several different Obas. Indeed, oral tradition tells us that '[t]here are three main moats or ditches (iya) surrounding the city . . . [the first two] dug by Oba Oguola' as a defensive measure. The third moat (ditch/iya) in the heart

Figure 11.4 Posted sign at a site of the Benin Moat, 2005. Plans are being made at Oba *Erediauwa*'s initiative to restore the walls of the moat.

Photo: The author

of the city was dug by Oba *Ewuare* about AD 1460' (Egharevba 1960: 85). These very tangible city (and forest) walls, thus, are intimately linked with intangible Benin cultural heritage – as well as archaeological research and dating.

Conclusions

Whatever the calculations made or comparisons drawn with engineering feats else-where – the walls of Great Benin City in the rainforest of south-west Nigeria remain a monumental achievement, as well as a political one. It required some centralized administration, a sizable labour force and sustained community effort. The walls attest to an indigenous state and urban civilization in the African rainforest – that originated and governed independently for more than 700 years.

The present deplorable condition of the Benin City walls today is a legacy of the British military assault on the kingdom in 1897. It represents a colonial record of neglect and a deliberate effort to crush Benin pride of place and culture. Benin resistance, however, continued in the absence of Oba *Ovonramwen* and even after the interregnum (from 1897 to 1914), until about 1920. The city itself was hated by the British because of the casualties sustained by the expedition in the fight to take over the city. Visitors described Benin City in the late 1920s as a 'forgotten wasteland' (Bacon 1897). Nor was there any longer an organized system of indigenous labour to repair the city walls after each rainy season.

Oba *Erediauwa* is a key player in restoring cultural identity and pride in Benin City. He has actively encouraged its beautification, designating plantings and flowers in public places. He is engaged in creating a virtual history book of Benin events, and in the process has changed the city's urban landscape with larger-than-life-size statues, created by living Benin artists. The statues prompt memory and give form to Benin oral tradition. They also lead visitors to ask after them. For example, a monumental statue of Benin's first Queen Mother, *Idia*, by the contemporary Benin sculptor, Gregory Agbonkonkon, watches over one of the main roads leading into and out of the city. *Idia* raised an army to assist her son, the king, and contributed to his success in winning the Idah wars to the north. She is known to this day as 'the only woman who went to war'. At another part of the city, on a hillock above Ikpoba Hill, there is a statue of the Benin warrior who sounded the alarm warning the city of an intended surprise attack. He stands on a pedestal at the centre of a traffic roundabout where several main roads converge.

These large-scale sculptures and the smaller art works are popular with visitors. The latter are made and sold commercially in Benin and beyond by the royal guilds to illustrate oral tradition. Some traditional pieces can be made only for the Oba of Benin. The translation of oral tradition into sculpture had its beginnings in the time of Oba *Akenzua II* (1933–1978), the father of the present Oba *Erediauwa*. In the 1950s, he decided to replace a tree planted in memory of a fifteenth-century Benin heroine with a cast bronze statue of the lady, *Emotan*. She is remembered as the humble market woman who saved the life of the great Oba *Ewuare*. In the 1990s, Oba *Erediauwa* made her shrine more elaborate, sheltering the statue from the elements. Oba *Akenzua II* was the first traditional ruler in the colonial days of Nigeria, to found a museum in his palace grounds.

The growing movement to identify and preserve Benin cultural heritage sites and the formation of groups wishing to recover looted art abroad is taking place outside of Benin City and Nigeria. Africanists, and scholars of anthropology, art history, history and other fields at universities and museums, most outside of Nigeria, have generated exhibitions, conferences and publications. They have illuminated and inspired widespread admiration of Benin art, history, art history and culture. Educated and affluent Benin businessmen and professionals who travel, live and work abroad have come to know of the high regard in which others in Europe, the Americas and Asia hold Benin art and culture. They have begun to use their fellowship associations formed in cities of the United Kingdom, Europe and the United States to lobby and support the Oba's efforts to retrieve and restore its treasures to Benin. Museum specialists and administrators interact together in national and international organizations to raise consciousness, establish best practices and set standards worldwide. They are influential professionals, belonging to international museum organizations, and the national committees of the 140 countries belonging to ICOM.

Long-time Benin expatriates support and come to identify with the Oba and the Palace, taking renewed pride in their history and cultural heritage. In recent years, Benin associations of expatriates have grown, especially in large cities in the United States of America and elsewhere. Some have become active in London, petitioning the British Government and museums for the return of Benin art looted from the Oba's Palace in 1897. These expatriate groups see site preservation of the Benin City walls as a way of revitalizing the city to attract businesses and tourists.

They maintain close ties with family, community and the palace in Benin City. A few return temporarily to Nigeria, to run for political office (state, local and national), as did a New York City businessman who ran for the office of Governor of Edo State. Other expatriates have been elected members of the local government area, of the central government, and as members of special state commissions, and served one or more national Constitutional Conventions. Many men (and some women) donate cash and materials to make improvements in their natal villages and communities, to refurbish or build a house, and to educate children or siblings. Some plan eventually to return home to Benin, to retire, and have begun building a house in the city or in another large town in anticipation. They use the networks they have built and the income they have generated abroad, to bring 'name' and prestige to themselves in Benin.

They also establish their status among the association members and in their local communities. The members seek consensus on the projects and support they will provide monetarily, and may assume new roles in the decision-making process. In Nigeria those living in proximity to the heritage sites often have no knowledge of the walls' history. Most are either unaware or uninterested in them, except for the utility they provide as a source of building blocks. Ironically, it is those who left the country, part of a virtual exodus of professionals and businessmen and women in the last two decades, who are taking an interest in preserving cultural heritage and rediscovering their Benin identity outside the country.

Whether or not these expatriate associations have the expertise and experience to do large-scale fund-raising is a major question. It is uncertain whether the federal NCMM that has been gravely underfunded in recent years is able and willing to bring together the resources needed in Benin City. Certainly, the fully restored medieval monument would enhance interpretation and provide the Benin and others, visitors and tourists with a total *experience*. Nonetheless, it may be possible to restore only some section or sections of the walls. What is uncertain is if local urban issues cited in this chapter create an imbalance in the push-and-pull exerted by the need to build for the future – without raising the past. It is for these reasons that private funding will have to be sought with the help of the World Monuments Fund. And its success or lack of it can be measured. The greatest threat to this heritage site, apart from weather, is not gentrification, but inertia.

Bibliography

Anderson, B. (1983) *Imagined Communities: Reflections on the origin and spread of nationalism*, London: Verso Press.

Bacon, R.H. (1897) *City of Blood*, London: Arnold.

Camara, A. (1999) 'Gorée: Dynamique D'un Musée Vers Ses Communautés', in *Musées et politique: Actes du Quatriéme colloque de l'Association internationale des musées d'histoires*, Quebec: Musée de la Civilization, 127–43.

Connah, G. (1972) 'Archaeology in Benin', *Journal of African History*, 13(1): 25–38.

Connah, G. (1975) *The Archaeology of Benin: Excavations and other researches in and around Benin City, Nigeria*, Oxford: Clarendon Press.

Darling, P.J. (1984a) *Archaeology and History in Southern Nigeria: The ancient linear earthworks of Benin and Ishan. Part i: Fieldwork and background information.* (Cambridge monographs in African archaeology 11). BAR International Series 215 (i) Oxford: British Archaeological Reports.

Darling, P.J. (1984b) *Archaeology and History in Southern Nigeria: The ancient linear earthworks of Benin and Ishan. Part ii: Ceramic and other specialist studies.* (Cambridge Monographs in African Archaeology 11). BAR International Series 215(ii). Oxford: British Archaeological Reports.

Egharevba, J. (1950) *Some Stories of Ancient Benin*, Lagos: Ribway Printers.

Egharevba, J. (1960) *A Short History of Benin*, 3rd edn, Ibadan, Nigeria: Ibadan University Press.

Fage, J.D. (1980) 'A Commentary on Duarte Pacheco Pereira's Account of the Lower Guinea Coastlands in His "Esmeraldo de Situ Orbis", and on Some Other early Accounts', *History in Africa*, 7: 47–80.

French, D. (1999) 'A Commonwealth Perspective', in *Musées et politique: Actes du Quatriéme colloque de l'Association internationale des musées d'histoires*, Quebec: Musée de la Civilization, 245–55.

Goodwin, A.J.H. (1957a) *History and Archaeology in Africa*, London: School of Oriental and African Studies.

Goodwin, A.J.H. (1957b) 'Archaeology and Benin Architecture,' *Journal of the Historical Society of Nigeria*, 1: 65–85.

Goodwin, A.J.H. (1963) 'A Bronze Snake Head and Other Recent Finds in the Old Palace at Benin', *Man*, 63: 142–5.

Hobsbawm, E.J. and Ranger, T. (1983) *The Invention of Tradition*, Cambridge: Cambridge University Press.

ICOM Recommendations (1970) 'Ethics of Acquisition'.

ICOM (2007) *ICOM Mission*. Available online at: http://icom.museum/mission.html (accessed 11 October 2007).

Kaplan, F.E.S. (1982) 'Towards a "Science" of Museology' in *Museological Working Papers*, No. 2. ICOFOM: Paris, 14–15.

Kaplan, F.E.S. (1996) 'Museum Anthropology', in D. Levinson and M. Ember (eds) *Encyclopedia of Cultural Anthropology*, Vol. 3, 813–17.

Kaplan, F.E.S. (1998) 'Nigerian Museums: Envisaging Culture as National Identity', in F.E.S. Kaplan (ed.) *Museums and the Making of 'Ourselves': The role of objects in national identity*, (First published in 1994), Leicester: Leicester University Press, 45–78.

Kaplan, F.E.S. (1999) 'Rethinking the Boundaries of National Identity' (Keynote address) in *Musées et politique: Actes du Quatriéme colloque de l''Association internationale des musées d'histoires*, Quebec: Musées de la Civilization, 59– 65.

Kaplan, F.E.S. (2004) 'Understanding Sacrifice and Sanctity in Benin Indigenous Religion, Nigeria: A case study', in J.K. Olupona (ed.) *Beyond Primitivism: Indigenous religious traditions and modernity*, London: Routledge, 181–99.

Kaplan, F.E.S. (2006) 'Making and Remaking National Identities', in S. Macdonald (ed.) *A Companion to Museum Studies*, Oxford: Blackwell Publishing, 152–69.

Knowles, L. (1999) 'Museums and Communities: Who needs whom most?' in *Museés et politique: Actes du Quatriéme colloque de l'Association internationale des musées d'histoire*, Quebec: Musée de la Civilization, 113–26.

Pinna, G. (2003) 'Intangible Heritage and Museums', *ICOM News*, 56(4).

Shaw, T. (1969) 'Further Spectrographic Analyses of Nigerian Bronzes', *Archaeometry*, 11: 85–98.

UNESCO (1978) *World Cultural Heritage Information Bulletin*, No. 18.

UNESCO (2007) *World Heritage List*. Available online at: http://whc.unesco.org/en/list (accessed 11 October 2007).

Vinson, I. (2001) 'Heritage and Museology: A new convergence', *Museum International*, 53(3): 211.

Whalen,T. (2000) 'Conservation in the New Century', *The Getty Conservation Institute Newsletter*, 15(1).

Willett, F. (1964) 'Spectrographic Analyses of Nigerian Bronzes', *Archaeometry*, 7: 81–3.

Willett, F. (1985) *African Art* (First published in 1971), New York: Thames and Hudson.

World Monuments Fund (2007) *100 Most Endangered Sites, 2008*. Available online at http://www.wmf.org/html/programs/watchlist2004.html (accessed 11 October 2007).

12

The past in the present: Towards a politics of care at the National Trust of Australia (WA)

Andrea Witcomb

> Progress we need; progress we will have. Stability we need; stability we will
> . . . I am not sure how this sentence ends, for the noise of the bull-dozer
> confuses me and the dust of falling buildings obscures my vision. And my
> children's historic roots seem to be being fed to the flames as casually as the
> mallee root is thrown on the evening hearth, to glow – and die in ashes.
> (Roberts 1961)

So wrote Hew Roberts, foundation member of the National Trust, in his preface to John and Ray Oldham's book, *Western Heritage*, first published in 1961. In expressing his sense of loss at the destruction of the historical landscape going on in Perth during the early 1960s, Roberts was articulating one of the central problems of the experience of modernity – how should we relate to the past? What role should the past play in the present and in the future?

At the time that he expressed his fears, Western Australia was going through a remarkable period of change: its population was growing exponentially, the long mining boom was just beginning and its new found confidence in the future was expressed through modernist town planning schemes, particularly for central Perth. The familiar landscapes around them were changing fast – old buildings were coming down to make way for new roads, car parks and skyscrapers and the river was losing its familiar contours through infill to build freeways and bridges.

This was not the first time that Perth had experienced a boom and the remaking of the city that accompanied it. The gold rushes of the 1890s had resulted in a new face for Perth which largely obliterated the physical traces of the first wave of European settlers. Nevertheless, the moment Roberts was referring to was palpably different. In the 1890s, the rebuilding expressed a confidence in the future of Perth and Western Australia, a feeling that the colony had finally achieved economic success and was here to stay. At that time, the past represented only the beginning, something that Western Australians were in the process of moving away from in order to build a better place. Development was the dominant ideology of the day, informing everything from economic policy to the beginnings of Western Australia's historiography.

By the late 1920s, enough time had passed for some elements within Western Australian society to feel confident enough of their forebears' success to want to begin to celebrate it by remembering and documenting it. The past, at this point became something from which to measure progress. Thus was born the Western Australian Historical Society whose job was to document that progress and celebrate those pioneers, often their own family forebears, who had made the present possible. Antiquarian in orientation, their version of history was intensely familial, parochial and protective of what Tom Stannage (1985) has described as the gentry tradition. For those contributing to the pages of the Society's journal, *Early Days*, the past was a romanticized landscape, built on an Arcadian tradition in which the pioneers revealed moral courage and physical strength in the face of hardship as well as opportunity. Their version of history was thus a monumentalist (Nietzsche 1957) one in which the past furnished the present with a source of moral values. When expressed in terms of heritage, the past was commemorated and memorialized, often through the erection of cairns, plaques and sometimes monuments (Davison 1989). The physical remnants of the past, however, other than documentary sources, were rarely preserved, as the prevalent sensibilities did not include a conscious desire to maintain traces of the past in the present (Healy 1994).

In the 1960s, however, the past came to represent more than a source of moral values. For some it became a haven from the present, a utopia. For them, the past was a 'foreign country' (Lowenthal 1985) for which they yearned with unabashed nostalgia. To others like Roberts though, it came to represent an anchor, a point of stability amidst the forces of change. For them, it was no longer sufficient to commemorate and memorialize the past. It was also important to preserve its physical traces as it was these that preserved a sense of place and identity. Inherent in this desire was a critique of ideologies of progress. This time, then, the threats to the built and natural environments posed by the next wave of development did not just signify welcomed progress. They also signified destruction and a loss of connection to a past and a place.

Such a step indicates a departure from standard approaches to the past within modernity which cannot be understood within a rationalist framework. For here the past is neither a stepping stone in a narrative of progress nor something to erase in the search for a future utopia. Instead it is a source of identity. From this perspective, what is lost in the attempts to break with the past is a sense of place, as the very threads of connection between past, present and future are severed making it impossible to actively remember. It is this approach to the past that underlines Roberts' arguments for the importance of maintaining connections to the past if society is to have stability. His cry against the bulldozer then, is one of the first indications that not everyone was happy with the modernist ethic taking shape at the time.

Expressed through a preservationist sentiment, critiques like that of Roberts formed the basis of what has come to be known as the heritage movement. It is thus not surprising that for many the debate over whether to preserve something or not is cast as an ideological one – those for and those against the values of progress. This, however, is a line of argument fraught with danger; for embedded in it, is a tendency not only to romanticize the past but also to become nostalgic for it, turning it into a lost utopia. The problem for the heritage movement has thus always been one of public representation – how can they portray themselves as anything other than nostalgic? The fight to gain public support then, is not only a fight to change the dominant values away from utilitarian perspectives on development and preservation towards a more holistic approach which takes into account cultural and social values. It is also a fight to prevent our relationship to the past from succumbing to either nostalgia or utilitarianism. How the past was understood and even fought for said much about conflicting identities and modes of being. At once a landscape of memories as well as hopes for the future, the past was one of the battlegrounds where differing understandings of what it was to be a modern citizen were fought out. The activities of the National Trust of Australia (WA) offer us the opportunity to chart these landscapes and set them against the context of their times.

In this chapter, I want to contrast two very different historical moments in the history of the Trust as a means to understanding vastly different conceptualizations of the past and its relevance to the present. My case studies focus on the Trust's involvement in two heritage battles – the battle for the Barracks Arch and the ongoing battle for the Burrup Peninsula – as a way of illuminating the role of the Trust in shaping public perceptions of the past by fostering expressions of heritage sentiment at the grassroots level. While the Trust used all of its social connections to operate at the formal political level within the corridors of government in both campaigns, the Trust also facilitated the involvement of 'ordinary citizens', believing that only public pressure can change political wills. I would argue that in the process of opening up a space for active forms of citizenship around debates for the preservation of particular sites, the Trust has contributed to the development of new understandings of community and provided a space for the performance of evolving forms of citizenship.

The battle for the Barracks Arch

The Barracks once housed the pensioner guards. Built by convicts between 1863 and 1867 and designed by Richard Roach Jewell, the building sat at the top of St George's Terrace, Perth's premier street. Unfortunately for it, its address was also right in front of the proposed new Parliament House and the Mitchell Freeway passing below it. The building was in the way of Perth's own version of a modernist city being planned by Gordon Stephenson and Alistair Hepburn, employees of Premier David Brand and Minister for Development Russel Dumas, who, as Lenore Layman (1982) argues, were the architects of the biggest development agenda Western Australia had ever had.

The Barracks represented an important network of buildings that symbolized the first major civic development in the colony after the initial settlement period. More importantly though, the site was part of Perth's psyche, a major landmark in its sense of place and identity. It was a building that was loved, as captured in Dorothy

171

Sanders' (1961: 173) fictionalized response to Gordon Stephenson's recommendation to demolish it in the 1955 Metropolitan Plan:

> A town planner from abroad had advised West Australians to remove that old historical building in order to allow a finer vista down the length of the Terrace from Parliament House. The Barracks were not architecturally beautiful, he had informed the citizens.
>
> This advice had been received in courteous silence. West Australians could not explain to a man from abroad that the Barracks held a beauty for them he would never be able to see with foreign eyes. That building stood for their history, their birth pangs. As a nation they had not come trailing clouds of glory from some other world. Their primordial memory was one of discovery ships, pioneer ships, convict ships, immigrant ships. The Barracks, relic of the birth of the nation, reminded the citizens they were not born of privilege but of hardship, endurance and the will to survive.

When it became increasingly clear that this intention to demolish the Barracks to make way for the Freeway to the north of the city was real, there was immediate public concern. The Buildings Committee of the National Trust made the Barracks an early focus of attention, advocating as early as February 1960 that the National Trust should join forces with the Historical Society and advocate its preservation to government (Council National Trust of Australia [WA], 10 February 1960).

The result was the birth of a spirited public campaign which worked behind closed doors through the corridors of power and through more open avenues such as public meetings, street protests and the media. These two approaches were symbolized by a decision of Council to work with the Historical Society to produce a pamphlet about the Barracks promoting the need for its preservation at the same time as seeking to influence the committee working on the Road Scheme (Council National Trust of Australia [WA], May 1961).

On 2 October 1961, the National Trust decided to print 5,000 copies of the pamphlet the Trust and the Historical Society had jointly produced (Council National Trust of Australia [WA]), distributing it to parliamentarians and members of a wide range of associations. The pamphlet asked Western Australians to consider whether the Barracks was '[t]o be reduced to rubble and forgotten ? . . . or to be preserved by citizen action for all our future citizens – and their tourist visitors?' As well as articulating the historical and architectural significance of the site, the pamphlet articulated the importance of the Barracks to Perth's sense of place, appealing to emotional as well as intellectual arguments by using the Barracks as a symbol of stability: 'a sense of being rooted is good for us' its authors said, 'in an age when restlessness and rootlessness seem to accompany rapid change. Standing where it has stood for three-quarters of our history, the Barracks gives a sense of time and stability'. The pamphlet also attempted to combat the perception that the Premier's decision was irreversible, pointing out its faith in the Premier's commitment to review the decision to raze the Barracks in 1964 and that therefore it was worthwhile to participate in public debate about the issue by signing the petition being circulated by the Historical Society. The result was a petition to the Premier for the preservation of the Barracks from 700 people (Gregory 2003: 120).

In the meantime, liaison between the Trust and the Historical Society had led to the formation of the Barracks Defence Council (BDF) at a public meeting in September 1961. This body also had representatives from other preservation bodies such as the Tree Society and associations such as the Citizen's Committee for the Defence of Kings Park, the WA Fellowship of Writers, the Women's Service Guild and the National Council of Women. A grassroots heritage movement was taking shape. While led by what one of the Trust's founders described as 'citizens of discernment' (Medcalf 2004), its tactics were thoroughly modern, using pamphlets, radio interviews, stickers and petitions to capture the public's imagination.

While the BDF and the Trust developed enough status to be invited to meetings with the Government and its committees, they failed to convince them. Prepared to compromise, the Trust began to argue only for the retention of the Barracks Arch, two towers and two wings (Council National Trust of Australia (WA) 1 April 1962). By mid-1963, the Premier relented a little by announcing that the wings of the Barracks would be demolished in 1966, but that the central archway and the two towers would be retained until the Government and the public could form a final opinion on whether this portion should, and could, be preserved.

As the final date for the destruction of the wings approached, the BDF and the Trust mobilized once again in a final attempt to save both the wings and the archway. The media became a great ally, conducting a series of public polls which clearly showed the majority of the public were in favour of retaining the Barracks Arch. Premier Brand's attempt to minimize the significance of these polls showed him and his Government up as autocratic. Numerous stickers for and against the preservation of the arch were produced, including one that simply stated 'preserve democracy' (Gregory 2003: 121). In his role as the President of the BDF Bishop Riley felt moved to side with the people, warning the Government that they were sacrificing the will of the people 'on the altar of an engineering Moloch' (Riley in Gregory 2003: 122).

If Premier Brand hoped that the removal of the Barrack's wings would lead to public recognition of the futility of leaving the remaining arch and two towers he was misguided. In a poll taken immediately after the destruction of the wings, the people of Perth once again proved their attachment to the site. If anything, they began to romanticize the arch, describing it as 'striking', 'mellow', 'picturesque' and 'elegant.' Brand's Government, however, thought that this was merely the rantings of a vociferous minority and did not reflect the views of the majority of the electorate. Most government ministers followed the Premier, who thought that 'the tendency to be influenced by our emotions should be set aside for the sake of town planning and the demands of the car' (Brand in Gregory 2003: 122). The citizens of Perth, however, continued to apply pressure.

Realizing that the protestors were not diminishing in numbers, the Government commissioned a Gallop poll on the issue. When the Gallop poll showed that the majority of people favoured the retention of the arch, Premier Brand decided to give Parliament the opportunity to vote on the issue, advising members of the Government that this would be a non-party issue. In a last minute attempt to sway the Government, the National Trust decided to send a telegram to every member of Parliament, asking them to vote in favour of retaining the arch. In a historic vote, before a crowded public gallery, the Legislative Assembly voted twenty-six to eighteen to reject Premier Brand's motion to remove the archway. The battle for the remaining vestiges of the Barracks was won.

The landscape the Trust was fighting for in this example was highly personal, local, familial. While this makes the battle an expression of antiquarianism (Nietzsche 1957), the aims cannot be simply understood as nostalgic in motivation. Shaped by the sense of threat posed by the Government's development ideology, the past suddenly became tangible as the landscape became invigorated though the activation of people's memories and associations. For perhaps the first time, the past became a source of community identity for the general population, affirming the right of settlers to the place, affirming a sense of belonging. In their attempt to express this sense of belonging, the people of Perth integrated the past into the present and made it part of their everyday lives in a very conscious and explicit manner. For the past had become a means to assert one's citizenship, one's right to comment on government policy and indeed, to attempt to change it. Heritage had become a right. Configured as heritage, however, the past was not a space where the relationship between European settlers and indigenous people could be explored. The past was a white past and it belonged only to whites.

Beyond a white past – The battle for the Burrup

By the 1990s and early 2000s, however, this erasure of the complexity of the past for a simple version of Australians' relationship to place was losing favour both within and without the Trust. Changes in Australian historiography which now devoted considerable space to events around the colonial frontiers (e.g. Attwood 1994, 1996; Green 1984, 1995; Reynolds 1987, 1995, 1996), legal developments such as the Mabo case which recognized indigenous land rights under common law in 1992 and the Wik judgment (1996) which followed it by recognizing the coexistence of native title on pastoral leases, the impact of the National Inquiry into the Separation of Aboriginal and Torres Strait Islander Children from their Families (1997) on the general public's understanding of indigenous lives in the twentieth century, the revelations around the Royal Commission into Aboriginal Deaths in Custody (1991) and the increasing opportunities for indigenous people to write and talk about their own experiences in both fiction and non-fiction genres contributed to a groundswell in the general public's understanding of their forebears complicity in the suffering of indigenous people as well as their own.

At the same time the Trust itself had become a professional body whose staff were informed not only by the new historiography but also by the new museology with its attention to the politics of representation. The Trust's Council also changed in composition, away from 'people of discernment' – that is, members of the cultural and social elite – towards professional historians and heritage experts. With the approval of Council, the staff, rather than volunteer committees, increasingly began to revise the interpretation of Trust properties, frequently including a more nuanced understanding of the indigenous presence within the history of settlement (Gregory and Witcomb 2007). At the same time, the Trust lost its privileged position within the heritage field, gained as a consequence of being the only heritage body in town for over thirty years. In 1990, for the first time in Western Australia, heritage legislation was passed and a Heritage Council with legislative powers over listed sites was established. Other grassroots associations had also emerged, often with specific interests such as Art Deco architecture or specific sites under threat from development. No longer the only defender of heritage, the Trust had to find a new role for itself.

A major part of this was an explicit attempt to engage with revisionist histories, especially contact history. This put the Trust at loggerheads with those within its membership who still subscribed to a pioneer mythology, particularly in the interpretation of properties. The management's response was to articulate and implement a policy of management with the volunteers rather than management by the volunteers (NTAWA 2001). Entire committees either resigned or were disbanded from above and professional staff engaged to lead the Trust's activities. While the reinterpretation of history at Trust properties was one of the first action points, the second was a renewed attempt to create a position for the Trust as a leader in the development and shaping of heritage consciousness. Nothing shows this better that the Burrup campaign which provided the Trust with an opportunity to renovate and reinvigorate its image as both a leader and a representative of public opinion in relation to heritage. The Trust's decision to intervene on behalf of Aboriginal people was also an explicit attack on the current state legislative system which separates indigenous from settler heritage under different regimes.

As with previous heritage battles, the enemy was the zealous development ideology of the Government who constantly prioritized economic and industrial development over heritage. But this time the focus was on a site of importance to indigenous communities. In fighting this battle, the Trust was clearly signalling a number of things: the desirability of balance between development and preservation, the need to be inclusive of indigenous communities, taking their heritage seriously and perhaps even more importantly, an attempt to win the battle on the grounds that the indigenous heritage on the Burrup Peninsula was significant for all Australians and indeed the world. Its definition of community had changed and it was clearly critical of conservative attitudes opposed to reconciliation. With the Burrup campaign, the Trust announced its progressive political aims, wanting to capture a new audience.

The Burrup peninsula is just to the north of Karratha on the north-west coast of west Australia. Formerly Dampier Island, it formed part of the Dampier Archipelago and is an area with a long history of human occupation. Its rock carvings – petroglyphs – blanket the landscape making it the world's largest open air art gallery. As Ken Mulvaney (2003) said in a 2003 Forum organized by the National Trust, the Burrup 'has in fact the greatest density, diversity of subject and style than anywhere in Australia and in fact anywhere in the World'. As well as rock art, the Burrup also contains shell middens and standing stone arrangements. Experts date the rock art as between 4,000 and 20,000 years old, making it the earliest known art site in the world (Bird and Hallam 2006).

While the existence of rock art in the area was known about as early as the nineteenth century, it was never seriously studied and was little understood. In the late 1960s, the area was identified for industrial purposes, largely in response to the discovery of iron ore in the Pilbara region. Three large deep water ports were built in the area to facilitate its export. By 1973, the state Minister for Development had identified the Burrup area for industry development purposes with no consultation as to its heritage significance and built a causeway to link the island with the mainland creating a peninsula (NTAWA 2006; Bird and Hallam 2006). Lack of consultation and research into the area's natural and indigenous heritage values continued into the 1980s and 1990s and facilitated the development of a number of industries in the area such as a salt production facility, a gas pipeline and a railway to carry iron ore (Bird and Hallam 2006). The recent discovery of further oil and gas reserves in the area has only increased industry's and the Government's interests in the area.

Despite a variety of archaeological studies done as part of each industrial project which clearly pointed to the heritage significance of the site, successive governments chose to prioritize the needs of industry above those of conservation. There was simply too much money and too many jobs at stake. While individual sites within the peninsula were registered under the Aboriginal Heritage Act of 1970, it was all too easy for the mining companies to get permission to either move or destroy sites in the path of their expansion under section 18 of this Act. As David Ritter (2003) has argued, no application under this Act has been refused. While no one knows how many sites were destroyed prior to 1972, it is estimated that as many as one hundred thousand petroglyphs have been destroyed since then. Given that the significance of the area resides in the relationships between the various sites and that no comprehensive survey of the entire island has yet been done, it is impossible to make good planning decisions based on *ad hoc* studies commissioned by the developers.

In 2002, the Federal Government denied outright native title to local groups. The State Government agreed to a conservation area covering 62 per cent of the Burrup, to be jointly managed with the native title claimants in exchange for unfettered access to existing industrial zones and their expansion into West Intercourse Island and the Maitland area to the south of Dampier. Native title in the industrial areas would be extinguished. This policy added to the existing worldwide concern that existing and future developments will impact negatively on the rock art and further destroy its ability to yield knowledge about the past.

The Trust became involved in the fight to stop industrial development in the Burrup in 2000. It aimed to inform the general public across Western Australia, nationally and internationally about the heritage values of the place in order to mount pressure on government to change its policy and develop an alternative location for industry. The Trust wanted one management plan for the place that balanced preservation with access and restricted development to the Maitland Industrial Estate (NTAWA 15 September 2006). It set about achieving this by building relationships with the local indigenous leaders, mounting a series of public forums in 2003 and 2006 using sponsorship from American Express and the World Monuments Fund, forming a relationship with the International Federation of Rock Art Organizations through its President Robert Bednarik, working through the National Trust movement throughout the world, fostering local grassroots associations intent on saving the Burrup and partnering with Get Up Australia for a Web-based petition. At the same time, it also worked through official channels. In 2002, the Burrup was placed on the National Trust's Endangered Places list. In 2003, it was placed on the top 100 Most Endangered World Monuments List, the only Australian site to ever be so identified. During 2003, the Trust also lobbied to have the place registered under the State Heritage Act which involved a legal challenge to the Heritage Council's understanding of its own Act. While successful in changing the Council's belief that indigenous heritage was not part of its remit, the State Government continues to delay the registration process. By 2004, the Trust was working with Robert Bednarik from the International Federation of Rock Art Organizations and the native title claimants to nominate the place for National Heritage Listing under the new Commonwealth Heritage Legislation. The Trust is also lobbying for World Heritage Listing.

Progress has been made as a result of the combined forces of this campaign. The area was placed on the National Heritage List in July 2007 by the Federal Government (Turnbull 2007) who also signalled its support for World Heritage Listing and invited the State Government to outline its position. The latter, however is not forthcoming in providing the necessary political commitment as yet. Until it does, it is not possible to develop such a nomination under the World Heritage Convention's rules, which require both government support and an appropriate management plan. However, a single management body is being developed that will identify the heritage significance of the area as a basis for future decision-making.

By way of conclusion, I want to focus on a theme that comes through again and again in this campaign: the connection between reconciliation and a sense of ethics. It is perhaps best summarized by Tom Perrigo, the Trust's CEO, when he argued in the 2006 Forum in Perth for the importance of accountability:

> We are going to be judged by the next generation and we are going to have to accept that we are accountable for whatever happens at the Burrup and we can't delegate that accountability, nobody can. Values change and values in the 60s drove a lot of this . . . how we as a population and the State Government as a government change with those values is going to be judged by the outcome of what's going to happen up here.

The Trust was in the business of changing mindsets by appealing to our humanity and creating a space for its expression. A responsible citizen, it implied, was one that recognized the development of the Burrup as a crime against humanity and who tried to stop it by becoming informed and acting on that information. Essential to that strategy was the presentation of information from scientific experts alongside addresses from indigenous elders to a mainly white audience. The importance of this strategy was well understood by the indigenous elders who used the opportunities the Trust provided through their organization of Public Forums to cast the significance of the campaign in terms of reconciliation. For example, David Daniels (2003) from the Ngarluma Yindjibarndi group described the importance of saving the Burrup rock art sites as 'about recognizing and living in harmony – that's what this is all about and if the white Australian can understand that the Black and the White can live together in harmony', then they can 'learn to change the constitution of the country so we can live in harmony'. The indigenous elders used these Forums to create a space in which white people could jointly own responsibility for the spiritual and cultural significance of the rock art simply by recognizing and supporting its significance for indigenous people. Thus, Wilfred Hicks (2003) took care to explain that:

> [w]e, the traditional owners of the lands between the George and Maitland Rivers, have a special duty also for the country, as the holders of its spiritual energies. On the Burrup that spiritual force is alive in the thousands of rock engravings that surround you here. They were placed there by our ancestors, and we receive from earlier generations the duty to protect them and must pass that on to our successors. The engravings are to us a spiritual source of energy – we can hear and see this energy when we are among them. It ties us to the land and the land to us. . . . So, because of that, while we come here today to stand firm with you, we also ask you to support us in the protection of our heritage and its spiritual aspects.

The impact was not only to let white audiences understand the significance of the area for contemporary indigenous communities who continue to maintain cultural practices there and who understand the cultural significance of a number of the sites. It was also to set up what James Clifford (1997) referred to as a 'contact zone' when discussing the opportunities museums that engaged with indigenous communities had. In using this term, borrowed from the work of Mary Louise Pratt, Clifford meant to open up an understanding of museums which both recognized and encouraged a way of working which was not premised on colonial power relations but on a shared platform of joint responsibilities. Taken to the work by the National Trust on the Burrup Campaign, the political dimensions of the ways in which the Trust facilitated the creation of a 'contact zone' are startling. Promoting an agenda of shared responsibilities was to contradict the Federal Government's earlier decision that native title no longer exists in the Dampier Archipelago. While the area's original inhabitants were decimated in the Flying Foam massacre in 1868, there are descendants and neighbouring groups with custodial responsibilities. In this context, it becomes impossible to argue that the area is only of archaeological significance. The Burrup becomes a zone of ethical responsibility where an opportunity for reconciliation exists. In that space is also an opportunity to rethink what it means to be Australian. For Robert Bednarik (2006), the fight to preserve the Burrup as a cultural landscape is, in large part, an ideological battle in which settler groups have to give up their tendency to 'other' indigenous heritage, as 'somebody else's culture'. It is only when indigenous heritage can come under the rubric of national heritage, he argues, that we can begin to practice reconciliation. The past the Trust is fighting for is not only more inclusive and reaching back to deep time – it is also a landscape in which it is possible, indeed necessary, to practice a politics of care for one another.

Acknowledgements

This chapter is part of a much larger project on the history of the National Trust of Australia (WA) funded under the Linkage Grant Scheme by the Australian Research Council and the National Trust of Australia (WA). I am grateful to Karl Clement Heynes, from the Trust, for his considerable help in providing access to a variety of materials concerning the Trust's Burrup campaign.

Bibliography

Attwood, B. (1994) *A Life Together, a Life Apart: A history of relations between Europeans and Aborigines,* Carlton, VIC: Melbourne University Press.
—— (1996) *In the Age of Mabo: History, aborigines and Australia,* St Leonards, NSW: Allen & Unwin.
Bednarik, R.G. (2006) *Australian Apocalypse: The story of Australia's greatest cultural monument,* Occasional AURA Publication, 14, Melbourne: Australian Rock Art Research Association, Inc.
Bird, C. and Hallam S.J. (2006) *Archaeology and Rock Art in the Dampier Archipelago: A report prepared for the National Trust of Australia (WA),* Perth: National Trust of Australia (WA).
Clifford, J. (1997) 'Museums as contact zones' in J. Clifford, *Routes: Travel and Translation in the Late Twentieth Century,* Cambridge, MA: Harvard University Press, 188–219.
Council of NTAWA (10 February 1960) *Minutes of Meeting.*
Council of NTAWA (May 1961) *Minutes of Meeting.*
Council of NTAWA (2 October 1961) *Minutes of Meeting.*
Council of NTAWA (1 April 1962) *Minutes of Meeting.*
Daniels D. (2003) Transcript from his presentation at the Dampier Rock Art Precinct Public Forum, 7 April 2003, State Theatre, Alexander Library, Perth, presented by the National Trust of Australia (WA).
Davison, G. (1989) 'The parochial past: Changing uses of Australian local history', in Paul Ashton (ed.), *The Future of the Past? Australian history after the bicentenary,* Nowra, NSW, Proceedings of the Royal Australian Historical Society Annual Conference with Affiliated Societies, 5–19.
—— (2000) *The Use and Abuse of Australian History,* Sydney: Allen & Unwin.
Green, N. (1984) *Broken Spears: Aborigines and Europeans in the southwest of Australia,* Perth: Focus Education Services.
—— (1995) *The Forrest River Massacres,* Fremantle, WA: Fremantle Arts Center Press.
Gregory, J. (2003) *City of Light: A history of Perth since the 1950s,* Perth: City of Perth.
Gregory, K. and Witcomb, A. (2007) 'Beyond nostalgia: The role of affect in generating historical understanding at heritage sites' in S.J. Knell, S. MacLeod and S. Watson (eds), *Museum Revolutions: How museums change and are changed,* London: Routledge, 263–75.

Griffiths, T. (1996) *Hunters and Collectors*, Melbourne: Cambridge University Press.

Healy, C. (1994) 'Histories and collecting: Museums, objects and memories', in K. Darian-Smith and P. Hamilton (eds), *Memory and History in Twentieth Century Australia*, Melbourne: Oxford University Press, 33–52.

Hewison, R. (1987) *The Heritage Industry: Britain in a climate of decline*, London: Methuen.

Hicks, W. (2003) Transcript from his presentation at the Dampier Rock Art Precinct Public Forum, 7 April 2003, State Theatre, Alexander Library, Perth, presented by the National Trust of Australia (WA).

Human Rights and Equal Opportunity Commission (1997) *Bringing Them Home: Report of the national inquiry into the separation of Aboriginal and Torres Strait islander children from their families*, Canberra: Human Rights and Equal Opportunity Commission.

Layman, L. (1982) 'Development ideology in Western Australia, 1933–1965', *Historical Studies*, 20 (October): 234–60.

Lowenthal, D. (1985) *The Past Is a Foreign Country*, Cambridge: Cambridge University Press.

Medcalf, I. (2004) *Oral History with Criena Fitzgerald*, Woodbridge Archive, National Trust of Australia (WA).

Mulvaney, K. (2003) Transcript from his presentation at the Dampier Rock Art Precinct Public Forum, 7 April 2003, State Theatre, Alexander Library, Perth, presented by the National Trust of Australia (WA).

Nietzsche, F. (1957) *The Use and Abuse of History*, trans. A. Collis, Indianapolis, IN: Bobbs-Merrill.

NTAWA (2001) *The National Trust of Australia (WA) Corporate Plan 2001–2005*.

NTAWA (15 September 2006) Submission by the National Trust of Australia (WA) on the Proposed Burrup Peninsula Conservation Reserve (PBPCR) Draft Management Plan, Perth, NTAWA.

NTAWA (2006) 'Rock Art Feature', *Trust News*, 34(4): 9–16.

Perrigo, T. (2006) Transcription of proceedings from 'The Heritage Values of the Dampier Rock Art Precinct Public Forum', 5 May 2006, State Library Theatre, Perth, Western Australia.

Reynolds, H. (1987) *Frontier: Aborigines, settlers and land*, Sydney: Allen & Unwin.

—— (1995) *Fate of a Free People*, Ringwood, VIC: Penguin.

—— (1996) *Aboriginal Sovereignty: Reflections on race, state and nation*, St Leonards, NSW: Allen & Unwin.

Ritter, D. (2003) 'Trashing heritage: Dilemmas of rights and power in the operation of Western Australia's Aboriginal heritage legislation', *Studies in Western Australian History*, 23: 195–208.

Roberts, H. (1961) 'Preface' in R. Oldham and J. Oldham, *Western Heritage: A study of the colonial architecture of Perth, Western Australia*, Perth: UWA Press, 1–2.

Royal Commission into Aboriginal Deaths in Custody (1991) Regional Report of Inquiry into underlying issues in Western Australia by Commission P.L. Dodson, Adelaide.

Sanders, D.L. (1961) *Monday in Summer*, London: Hodder and Stoughton.

Stannage, T. (1985) *Western Australia's Heritage: The pioneer myth*, Monograph Series No. 1, University Extension, Nedlands, WA: The University of Western Australia.

Turnbull, M.B. (2007) 'Inclusion of a place in the National Heritage List', *Commonwealth of Australia Gazette Special*, S127 (3 July). Available online at: http://www.burrup.org.au/Gazette.pdf (accessed 26 May 2008).

13

Yorùbá identity and Western museums: Ethnic pride and artistic representations

Anna Catalani

The encounter between different societies is often problematic and can take the form of a cultural clash, especially if it happens during postcolonial times, when specific stereotypes have deepened within social constructions and assumptions.[1] This chapter is based on the idea that 'the connection between past and future may be more fragile than is generally assumed [and definitely] it requires deliberate actions to maintain social organizations and cultural traditions' (Leeds-Hurwitz 1993: xxii). Specifically, it deals with the way Yorùbá people living nowadays in Great Britain relate to, interpret and classify their traditional ceremonial objects, as displayed in museums.[2]

The chapter is organized into two main sections and is based on the author's PhD research, carried out between April 2002 and January 2004, among the communities of Yorùbá immigrants living in Leicester and Nottingham.[3] The first section will consider the historical and social changes that have occurred in the interpretation and definition of non-Western objects (with a specific focus on African/Yorùbá objects). The second section will focus on some of the results of the research. It will present the perception of Yorùbá people towards contemporary Yorùbás and traditional Yorùbá objects, within a postcolonial society and a postcolonial institution, such as the museum.

Museums and the 'other' cultures 1890–2005: From ideals of power and possession to intercultural bridges

In Yorùbá tradition, every time a new king was elected by his tribe, he was requested to open one of the carved gourds presented to him during the coronation ceremony. The contents of the chosen gourd, (e.g. salt, sugar, nuts or pepper) foretold to the community what style of reign was just beginning. Usually, the gourds used for this kind of ceremony were finely carved with symbolic geometric designs, which defined – in conformity with the Yorùbá cosmology and religious beliefs – the boundaries and the indissoluble bonds between the world of the spirits and the world of the living.

During the age of high imperialism (1850–1914), in order to satisfy the desire for possessions of many politicians, scholars and missionaries, thousands of non-Western objects – like the Yorùbá gourd of the example – were brought to Europe and started to fill the glass cases of public museums, as well as the stores of private collectors. As a consequence, non-Western material culture (and the people who produced it) became symbols of Western social and economic ideologies. In the early nineteenth century, Britain had already achieved significant political and expansionist successes,[4] but it was only with the completion of the Suez Canal (1869) that the British Empire started effectively to expand its supremacy to other states of the African continent.[5] While the British colonizers were securing different African territories, back in Britain the Government was focused on the 'attempt to shape a world system which both expressed and reinforced the gentlemanly order at home' (Hopkins 1988: 6). Indeed, the British Government was aiming at the construction and the propaganda of the idea of the 'Africans', ghettoized into the negative category of 'the others'. Without any doubt, in the last decade of the nineteenth century, the idea of the non-Western other, understood as different, unusual and uncivilized, started to be more consistently formed and publicized, as did the idea of the superiority of the Western race (Danaher *et al.* 2000). The public image of the uncivilized 'other', who did not fit into the social and aesthetic Western canons, became a necessary persona to justify colonialist conquests. The complex and different cultural system which formed non-Western societies was ignored and misunderstood by the West: in this nineteenth-century marketing strategy, cultural diversity was superficially extrapolated, exotically flattened and reshaped, in order to feed the Western imagination and to strengthen the idea of the superior Western civilization.

As public institutions, museums did not escape from this propaganda. On the contrary, exhibitions became pivotal centres of the colonial policy. Indeed, due to their public nature, museums became powerful means to promote imperialist interests and colonial responsibilities. As Black observes, 'within the museum's walls, the other serve[d] to reflect the self's glory' and 'the museum fed the curiosity of its visitors ... and could satisfy the appetite for novelty as well as for nostalgia'. This happened at, for instance, the *Stanley and Africa Exhibition* (1890), set in the Victoria Gallery in London by Henry Morgan Stanley, and where each visitor, as an explorer, had to make his/her way through the jungle of objects, portraits and collections (Black 2000: 26; Coombes 1994).[6]

During this period, a mass process started that, for several decades, would rank and re-represent non-Western cultures as subcultures that needed to be subjugated in order to be civilized: non-Western people became the target for anthropological research, as well as a sort of social panacea, useful to reinforce the idea of Western superiority. For instance, H. Huxley and J. H. Lamprey, the inventors of the standard measuring-grid, were recommending that 'all aboriginal subjects [should] be photographed naked, their bodies posed in such a way that the viewer could make unimpeded cross-comparison with the anatomy of other racial groups' (Maxwell 1999: ix). In addition, with reference to colonial responsibilities, museums started to be conceived more as 'instructive amusements', necessary for the 'mental and moral health of the [Western] citizens' (Bennet 1995: 19). As a consequence, by 1890 the museum scene was flourishing with national and international exhibitions that, besides the educational and power-image advantages, raised the perspective of commercial benefits and recreational environments. Therefore, from cabinets of intellectual curiosities, museums became worlds of curious mysteries, where academic science and popular fantasy were married perfectly.[7] There was a clear ambition to surprise the visitors and imperialistically to construct their experience and understanding: 'by mapping out the world, museums became synonymous with culture and education' (Black 2000: 26). For instance, in June 1904, Henry Balfour, the first curator of the Pitt Rivers Museum, speaking of museums in Britain said, 'I believe that ... [there] will arise institutions, which, even though they may be small, will take a definitive plan among the teaching units of our countries' (Balfour 1904: 398).

A catalyst of this change was the Education Act, in 1902, which contemplated the educational potential of museums – by soliciting school visits to museums – and generated debates concerning ethnographic collections as educational resources. As a consequence, most museums adapted and redefined 'their public image, in terms of educational prerogative' (Coombes 1994: 112). Ethnographic collections started to be displayed on the basis of the comparative approach, which served didactic purposes, through a prompt assessment of objects' similarities and differences.[8] For example, between 1895 and 1916, the Arnold Ridyard Collection at the Liverpool Museum counted around 6,500 objects, mainly from West and Central Africa. During these years, the collection was initially organized according to taxonomic principles but then, due to a dramatic rise in the number, specimens were ordered according to their ethnographic group (Tythacott 2001).[9] After the age of voracious collecting, there was a deeper Western understanding and a more accepting attitude towards the objects and towards the people who made such objects. This was because people started to understand the new objects and their cultures better, after having had them around for a long time. Undoubtedly, the transformation of the perception of non-Western material culture determined new ways to conceive and represent ethnographic collections and non-Westerners, within the Western museum context.

Over the past two centuries, museums have certainly made significant attempts to review their social role and have changed remarkably their attitude towards non-Western cultures and their objects. Indeed, if in the past ethnographic collections were conceived and represented as the material culture of disappearing societies, mainly preserved for the benefit and education of future generations, today the scene is markedly different (Peers and Brown 2003). Ethnographic collections are no longer interpreted as colonial trophies – although museums acknowledge that they are the result of the 'great age of museums collecting' (Peers and Brown 2003: 1) – and they are no longer portrayed as tangible proofs of disappearing and lost societies, which need to be displayed in a comparative, educational order (Simpson 1996). Since the middle of the twentieth century, Western exhibitions of non-Western material culture have gone through interesting changes: from a functionalist approach, museum displays have moved towards a more material-culture focus – intended to enhance and celebrate cultural diversities – to a people's interpretation focus.

183

Indeed, nowadays, Western museums are making considerable efforts to actively involve the source communities,[10] after recognizing them as the direct heirs of ethnographic collections and after acknowledging that the memories of indigenous people and their descendents, related to their material culture, may be significantly different from those of Westerners (Cummins and Arinze 1996). Museum professionals are trying to be more aware (and to express this awareness in exhibitions) of the different perceptions and senses of identity of non-Western people, living outside their original country, in relation to their material culture displayed in museums (Szekeres 2002). Museums aim constantly to foster more interactive and cooperative dialogues between the museum and the descendants of the people who originally created these objects: only in this way, in fact, can the relationship between the host country, the 'adoptive' people and the original heirs lead to a feasible, cultural transmission of shared histories and traditions within the museum context.

However, in relation to African material culture displayed in Western museums, it is interesting to note that Western colonial stereotypes of the past have produced today a unique way to make African objects culturally acceptable. The interpretation of African material culture in museums has mainly shifted from the socially recognized category of ethnographic specimens to that of artistic pieces. For example, in the *African Worlds Gallery* at the Horniman Museum, it is possible to find contemporary art objects, displayed close to the ethnographic objects that have been the source of the artistic inspiration. And indeed, exhibited in one of the displays, there is a painting by the Yorùbá artist Ademola Akintola, which represents an Ifa divination tray.[11] In this specific museum case, the Yorùbá divination tray has become a colourful piece of African art and, as such, it has probably become more intellectually accessible to the Western public.

Furthermore, when considering African material culture in Western museums, it seems that the uniqueness of the different African groups has been progressively absorbed within a sort of pan-Africanism. This is a consequence of the colonial period and of the Western approach to non-Western countries: a sort of flattening categorization that, for instance, has opposed the West to Africa. Bearing this in mind, if we tailor this idea of categorization to the Yorùbá group, a good example is provided by the Sainsbury Galleries at the British Museum in London. When entering the Sainsbury Galleries, visitors are presented with impressive, artistic displays of ceremonial masks, pottery, religious objects of different African regions and groups. In order to appreciate the exhibits, visitors require a high level of knowledge of African culture. Yorùbá objects are immersed in this jungle of concepts, images and geometries and their cultural uniqueness is absorbed into highly artistic and aesthetized displays (Pole 2001).

But what is the perspective of African people towards Western museum displays? How do members of the African Diaspora (and specifically, of the Yorùbá Diaspora) relate to their traditional heritage in museum displays? How much have past stereotypes affected this relationship? The next part of this chapter will present the views of some members of the Yorùbá Diaspora living in Britain towards their traditional objects, presented in Western museums.

Yorùbá pride and artistic displays

So far, the chapter has presented how, shaped by political and social ideals, Western museums over the centuries 'have amassed, archived, and displayed [non-Western] objects while often ignoring or distorting their cultural meaning' (Edward and Sullivan 2004: xv, xvi). The case of non-Western traditional objects (and specifically of religious and ceremonial objects) is an interesting one. This is because in Yorùbá society, religion is the foundation and the all-governing principle of life: it is the base to every activity and gives meaning to everything, including everyday objects (Bo?laji 1973).

This part of the chapter will present an overview of the ways Yorùbá people, members of the Yorùbá Diaspora in Britain, relate to their traditional religious objects, displayed in Western museums. It will not, however, discuss the notion of religion among Yorùbá diasporic groups, since this is not the focus of the paper. Instead, the following part will centre on the idea that 'the social world is a rich and complex place, with frequent subtleties of implication' and also that 'people are ultimately responsible for creating the meaning they use, [meaning which is] often conveyed through minor details of everyday [verbal and non-verbal] behaviour' (Leeds-Hurwitz 1993: xvi).

This section is based upon the fieldwork of the author's PhD research, carried out among some members of the diasporic Yorùbá communities in Leicester and Nottingham, between 2002 and 2004.[12] The main research methods used for this part of the study were individual interviews and focus groups. Sixteen individuals, aged between 21 and 60 years old, took part in the research.[13] At the time of the research, most of the participants were residents in Britain. All the Yorùbá participants were immigrants, living in Leicester and Nottingham, and they were therefore all members of the Yorùbá Diaspora.[14] Names, addresses and contact details of the people were gathered through the help of a local museum,[15] local churches (attended mainly by Nigerians) and through word of mouth among the local Yorùbá community.

The majority of the participants were Christians, of the Born-Again Christian community.[16] The author's initial intention was to involve a larger and more assorted sample of Yorùbás. However, to engage with and involve Yorùbá people in this research proved to be extremely difficult and challenging. These difficulties were faced in the beginning of the research and they were mainly due to the mistrust and reticence of Yorùbá people towards the researcher (an outsider to the Yorùbá community) and the research topic (traditional African religion, which they had rejected because they had converted either to Christianity or to Islam). Nevertheless, these issues helped the author in understanding better the participants' ideas of Yorùbá identity within British society, their personal knowledge of and relationship with their traditional religious objects and their experience and understanding of Western museums.

Yorùbá identity within British society

As mentioned above, the participants were members of the Yorùbá Diaspora in Britain.[17] Among a diasporic group, the construction of a communal identity is essential. This communal identity helps to define the diasporic group as a distinct social and cultural constituent of the host community. Therefore, among diasporic groups, the notions of culture and traditions become fluid and constructed and a process of continual redefinition of their communal identity is implied, as well as 'self-conscious appropriations and rejections of elements of traditions' (Dudley 2002: 143). This is done in order both to strengthen the sense of the communal identity and to make more evident the differences from people outside the diasporic group.

In relation to the concept of communal identity among diasporic groups, the researcher aimed to investigate the idea of Yorùbá communal identity among members of the Yorùbá Diaspora, within the context of contemporary British society. All the Yorùbá participants showed a very strong sense of identity: they all highlighted the idea of Yorùbá identity (Yorùbáness) and of the pride associated with it. As one of the participants explained, it is 'a great thing to be Yorùbá [and] it is something to be proud of, because Yorùbá is a rich culture'. However, during the discussion it became clear that a contemporary definition of the word 'Yorùbá' is quite difficult: in fact, it is a complex concept indicating a culture, a nationality, a country within a country and a body of religions.

In addition, members of the Yorùbá Diaspora seem to have reacted to the adoptive British society by strengthening their tribal pride and by feeling special in the name of their origins. Indeed, within the host society, diasporic Yorùbá groups have tried to re-define themselves by underlining their divine and mythical origin. For example, a female participant stated that Yorùbá people are the people of Oduduwa, 'the descendants of Oduduwa, the progenitor of the Yorùbás': she emphasized that Yorùbás are the 'children of a king' and, even back in Nigeria, people of other ethnic groups are very respectful to individuals with Yorùbá origins.[18]

Personal knowledge of traditional Yorùbá religious objects

In the conditions of uncertainty and vulnerability typical of diasporic movements, objects understood as 'private mementos may take the place of interpersonal relations as a depository of sentiment and cultural knowledge' (Parkin 1999: 31). In the context of this chapter, the importance of this concept is evident. Indeed, the chapter argues that, once moved from their original place into a new environment, cultural objects may assume new meanings and values.[19] Through them, diasporic groups tend to strengthen their sense of communal identity or assume a new cultural distinctiveness. On the basis of this, the researcher intended also to investigate the extent to which traditional religious Yorùbá objects were regarded by members of the Yorùbá Diaspora as depositories of Yorùbá cultural knowledge, as well as the extent of the influence of Western stereotypes towards cultural objects.

As mentioned, the discussions included the presentation of some pictures of traditional, religious and ceremonial Yorùbá objects. Almost all the participants were reluctant to speak about such artefacts, because of their new faith and because they looked upon traditional beliefs and traditional religious objects only as part of their past.[20] Therefore, the comments provided on the images were strongly influenced by the participants' religious background. Nevertheless, they appeared still to believe in the power of traditional religious objects and in the consequences they could incur by having to deal with such items. This suggests that the relation of members of the Yorùbá Diaspora towards their traditional religious artefacts has been influenced by Western, religious stereotypes. As von Laar states:

> for many centuries, Westerners have tried to impose their own ideas of what Christianity should be, often backed up by the forces of colonial political power and the imposition of patterns and models in line with the fashionable ideologies of Europe.
>
> (von Laar 2006: 8)

It was evident, during the discussions, that the adoption of new faiths and resettlement into a new context has changed the Yorùbás' perception of and attitude towards traditional, religious and cultural objects: outside their homeland, the new (social and religious) context has created a new, unsympathetic view of their cultural heritage. In relation to this, participants added that traditional religious objects have become meaningless to them (although they acknowledged the power and effectiveness of some objects) because they have been exposed to public viewing. In Nigeria, such objects are not meant for display but for private and initiated worshipping.

The Yorùbás and their experiences of museums

Museums are social and educational institutions that reflect, to a certain extent and in a distinctive way, the needs and tendencies of the societies that host them. In the first part of this chapter, we saw how, in the past, the ideas of non-Western cultures were shaped according to historical, social and political European terms and stereotypes.[21] However, as societies change, so do museums and the approach taken to interpreting non-Western collections. On the contemporary museum scene, professionals are making considerable efforts to be more aware of the different identities of non-Western people, in relation to their objects displayed in museums. On the other hand, Western museum representations of African (and in this case of Yorùbá) material culture are still very much pan-Africanist, artistic interpretations.

The intention of the research was to take account of the voices of Yorùbá people in relation to their traditional objects displayed in museums and to investigate their idea of museums. In fact, the Yorùbá participants were also asked about their individual experiences in museums (both African and Western) displaying Yorùbá objects – specifically, traditional religious objects. From the responses, it was evident that the display of Yorùbá material in Western museums was a sensitive issue for them. Indeed, although they seemed to be generally pleased that their culture has been exhibited (and thus acknowledged) in museums, at the same time they felt deprived of a past and heritage that was brought to the West

187

as exchange merchandise or as trophies and became part of artistic and pointless displays. As one of the participants explained:

> for the people who brought [these objects] here, these objects did not mean anything to them; they just got them for artistic display . . . but for us, these objects have a value . . . and to have them in a country or in a context that is not their own does not make any sense.

Museum displays, in fact, were described generally as pointless by the participants because most of the artefacts exhibited have a spiritual life of their own and 'in [the original] traditional society, these objects were separated from daily life, kept in private places and accessed only by those capable of managing their power' (Haakanson and Steffian 2004: 156). All the participants wished the repatriation of the items (since people back in Nigeria do not have many opportunities to see such objects any more) or, at least, for a more evident and active involvement of Yorùbás in the display setting and presentation. In order to ensure visitors realize the complexity and beauty of Yorùbá culture and in order to obtain the correct names of and information about the objects presented, participants suggested that Western curators should study this kind of artefact in its own original context, namely Nigeria. These suggestions and comments highlighted an understanding of museums as 'static, monolithic institution[s] at the center of the power' (Witcomb 2003: 89) rather than open and interactive spaces for debate and cultural exchanges. Indeed, from the research it was evident that Yorùbá participants indicated an urgent need and wished for a stronger cooperation and dialogue between museum curators and non-Western people.

Concluding thoughts

We must now turn to some concluding thoughts. This chapter has been concerned with traditional Yorùbá material culture displayed in Western museums and the ways members of the Yorùbá Diaspora relate to it. The chapter aimed to present briefly the historical and social changes that have occurred in the interpretation and definition of African material culture in Western society and museums. It has discussed how the Western museum interpretation of African objects has changed over the last two centuries: from curiosities which enhanced colonialist politics, to scientific specimens useful for educational purposes; and from artistic pieces to three-dimensional cultural links.

The chapter has then continued by presenting some results of the author's PhD research, carried out among some Yorùbá diasporic groups of Leicester and Nottingham. It has aimed to describe the contemporary Yorùbá perception towards their traditional religious objects, displayed within a postcolonial institution, such as the museum. From the research, it emerged that members of the Yorùbá Diaspora living in Britain are trying to proudly strengthen their sense of communal identity (Yorùbáness) within the hosting society. In addition, members of the Yorùbá Diaspora seem to have been influenced by Western stereotypes, in terms of their relation towards their traditional religious objects. This attitude is the result of the fact that their local traditions have been too often misunderstood by the Westerner and have been associated with the stereotypes of primitive and uncivilized. Finally, the chapter has explained that Yorùbá immigrants still nourish a sort of mistrust for the museum: indeed, the Yorùbá participants made it clear that, although they were pleased to see their cultural objects presented in museums, at the same time they felt deprived of their heritage, which had become part of artistic displays.

The chapter, therefore, intended to underline that, nowadays, members of the Yorùbá Diaspora have an uneasy relation towards their material culture displayed in museums. This is because they cannot identify themselves with the ways their culture and objects are presented in museums. Indeed, it is not Yorùbá identity or traditional Yorùbá religious objects that are present in museum, but what museum professionals and Western visitors need and want to be displayed. As a consequence, it just so happens that the 'interests of the community should coincide with those of government' (Witcomb 2003: 85), rather than the opposite.

Acknowledgements

The author wishes to acknowledge the helpful suggestions of Dr Konstantinos Arvanitis, Professor Susan Pearce, all Yorùbá participants and the AHRC (funding body for this research between October 2003 and October 2005).

Notes

1   Postcolonialism is a complex concept. However, in the context of this chapter, with the terms 'postcolonialism' and 'postcolonialist', the author will refer to 'an intellectual effort at managing the aftermath of the colonial past in an era when official political relations of colonialism had all but ended' (During 2000: 388).
2   The word 'Yorùbá' describes both a language and an ethnic group living across Nigeria and the Republic of Benin.
3   Anna Catalani was an AHRC scholar between October 2003 and October 2005.
4   These achievements included the capture of the Cape of South Africa and the control of different ports along the African coast.
5   In 1901, Nigeria became a British protectorate and Yorùbáland was officially colonized by the British Empire.
6   Henry Morgan Stanley (1841–1904) was a foreign correspondent for the New York Herald. In 1871, he was sent on an expedition to Africa to find the Scottish missionary David Livingstone. From his journey, he brought back a remarkable amount of objects, which were organized in a five-section exhibition, enriched by maps and detailed charts, geographical information, and information on rainfall, population, religions and minerals distribution (Coombes 1994).
7   It is important to mention also the missionaries' exhibitions and collections, which became a way to support the colonialist ambition of power by stimulating pitiful feelings towards the uncivilized and idol-worshipping Africans (Ajayi 1965; Coombes 1994).

8   Other examples of the comparative approach in museum displays of the time are provided by the Royal Albert Museum (Exeter), the Horniman Museum (London) and the Pitt Rivers Museum (Oxford).

9   Arnold Ridyard (1853–1924) was a shipping engineer from Liverpool with a particular interest in Central African power figures.

10 According to Laura Peers and Alison Brown, the term 'source communities . . . refer both to these groups in the past when the artefacts were collected, as well as to their descendants today'; and again 'source communities have come to be defined as authorities on their own cultures and material heritage' (Peers and Brown 2003: 21).

11 The term Ifa indicates a system of divination in Yorùbá religion.

12 It is fair to say that the sample of Yorùbá people interviewed for this research does not claim to represent the whole diasporic Yorùbá population. However, these Yorùbá people do give a 'close-up, detailed [and] meticulous view of particular units, which may constitute processes, types, categories, cases or examples which are relevant to or appear within the wider universe' (Mason 1996: 92).

13 Six women and ten men.

14 Overall, the author carried out three focus groups and three individual interviews organized around four main themes: definition of being Yorùbá, knowledge of traditional Yorùbá religions, knowledge of the purpose of traditional Yorùbá religious objects and individual museum experience. Initially, the author intended to carry out only focus groups. However, due to personal commitments, it was not possible for some of the participants to take part in group discussions: in these cases, therefore, it was necessary to carry out individual interviews. During the discussions and interviews, pictures of some traditional Yorùbá religious objects were shown to the participants, who could comment on them and provide any kind of information about them. All the objects in the photographs belonged to a Nigerian collection of the eighteenth century, hosted in the Brewhouse Museum, Nottingham. Participants agreed to take part in the research, provided that they did not have to see or to deal directly with the objects but only with images of the objects, considered not as real or harmful as the objects themselves.

15 The Brewhouse Yard Museum in Nottingham. The museum had an ongoing cooperation with an African artist from the art centre 'Emaca' (Nottingham) who, at the time of this research, suggested the author to contact a Yorùbá person, owner of an African Shop in Nottingham.

16 The term 'Born-Again Christian' is used in branches of Protestant Christianity. One participant was a Muslim and another participant was a traditional believer.

17 After 1965, the term 'Diaspora' started to be used to define dispersed ethnic groups. According to Tölöyan, nowadays 'Diaspora' exists in three overlapping but distinct forms: first diasporas exist as 'actual social formations made up of individuals, extended families, small groups and the relations conducted between them . . . Second, diasporas exist as multiple imagined communities. That is to say, they are constantly articulated by their own individual and institutional members, who construct and disseminate numerous representations of what they are, what their diasporic experience feels like and what it means or it should mean. . . .; the third form of diasporic existence is wholly discursive' (Tölöyan 2003: 56).

18 Oduduwa is the mysterious and divine founder of the Yorùbás.

19 The category 'cultural objects' includes also religious objects, which have been the example for this chapter.

20 Eleven participants were of the Christian faith; one of them was of the Islamic faith and only one said to be a traditional believer.

21 Including African culture and specifically Yorùbá culture.

Bibliography

Ajayi, J. F. A. (1965) *Christian Missions in Nigeria 1841–1891: The making of a new elite*, London: Longman.

Balfour, H. (1904) 'The relationship of museums to the study of anthropology', *Museum Journal*, 3: 396–408.

Bennet, T. (1995) *The Birth of Museum. History, theory, politics*, London: Routledge.

Black, B. J. (2000) *On Exhibit. Victorians and their museums*, Charlottesville, VA: University Press of Virginia.

Bolaji, I. (1973) *African Traditional Religion: A definition*, Maryknoll, NY: Orbis Books.

Casely-Hayford, A. (2002) 'A way of being: Some reflections on the Sainsbury African Galleries', *Journal of Museum Ethnography*, 14: 113–27.

Coombes, E. C. (1994) *Reinventing Africa: Museums, material culture and popular imagination in late Victorian and Edwardian England*, New Haven, CT: Yale University Press.

Cummins, A. and Arinze, E. (1996) 'Retrospective curatorship: Indigenous perspectives in postcolonial societies', in C. Turner *et al.* (eds) *Curatorship: Indigenous perspectives in postcolonial societies: Proceedings of a symposium*, Alberta: Canadian Museum of Civilization with the Commonwealth Association of Museums and the University Victoria, 2–4.

Danaher, G., Schirato, T. and Webb, J. (2000) *Understanding Foucault*, London: SAGE.

Dudley, S. (2002) 'Diversity, identity and modernity in exile: "Traditional" Karenni Clothing', in A. Green and R. Blurton (eds) *Burma: Art and archaeology*, London: British Museum Press, 143–51.

During, S. (2000) 'Postcolonialism and globalization: Towards a historicization of their interrelation', *Cultural Studies*, 14: 385–404.

Edwards, A. and Sullivan, L. E. (2004) 'Stewards of the sacred: Museums, religions, and cultures', in L. E. Sullivan and A. Edwards (eds) *Stewards of the Sacred*, Washington, DC: American Association of Museums in cooperation with the Center for the Study of World Religions, Harvard University, ix–xxi.

Haakanson Jr, S. and Steffian, A. F. (2004) 'The Alutiiq Museum's guidelines for the spiritual care of objects', in L. E. Sullivan and A. Edwards (eds) *Stewards of the Sacred*, Washington, DC: American Association of Museums in cooperation with the Center for the Study of World Religions, Harvard University, 155–66.

Hopkins, T. (1988) 'British imperialism. A review and a revision', *Refresh*, 7: 5–8.

Leeds-Hurwitz, W. (1993) *Semiotics and Communication: Signs, codes, cultures*, Hillsdale, NJ: Laurence Erlbaum Associates.

Mason, J. (1996) *Qualitative Researching*, London: Sage.

Maxwell, A. (1999) *Colonial Photography and Exhibitions. Representations of the 'native' and the making of European identities*, London: Leicester University Press.

Parkin, D. (1999) 'Mementoes as transitional objects in human displacement', *Journal of Material Culture*, 4: 303–20.

Pearce, S. M. (1990) *Archaeological Curatorship*, London: Leicester University Press.

Peers, L., and Brown, A. K. (2003) 'Introduction', in L. Peers and A. K. Brown (eds) *Museums and Source Communities*, London: Routledge, 1–16.

Pole, L. (2001) 'Distant voices', *Museums Journal*, 101: 48.

Simpson, M. A. (1996) *Making Representations: Museums in the postcolonial era*, London: Routledge.

Szekeres, V. (2002) 'Representing diversity and challenging racism: The migration museum', in R. Sandell (ed.) *Museums Society, Inequality*, London: Routledge, 142–52.

Tölöyan, K. (2003) 'The American model of diasporic discourse Diasporas', in R. Münz and R. Ohliger (eds) *Diaspora and Ethnic Migrants. Germany, Israel and PostSoviet Successor States in comparative perspective*, London: Frank Cass, 56–74.

Tythacott, L. (2001) 'From the fetish to the specimen: The Ridyard African Collection at the Liverpool Museum', in A. Shelton (ed.) *Collectors. Expressions of Self and Other*, London and Coimbra: Horniman Museum and Museu Antropologico da Universidade de Coimbra, 157–180.

von Laar, W. (2006) 'Introduction', in A. Droogers, C. van der Laan, and W. van Laar (eds) *Fruitful in this Land. Pluralism, Dialogue and Healing in Migrant Pentecostalism*, Zoetermeer and Geneva: Boekencentrum and WCC Publ., 7–16.

Witcomb, A. (2003) *Re-imagining the Museum. Beyond the mausoleum*, London: Routledge.

Index

Note: page numbers in *italic* refer to illustrations

African art and cultures 183, 184, 187, 189; British colonialism 182; museum objects 182–3; pan-Africanization 184, 187, *see also* Benin; Nigeria; Yorùbá
Agbonkonkon, Gregory 165
Akintola, Ademola 184
Anderson, Benedict 143
Art on Tyneside exhibition (AOT) 29, 33–45, *35, 36*; architecture 36, *37*; 'Border Warfare' Room 34–5, *34*; difficult past 43–4; place identity 40, 41; Twentieth Century Room 39; Tyne Bridge 37, *38*; video presentation 39–40
Arts and Exhibitions International 99, 100, 101
Ashworth, G.J.: (2007) 15; and Graham B. (2005) 16, 17
Australia, Western Australia: Aboriginal Heritage Act 176; Heritage Council 175, 177; heritage movement 169–71; Perth, historical background 169–70; white and indigenous heritage 174, *see also* Barracks Arch; Burrup Peninsular; National Trust of Australia (WA)

Balfour, Henry 183
BALTIC Center for Contemporary Art, Gateshead 32, *33*
Barracks Arch, battle for 171–4; Barracks Defence Council (BDF) 173–4; Bishop Riley'support 173; Historical Society 172, 173; nostalgia vs utilitarianism 171; opposition to Government 173–4; place and identity 170, 171, 172, 174; preservation of the past 170–1
Beal, J. (2000) 43–4
Bednarik, Robert 177, 178–9
Benin 160–1, 162; art and culture 160, 165; culture suppressed 161, 162, 165; expatriate community 165–6; Festival of Ewere *163*; identity 165, 166; looted art 165, 166; the moat 163–4, *164*; National Museum 161; Oba Erediauwa *163*, 164, 165; the Oba's Palace 157, 160–1

Benin City, heritage and identity 157, 158–60, 162; versus religious evangelism 156, 157–8, 157, 162
Benin City Walls 161, *161*, 162, 164–5, 166; British colonial administration 160–1, 162, 165; construction of 163; World Heritage site 158, 159, 165
Birmingham Centre of Contemporary Cultural Studies 114
Black, B.J. (2000) 182
Bodnar, J. (1992) 111
Bourdieu, Pierre (1984) 148
Boylan, P. (1992) 52
Brand, David 171, 173, 174
Britain, cultural diversity 17, 18, 19–20, 24
British colonialism 182
Britishness 17, 18–19, 20, 21, 23–4, *see also* Englishness
Brown, Gordon 17–18, 24
Burke, Thomas 135
Burrup Peninsular: conservation vs. industry 175, 176–7; indigenous leaders 177, 178; National Trust strategies 175, 176–9; National and World Heritage listing 177; native title/State Government 176, 178; responsibility of whole community 175, 177–9; rock art 175–6, 177; State Heritage Act 177; world significance of 175–6, 177
Buttimer, A. (1980) 50

Casey, Bishop Eamon 133
Cavendish, Lord Frederick 135, 136, 137
Charlton, John, 'The Women', painting 36, *38*
Charteris, Lord 16, 22
China: Liuzhi ecomuseum principles 53, 54; the Soga Miao Ecomuseum 53–4, *54*
Cleary, Father Michael 133
Clifford, Barry 99, 100
Clifford, James (1997) 178
Clifford, S. and King, A. (1993) 50

Coalition of African American Organizations 99
Colonial Williamsburg 96, 143, 144, 145, 146
Common Ground 50, 51
Connah, G. (1975) 162, 163
Connerton, Paul (2008) 105, 115
Cook, Robin 25
Corsane, G. and Holleman, W. (1993) 52
Cortemilia, ecomuseum regeneration 57–61;
   disadvantaged area 58, 61; empowerment of
   community 59, 60–1; farm, vineyard and
   orchard 59, 60; functional buildings 59–60;
   restoration of terraced landscape 58–9
Culture Online (UK) 21

Daniels, David 178
Danziger, K. (1997) 31
Darling, P.J. (1984) 162, 163
Davis, P. (1999) 50, 52
Dicks, Bella (2003) 16
digital heritage 16, 26; ICONS of England 20–7
Dixon, J and Durrheim, K. (2000) 32
Dorment, Richard 42
Dumas, Russel 171

ecomuseums: China 53–4; community
   involvement/initiative 57, 62; concept of 49,
   51, 52–3, 56, 61; Crete 47–9; France 56–7;
   Italy 57–61; Japan 54–6; local distinctiveness
   49–51; and local identity 57, 61–2
Elkins, J. (2002) 45
Englishness 18, 19, 20–1, 23–4; national symbols
   22, *see also* Britishness
Enola Gay aircraft 94, 102
envisaged audience 30–1, 42
Esteves, Ribau 109
ETHNOS (2005) 21

Farrell, James T. 137–8
Fleming, David 41, 42
forgetting 105–6; negative aspects 106; politics of
   117; social significance of 115, 117, 118, 119,
   see also memory
Foster, Norman 32
France, Écomusée Saint Dégan 56–7, 57
Fronikakis, Basil 47
Fronimakis, Vasilios 48

Gateshead on Tyne, quayside 32, 33
Gavalochori Museum, Crete 47–9, 48;
   community initiative 47–9
Geertz, Clifford (1973) 80
Germany, Nazi past 95
Giern, T.F. (1999) 45
Gjestrum, John Aage 53
Glaser, Hermann 97
Gotman, Anne (1990) 113

Graham, B. 16, 17; *et al.* (2000) 130
Gross, Jan Tomasz, *Neighbors* (2000) 123–4,
   125, 126
Gupta, D. (2005) 118

Haartsen, T. *et al.* (2000) 32
Hall, Stuart (2005) 16–17, 20, 24
Healy, Tim 39–40
Hemings, Sally 96, 151–2
Hepburn, Alister 171
heritage 15, 16, 22–3, 74, 76–7, 130; activations
   67, 79–81; collective 76–7; commercialization
   of 80; cultural 76–9, 159; as ethical space 103;
   genius and art 77, 78; and identity 80, 93;
   intangible 159; international organizations
   159, 160, 166; local 74, 82–3, 84; national 17;
   natural 78, 159; and power 79–80; and science
   81–2; shortage/obsolescence 77, 78; sites 158;
   social construction of 67, 78, 79; socio-cultural
   aspects 63, 76; socio-political function 130, *see
   also* museums
heritage controversies 94–6, *see also* Nuremburg;
   slave heritage controversy
Heron, P. (1991) 61
Hicks, Wilfred 178
Hooper-Greenhill, E. (2000) 71
Hudson, Kenneth 41
Huyssen, Andreas (1994) 43

ICONS of England website 20–7; Atlas 23
identification 144–6
identity 143, 144–5, 158; collective 117; local 41,
   74; non-Western peoples 184; place 29–30, 43;
   politics 93
Ílhavo, cod capital of Portugal 109–14; change
   and identity 109; community silence and
   survival 111, 112, 115; maritime museum
   110–12, 113; politics/maritime identity
   109–10; social tensions silenced 111, 113, 114
International Council of Museums (ICOM) 15,
   80, 159, 160
International Federation of Rock Art
   Organizations 177
Ireland: the Invincibles 135, 138; national identity
   129, 131, 138, 139; Roman Catholic Church,
   power of 132, 133, *see also* Phoenix Park,
   Dublin
Italy, Cortemilia, ecomuseum regeneration 57–61

Japan, Miura Peninsula ecomuseum 54–6;
   Kamiayama-guchi, rice terraces 55, 55;
   Yokosuka City museum 55
Jefferson, Isaac 146–7, 148
Jefferson, Thomas 96, 147, 148; at Monticello
   148–54; Sally Hemings 151–2
Jewell, Richard Roach 171

Jordan, Daniel 146
Jordan, Jennifer (2006) 102
Judt, T. (2005) 117

Kanagawa Foundation for Academic and
  Cultural Exchange (K-Face), Japan 54
King, A. 50
Kirschenblatt-Gimblett, B. (1998) 45
Kohl, Helmut 95

Lammy, David 15, 19, 25, 26
Larkin, Jim 138
Layman, Lenore (1982) 171
Lefebvre, H. (1991) 130
local: distinctiveness 43, 49–50, 51; heritage 74,
  82–3, 84; identity 41, 74
local heritage activation 83–5; structure of
  forces involved 84, 85
Loures, Portugal, heritage and museums 66–74;
  Casa do Adro 68–9; Ceramics Museum of
  Sacavém (CMS) 64, 70, 72; identity 67, 70, 75;
  inclusion/accessibility 70, 71, 72–3; industrial
  heritage 65, 70–1; local culture and politics
  68–9, 74; Municipal Museum of Loures
  (MML) 64, 69–70, 72; Wine Museum 70
Lübbe, Herman 43

MacDonald, S. (2002) 31
Margalit, A. (2002) 119
maritime heritage, Portugal 107–9; cod fishing
  and consumption 107–8; collapse of cod
  industry 108, 109, 112, 113; *Faina Maior*
  tradition 108, 110, 113; idealization of 108,
  111, 113, 114; private voices 112–14; public
  silences 110–12; Salazar government 106,
  107–8, 111, 112; working conditions
  108, 111, *see also* Ílhavo, cod capital
  of Portugal
Marques, Francisco Correia 110, 113
Meinig, D.W. (1979) 49
memory 105–6, 129; collective 117; and
  democracy 118–19, 121; excluded memories
  93; and identity 106, 115; interventions 94–5,
  96, 98; politics 101, 117, 126; social
  remembering 117–19; studies 105–6,
  see also unsettling memories
Millard, John 33, 40, 42, 43, 44
minorities, heritage niche 93
Monticello 96, 143, 144, 145, 146; identity
  segregation 147–8; racial identification 153–4;
  racism 150–1; slave centred exhibit 152–3;
  slave quarters 147, 148–9, 150; white identity
  154; Woodson family 152–3
Mulvaney, Ken (2003) 175–6
Murtas, Donatella 57, 58, 60
Museum Center, Cincinnati, US 101

Museum of Science and Industry (MOSI), Tampa,
  Florida 99, 100
museums: as cartographic spaces 45; flexibility
  71, 73; and heritage 68, 74, 80–1; history of
  51–2, 182–4; and identity 64, 75; International
  Council of Museums (ICOM) 80; local culture
  and politics 68–9, 74; new thinking 40, 41,
  51–2, 71, 178, 183–4, 187; non-Western
  traditional objects 185; offsetting local
  disadvantage 43–4, 74, *see also* ecomuseums;
  Loures, Portugal, heritage and museums; Tyne
  and Wear Museums

National Air and Space Museum, Washington,
  DC 94
national identity 18, 130, 138, 143, 145–6
National Maritime Museum, UK 102
National Museum of African History and
  Culture, US 96
National Museum of Slavery, US 96
National Trust of Australia (WA) 171; the
  Barracks, Perth 172–4; Burrup campaign 175–9;
  new focus 174–5; professionalization 174–5,
  see also Barracks Arch; Burrup Peninsular
National Trust movement 177
National Underground Railroad Freedom
  Center,Cincinnati US 95, 101
Newcastle upon Tyne: Discovery Museum 30;
  Laing Art Gallery 29, 33, 41, 42, 44; quayside
  32, *see also* Art on Tyneside exhibition
Nigeria: ethnic groups 157; National Commission
  for Museums and Monuments (NCMM) 156,
  166; Yorùbá people and culture 186, 187, 188,
  see also Benin; Yorùbá
Nora, Pierre (2002) 115
Norman, John 101
Nuremberg, Germany, heritage controversy 95,
  96–9; citizens protest initiative 97–8; memory
  interventions 96, 98; Nazi past 96–8

Oldham, John and Oldham, Ray *Western
  Heritage* 169
Olick, J.K. and Levy, D. (1997) 117

Paião, Aníbal 113, 114
Peckham, Robert Shannon (2003) 103
Peron, J. (1984) 56
Perrigo, Tom 177
Phillips, Trevor 18
Phoenix Park, Dublin, a national space 131–2,
  139; memory and meaning 134, 138, 139;
  Papal Visit (1979) 132–4, 138–9; Phoenix Park
  Murders 132, 135–8, 139; the Pope's cross
  132–3, 138–9; Roman Catholic Church, power
  of 132, 133; unofficial memorials 136–8, 139;
  Visitor Center 135–6

place: identity 29–30, 41, 43; perceptions of 31–2; sense of 49–50

Poland: anti-Semitism 125, 126; forced forgetting 120; the Holocaust 125, 126–7; identity crisis 125–6; Institute of National Remembrance 124; Jedwabne 124–5, 126; memory and forgetting 117, 126; national identity 117, 123–4; policy of forgiveness 121, 123; policy of lustration 121, 122, 126; Polish-Jewish relations 117, 120, 121, 124; postcommunist politics 121–4; relationship to Russia 120; World War II 120–1, 124

Portugal 64, 66; local culture and politics 68–9, 74, *see also* Ílhavo; Loures; maritime heritage

Pratt, Mary Louise 178

public silence 106, 110–12, 115

Ransom, James 99, 100

Reagan, Ronald 95

Relph, E.E. (1976) 50

remembering *see* memory

Renan, Ernst 118

Renton, Tim 40

repatriation of non-Western art 188

Ricoeur, P. (1999) 119

Ritter, David (2003) 176

Rivard, R. (1984) 52

Roberts, Hew 169, 170

Rowles, G.D. (1983) 31

Sage Gateshead, Concert Hall 32, *33*

Samuel, R. (1994) 129

Sanders, Dorothy (1961) 171–2

Scotland/Scottishness 17, 19

slave heritage controversy 99–102; minority intervention 102; pirate heritage 99–101; prioritization of memories 100–1; ship-wreck the *Whydah* 99–101

slavery in the US 95–6, 143, 146–7, 148, *see also* Monticello

Smith, Laurajane (2006) 16, 22

Stannage, Tom (1985) 170

Stephenson, Gordon 171, 172

Stilianakis, George and Maria 48

Stone, L. and Muir, R. (2007) 18, 24

Todorov, T. (2003) 119

Tornquist-Plewa, B. (2003) 126

Turner, Victor (1974) 94

Tyne and Wear Museums (TWM) 33, 40, 42, 44

UNESCO 158, 159, 160

United States: culture/identity 143–5, *see also* Monticello; slavery in the US

unsettling memories, incorporation of 99, 102–3, *see also* heritage controversies

Verdú, V. (2003) 80

von Laar, W. (2006) 187

Western Australian Historical Society 170

World Monuments Fund 160, 167, 177

Yelvington, Kevin, Goslin, Neill and Arriaga, Wendy (2002) 100

Yorùbá art, history and tradition 181, 184, 185, 186, 188, *see also* African art and cultures

Yorùbá Diaspora in Britain: communal identity 185–6, 188; heritage devalued out of context 188, 189; museum presentation of artefacts 184, 185, 187–8, 189; religion and Western stereotypes 186–7, 188–9